GRAMMARS OF CREATION

Also by George Steiner

Errata: An Examined Life

No Passion Spent

*In Bluebeard's Castle: Some Notes Towards
the Redefinition of Culture*

*Antigones: How the Antigone Legend Has Endured
in Western Literature, Art, and Thought*

Tolstoy or Dostoevsky: An Essay in the Old Criticism

The Death of Tragedy

*Language and Silence: Essays on Language, Literature,
and the Inhuman*

After Babel

GRAMMARS OF CREATION

Originating in the Gifford Lecures
for 1990

George Steiner

YALE NOTA BENE

YALE UNIVERSITY PRESS   NEW HAVEN AND LONDON

First published as a Yale Nota Bene book in 2002.
Hardcover edition first published by Yale University Press in 2001.

For information about this and other Yale University Press publications,
please contact:

U.S. office	sales.press@yale.edu
Europe office	sales@yaleup.co.uk

Printed in the United States of America

Library of Congress Control Number: 2002105840

ISBN 0-300-09729-8 (pbk.)

A catalogue record for this book is available from the British Library.

10 9 8 7 6 5 4 3 2 1

ACKNOWLEDGEMENTS

My thanks are due to the Electors who did me the honour of inviting me to deliver the Gifford Lectures for 1990. During those taxing but rewarding weeks, the University of Glasgow was unfailingly hospitable. Professor Alexander Brodie's gently ironic witness and comments proved invaluable. Without the hectoring generosity and friendship of the late Professor Robert Carroll, the recasting of those lectures into this book might never have come about.

Its material arises very directly from work in the doctoral seminar in Comparative Literature and Poetics which I had the privilege of directing at the University of Geneva during a quarter of a century. The voices of its participants, many of whom returned year after year, are present throughout the argument. Students became friends and colleagues. This is true most particularly of Aminadav Dyckman whose scholarly scruple, linguistic range and critical acumen gave to the later years of the seminar much of its tenor. It is to him and to all "around that table" that this book is dedicated.

Heartfelt thanks also to Roger Cazelet of Faber and Faber and to Margaret Otzel of Yale University Press for their editorial authority.

George Steiner
Cambridge, April 2000

I

We have no more beginnings. *Incipit:* that proud Latin word which signals the start survives in our dusty "inception." The medieval scribe marks the opening line, the new chapter with an illuminated capital. In its golden or carmine vortex the illuminator of manuscripts sets heraldic beasts, dragons at morning, singers and prophets. The initial, where this term signifies beginning and primacy, acts as a fanfare. It declares Plato's maxim —by no means self-evident—whereby in all things natural and human, the origin is the most excellent. Today, in Western orientations—observe the muted presence of morning light in that word—the reflexes, the turns of perception, are those of afternoon, of twilight. (I am generalizing. My argument, throughout, is vulnerable and open to what Kierkegaard called "the wounds of negativity.")

There have been previous senses of ending and fascinations with sundown in Western culture. Philosophic witness, the arts, historians of feeling report on "closing-times in the gardens of the West" during the crises of the Roman imperial order, during the apocalyptic fears at the approach of the first millennium A.D., in the wake of the Black Death and the Thirty Years' War. Motions of decay, of autumn and failing light have always attached to men and women's awareness of physical ruin, of common mortality. Moralists, even prior to Montaigne, pointed out that the newborn infant is old enough to die. There is in the most confident metaphysical construct, in the most affirmative work of art a *memento mori*, a labour, implicit or explicit, to hold at bay the seepage of fatal time, of entropy into each and every living form. It is from this wrestling-match that philosophic discourse and the generation of art derive their informing stress, the unresolved tautness of which logic and beauty are formal modes. The cry "the great

god Pan is dead" haunts even those societies with which we associate, perhaps too conventionally, the gusto of optimism.

Nevertheless, there is, I think, in the climate of spirit at the end
of the twentieth century, a core-tiredness. The inward chronometry, the contracts with time which so largely determine our consciousness, point to late afternoon in ways that are ontological—
this is to say, of the essence, of the fabric of being. We are, or feel
ourselves to be, latecomers. The dishes are being cleared. "Time,
ladies and gents, time." Valediction in the air. Such apprehensions are the more compelling because they run counter to the
fact that, in the developed economies, individual life-spans and
expectancies are increasing. Yet the shadows lengthen. We seem
to bend earthward and towards night as do heliotropic plants.

A thirst for explanation, for causality, inhabits our nature. We
do want to know: Why? What conceivable hypothesis can elucidate a phenomenology, a structure of felt experience, as diffuse,
as manifold in its expressions, as that of "terminality"? Are such
questions worth asking seriously, or do they merely invite vacu-
ous high gossip? I am not certain.

Inhumanity is, so far as we have historical evidence, perennial. There have been no utopias, no communities of justice or
forgiveness. Our current alarms—at the violence in our streets,
at the famines in the so-called third world, at regressions into
barbaric ethnic conflicts, at the possibility of pandemic disease—
must be seen against the background of a quite exceptional moment. Roughly from the time of Waterloo to that of the massacres
on the Western Front in 1915–16, the European *bourgeoisie* experienced a privileged season, an armistice with history. Underwritten by the exploitation of industrial labour at home and colonial

rule abroad, Europeans knew a century of progress, of liberal dispensations, of reasonable hope. It is in the afterglow, no doubt idealized, of this exceptional calendar—note the constant comparison of the years prior to August 1914 with a "long summer"— that we suffer our present discomforts.

When, however, allowance is made for selective nostalgia and illusion, the truth persists: for the whole of Europe and Russia, this century became a time out of hell. Historians estimate at more than seventy million the number of men, women, and children done to death by warfare, starvation, deportation, political murder, and disease between August 1914 and "ethnic cleansing" in the Balkans. There have been hideous visitations of pestilence, famine, and slaughter before. The collapse of humaneness in this twentieth century has specific enigmas. It arises not from riders on the distant steppe or barbarians at the gates. National Socialism, Fascism, Stalinism (though, in this latter instance, more opaquely) spring from within the context, the locale, the administrative-social instruments of the high places of civilization, of education, of scientific progress and humanizing deployment, be it Christian or Enlightened. I do not want to enter into the vexed, in some manner demeaning, debates over the uniqueness of the Shoah ("holocaust" is a noble, technical Greek designation for religious sacrifice, not a name proper for controlled insanity and the "wind out of blackness"). But it does look as if the Nazi extermination of European Jewry is a "singularity," not so much in respect of scale—Stalinism killed far more—but motivation. Here a category of human persons, down to infancy, were proclaimed *guilty of being*. Their crime was existence, the mere claim to life.

The catastrophe which overtook European and Slavic civilization was particular in another sense. It undid previous advances. Even the ironists of the Enlightenment (Voltaire) had confidently predicted the lasting abolition of judicial torture in Europe. They had ruled inconceivable a general return to censorship, to the burning of books, let alone of heretics or dissenters. Nineteenth-century liberalism and scientific positivism regarded as self-evident the expectation that the spread of schooling, of scientific-technological knowledge and yield, of free travel and contact among communities would bring with them a steady improvement in civility, in political tolerance, in the mores of private and public business. Each of these axioms of reasoned hope has been proved false. It is not only that education has shown itself incapable of making sensibility and cognition resistant to murderous unreason. Far more disturbingly, the evidence is that refined intellectuality, artistic virtuosity and appreciation, scientific eminence will collaborate actively with totalitarian demands or, at best, remain indifferent to surrounding sadism. Resplendent concerts, exhibitions in great museums, the publication of learned books, the pursuit of academic research both scientific and humanistic, flourish within close reach of the death-camps. Technocratic ingenuity will serve or remain neutral at the call of the inhuman. The icon of our age is the preservation of a grove dear to Goethe within a concentration camp.

We have not begun to gauge the damage to man—as a species, as one entitling himself *sapiens*—inflicted by events since 1914. We do not begin to grasp the co-existence in time and in space, a co-existence sharpened by the immediacy of graphic and verbal presentation in the global mass media, of Western superfluity and the starvation, the destitution, the infant mortality which now batten on some three-fifths of mankind. There is a dynamic

of clear-sighted lunacy in our waste of what is left of natural resources, of fauna and flora. The South Col of Everest is a garbage dump. Forty years after Auschwitz, the Khmer Rouge buries
alive an estimated hundred thousand innocent human beings.
The rest of the world, fully apprised of the fact, does nothing.
New weapons soon start flowing from our factories to the kill-
ing fields. To repeat: violence, oppression, economic enslavement
and social irrationality have been endemic in history, whether
tribal or metropolitan. But this century has, owing to the magnitude of massacre, to the insane contrast between available wealth
and actual *misère*, to the probability that thermonuclear and bacterial weapons could, in fact, terminate man and his environment,
given to despair a new warrant. It has raised the distinct possibility of a reversal of evolution, of a systematic turn-about towards
bestialization. It is this which makes Kafka's *Metamorphosis* the
key-fable of modernity or which, despite Anglo-Saxon pragma-
tism, renders plausible Camus's famous saying: "The only serious philosophical question is that of suicide."

What I want to consider briefly is something of the impact of
this darkened condition on grammar. Where I take grammar to
mean the articulate organization of perception, reflection and experience, the nerve structure of consciousness when it communicates with itself and with others. I intuit (these are, of course,
almost wholly conjectural domains) that the future tense came
relatively late into human speech. It may have developed as late as
the end of the last Ice Age, together with the "futurities" entailed
by food-storage, by the making and preservation of tools beyond
immediate need, and by the very gradual discovery of animal-
breeding and agriculture. In some meta- or pre-linguistic register, animals would appear to know presentness and, one sup-

poses, a measure of remembrance. The future tense, the ability to discuss possible events on the day after one's funeral or in stellar space a million years hence, looks to be specific to *homo sapiens*. As does the use of subjunctive and of counter-factual modes which are themselves kindred, as it were, to future tenses. It is only man, so far as we can conceive, who has the means of altering his world by resort to "if"-clauses, who can generate clauses such as: "if Caesar had not gone to the Capitol that day." It seems to me that this fantastic, formally incommensurable "grammatology" of verb-futures, of subjunctives and optatives proved indispensable to the survival, to the evolution of the "language-animal" confronted, as we were and are, by the scandal, by the incomprehensibility of individual death. There is an actual sense in which every human use of the future tense of the verb "to be" is a negation, however limited, of mortality. Even as every use of an "if"-sentence tells of a refusal of the brute inevitability, of the despotism of the fact. "Shall," "will," and "if," circling in intricate fields of semantic force around a hidden centre or nucleus of potentiality, are the pass-words to hope.

Hope and fear are supreme fictions empowered by syntax. They are as indivisible from each other as they are from grammar. Hope encloses a fear of unfulfilment. Fear has in it a mustard-seed of hope, the intimation of overcoming. It is the status of hope today which is problematic. On any but the trivial, momentary level, hope is a transcendental inference. It is underwritten by theological-metaphysical presumptions, in the strict sense of this word which connotes a possibly unjustified investment, a purchase, as the bourse would say, of "futures." "Hoping" is a speech-act, inward or outwardly communicative, which "presumes" a listener, be it the self. Of this act, prayer is an exemplary case. The theological foundation is that which allows, which requires the desideratum, the forward venture and intent to be addressed to divine hearers in "the hope," precisely, of support or, at the least, understanding. The metaphysical re-insurance is that of a rational organisation of the world—Descartes must gamble on the supposition that our senses and intellect are not the toys of a malignant deceiver—and, even more importantly, on a morality of distributive justice. Hope would be meaningless in a wholly irrational order or in one of arbitrary, absurdist ethics. Hope, as it has structured the human psyche and behaviour, is only trivially operative where reward and punishment are determined by lottery (gamblers' hopes at roulette are exactly of this vacant order).

The formally religious subscription of the act of hope, direct resort to supernatural intervention, has weakened almost continually in Western history and individual consciousness. It has atrophied into more or less superficial ritual and inert figures of speech. Unthinking, one still "hopes to God." The philosophical edifice of hope is that of Cartesian rationality (where, most subtly, the theological drifts, like sand in an hour-glass, into the metaphysical and the scientific). It is that of Leibniz's optimism and, most eminently, of Kantian morality. A shared pulse of progress, of meliorism, energizes the philosophic-ethical enterprise from the early seventeenth century to the positivism of Comte. There are dissenters from hope, visionaries made desperate such as Pascal or Kierkegaard. But they speak from the margin. The prevailing motion of spirit makes of hope not only a fuel for political, social, and scientific action, but a reasonable mood. European revolutions, the improvement of social justice and material well-being, are crystallizations of hoped-for futurity; they are rational advents to tomorrow.

Out of Mosaic and prophetic Judaism grew two major branches or "heresies." The first is that of Christianity, with its promise of God's kingdom to come, of reparation for unjust suffering, of a Last Judgement and eternity of love through the Son. The future tense of the verb inhabits nearly every saying of Jesus. He is, for his followers, hope made flesh. The second branch, largely Jewish in its theoreticians and early proponents, is that of utopian socialism and, most signally, of Marxism. Here the claims on transcendence are made immanent, the kingdom of justice and equality, of peace and prosperity, is proclaimed to be of this world. With the voice of Amos, socialist idealism and Marxist-Leninist communism cry anathema on selfish wealth, on social oppression, on the crippling of countless common lives by insensate greed. The desert marches on the city. After the bitter struggle (after Golgotha) comes "the exchange of love for love, of justice for justice."

The twentieth century has put in doubt the theological, the philosophical, and the political-material insurance for hope. It queries the rationale and credibility of future tenses. It makes understandable the statement that "there is abundance of hope, but none for us" (Franz Kafka).

It is not the cant-phrase "the death of God," in fact predating Nietzsche and to which I am unable to assign any arguable meaning, that is pertinent. The determinant of our current situation is more embracing. I would call it "the eclipse of the messianic." In Western religious systems, the messianic, whether personalized or metaphoric, has signified renovation, the end of historical temporality and the coming in glory of an after-world. Over and again, the future tense of hope has sought to date this event (the year 1000 or 1666 or, among present-day chiliastic sects, the imminent turn of our millennium). In a literal sense, hope has sprung eternal. Western faiths are redemption-narratives. But the messianic is no less instrumental in secular programmes. For anarchist and Marxist imaginings of futurity, it will be represented by the "withering away of the state." Behind this figure, lie Kant's argument on universal peace and the Hegelian thesis of an end to history. In a paradoxical regard, the messianic can be independent of any postulate of God: it stands for man's access to perfectibility, to a higher and, presumably, enduring condition of reason and of justice. Again, on both the transcendental and the immanent levels of reference—these two being always closely related in a dialectical reciprocity—we are undergoing a radical displacement. Who except fundamentalists now awaits the actual coming of a Messiah? Who except literalists of a lost communism or anarcho-socialist Arcadia now awaits the actual re-birth of history?

Inevitably, this eclipse of the messianic presses on the future tense. The notion of the *Logos*, at once central and resistant to paraphrase, or of what is today called "grammatology" (the *Logos* inheres in this word), are relevant. The "Word" that was in the "beginning," for the pre-Socratics as well as for St. John, comprised a generative, dynamic eternity out of which time could spring forward, a present indicative of "to be" pregnant (in an almost material sense) with "shall" and "will." Future tenses are an idiom of the messianic. Take away energizing anticipation, the luminous imperative of waiting, and these tenses will be end-stopped. "Life-expectancy" is, then, no longer a messianic-utopian projection, but an actuarial statistic. Such pressures on the incipience of meaning and communication in the individual and collective sub-conscious, on the means of articulate speech, are gradual. Figures of daily discourse, totally devoid of concrete truth—"sunrise" for example—will persist like domestic ghosts. Except in masters of poetry and of speculative thought, language is conservative and opaque to nascent intuitions (hence the need for mathematical and logically formal codes in the swiftly moving sciences). But just as the almost imperceptible tectonic movements in the deeps of the earth sever and re-shape continents, so the forces emanating from the eclipse of the messianic will find manifest expression. Grammars of nihilism flicker, as it were, on the horizon. Poets put it succinctly. Unless I misread, ours are "Those Evenings of the Brain" (Emily Dickinson).

2

Valedictions look backward. In our age of transition to new mappings, to new ways of telling the story, the natural and the "human" sciences (*sciences humaines*) present a spiralling motion. It is that of which Nietzsche's "eternal return" and Yeats's "great gyres" are images. Knowledge proceeds forward technically, in its methods, in the ground it covers. But it seeks out origins. It would identify and grasp the source. In this movement towards "primacy," different sciences, different bodies of systematic inquiry, draw strikingly close to each other.

Cosmology and astrophysics are proposing models of the birth of our universe with a scenic sweep and speculative flight far closer to ancient or "primitive" creation-myths than they are to mechanistic positivism. Just now, the hypothesis of "continuous creation," of the provenance of matter out of interstellar "dark matter" or nothingness, is out of favour. Some kind of "big bang" is thought to have detonated our cosmos around fifteen billion years ago. Background radiation and the compaction of "lumps" into new galaxies are held to be spoors of this *incipit*. In a sovereign paradox, the further the horizon of radio-astronomy, of the observation of nebulae at the "edge of the universe," the deeper our descent into the temporal abyss, into the primordial past in which expansion began. The crux is indeed the concept of a beginning. Continuous-creation models dispense with the problem. They adduce eternity, a *perpetuum mobile* such as was dreamt of by medieval alchemists and makers of automata. In the physics of the "big bang" and of the possible transit "through" black holes into mirror-universes—though mathematically rigorous, the entailed similitudes are those of wildest fable and surrealism—the time-notion is Augustinian. Our current *magi* tell us that it is, *stricto sensu*, absurd, without meaning, to ask what was before the initial nanoseconds of the "bang." There was nothing. Nothingness excludes temporality. Time and the coming into being of being are quintessentially one (exactly as Saint Augustine taught). The present of the verb "to be," the first "is," creates and is created by the fact of existence. Though the conditions of "strangeness" and "singularity"—terms that reach as probingly into metaphysics or poetics as they do into the physics of cosmology—during the initial particle of time may still escape our computations, late-twentieth-century science is now "within three seconds" of the start of this universe. The creation-story can be told as never before.

In this story, the evolution of organic life comes late. Here also the energies of insight press on origination. The question as to the origin and evolution of self-replicating molecular structures occupies palaeontology, biochemistry, physical chemistry, and genetics. Life-forms more and more rudimentary, nearer and nearer to the threshold of the inorganic, are being discovered or modelled. The study of DNA (where the double helix is itself an icon of the spiralling pattern in today's sciences and systems of sensibility) leads back to the inception of ordered vitality, of the encoding of developmental possibilities. This "re-duction" or leading backward in the etymological sense has brought with it the likelihood that genetic material, capable of self-reproduction, will be created in the laboratory. The Adamic act, the making of the Golem are rationally conceivable. I will, in this study come back to what could prove to be not only a new chapter, but a change of language in the grammars of creation.

THE QUEST for point zero in astrophysics, for the ultimate foundation of organic life in molecular biology, has its counterpart in the investigations of the human psyche. Freud himself privileged the comparison with archaeology, with the methodical excavation of successive strata of consciousness. Depth psychology, in the Jungian programme, seeks to go even deeper. Its image could be that of probes into those marine trenches in the ocean floor, vents into the final deeps in whose turbulent volcanic heat emerge anaerobic life-forms and proto-organic shapes. We sense that the pre-history of the first person singular, of the organization of the ego, must have been long and conflictual. Autism and schizophrenia, as we now know them, may well be vestiges of this uncertain evolution, markers of a complex beginning as are background-radiations in cosmology. Myths are replete with motifs which point towards the prolonged opaqueness of the individual self to itself, to the fragility and terror of the borderlines to be drawn between the "I" and the other. In progressive interplay, neurophysiology, genetics, neurochemistry, the study of artificial intelligence and psychology, analytic and clinical, are

edging towards the earliest sediments of mental being. The sub-
conscious, even, conceivably, the outlying regions of the unconscious—of that first long night in us—is being drawn towards
observation. This rising out of chaos is mimed perfectly in the
celebrated initial chord of Wagner's *Ring*. Whose resonance, simultaneously radiant and ominous, poses the question: As we
comb the deeps, what monsters are we trawling?

To seek out the instauration of human consciousness is to
explore the birth of language. After the ebbing of theological-
mystical paradigms, still functional in Hamann and in Herder
at the close of the eighteenth century, the whole topic of the origins of language becomes suspect. Comparative philology and
the rise of modern linguistics regard the search for a "first language" as more or less fatuous. Meditations on "Adamic speech,"
attempts to discover what tongue would be used by children isolated from society, were the pursuit of cranks. During these past
two decades, the scene has altered dramatically. Anthropology
and ethno-linguistics are arguing for the probable existence not
only of a small number of language-nodes from which all subsequent tongues derive but for the possibility of one *Ur-Sprache,*
that primal speech which positivist linguistics and cultural history had rejected as a fantasm. *Ur,* this untranslatable German
prefix, connoting immensities of retrospection and the location
of an absolute "first" or "prime," is becoming the code-word, the
signature-tune in our new manuals.

Arrestingly, as on a spiral staircase, descent into the past
and the ascent of knowledge meet in ambiguous intimacy. Archaic religious-mythological figurations re-emerge, barely concealed. Marx's 1844 manuscripts infer some catastrophic event
in the genesis of society which provoked the deployment of class-

enmity, of social exploitation and the cash-nexus. In the Freudian legend of the structuring of the human psyche, familial and social relations arise from the primal murder of the father by the horde of his sons. (It is as a master of myth, as a teller of tales latent with secondary stories and extrapolations, that Freud will endure.) In the anthropology of Lévi-Strauss, so direct if recalcitrant an heir to Frazer, the domestication of fire makes man "transgress" into culture; it severs him from nature and impels him towards the solitude of history. Quite obviously, these scenarios of explanation are borrowed from that of Original Sin, of the Fall of Man out of the sphere of innocent grace into that of tragic knowingness or historicity. As we seek out the "lost" beginnings of our universe, of our organicity, of our psychic identity and social context, of our language and historical temporality, this search, this "long day's journey into night" (to borrow the title of one of the representative masterpieces in recent literature), is not neutral. It tells, as Hegel famously taught, of sundown. It adumbrates intuitions of some primal error. It manifests what is, as I have tried to suggest, the most deep-seated of the many crises or revolutions we are experiencing: that of the future tense. The utopian, messianic, positivist-meliorist "futures" presumed, blueprinted in the Western legacy from Plato to Lenin, from the Prophets to Leibniz, may no longer be available to our syntax. We now look back at them. They are monuments for remembrance, as obstinately haunting as Easter Island stone faces, on the journey into our outset. We now remember the futures that were.

In one sense, therefore, this book is an *in memoriam* for lost futures and a stab at understanding their transmutation into something "rich and strange" (though the "richness" is, perhaps, in doubt). In another sense, I want to consider the word and con-

cept "creation" at a moment when Western culture and argument
are so fascinated by origins. "Creation" is cardinal in theology,
in philosophy, in our grasp of art, music, and literature. My inquiry is founded on the assumption that the semantic field of this
word is most active and questionable where religio-mythological
narratives of the origins of the world, in *Genesis,* for example, or
in Plato's *Timaeus,* press upon our attempts to understand the
coming into articulate being of philosophic visions and poetics.
How do stories of the inception of the *Kosmos* relate to those
which recount the birth of the poem, of the work of art or melody?
In what regards are theological, metaphysical, and aesthetic conceptions of conception kindred or divergent? Why is it that Indo-
European languages allow, indeed solicit, the sentence: "God created the universe," whereas they flinch at the sentence: "God
invented the universe"? The intricate play of differentiation and
overlap between "creation" and "invention" has been little explored. Does the eclipse of the messianic infirm the concept of
philosophic and poetic creation even as deconstructive and "post-
modern" theories subvert that of the "creator"? Or, more drasti-
cally: What significance attaches to the notion of the creation of
expressive and executive forms, which we call "art" and, I believe,
"philosophy," if the theological possibility, in the larger sense, is
put in the dustbin (Samuel Beckett's *Endgame* is an allegory of
precisely this question)?

Walter Benjamin dreamt of publishing a book composed entirely of quotations. I lack the necessary originality. Juxtaposed,
quotations take on novel meanings and enter into mutual debate.
Let me cite some of the cairns on a taxing journey. The crux is that
of a query as old as pre-Socratic thought, but given canonic formulation by Leibniz: "Why is there not nothing?" Hegel's reflections on "beginnings" in the *Science of Logic* are indispensable.

He evokes a characteristic "modern discomfort (*Verlegenheit*) in the face of a beginning." Almost disturbingly, Hegel assigns to God alone the "undisputed right to be made a start" (*daß mit ihm der Anfang gemacht werde*). Like the *Odyssey,* of which his analytic process is so often an analogue, Hegel knows that every voyage towards a source is a homecoming. Wherever possible, I want the "makers" to speak for themselves. Paul Celan, in a letter of 1962: "I have never been capable of *inventing.*" What light is thrown on the implicit demarcation by Roman Jakobson's dictum: "Every serious work of art tells of the genesis of its own creation"? Too often, the material I must advert to is forbidding in its stature, in its contempt for parasitic comment or paraphrase. Martin Heidegger's warning is apposite: "to remain small when confronting the secret terror (*geheime Furchtbarkeit*) of the presence of all that is beginning (*Gestalt alles Anfänglichen*)." Spoken in 1941, this monition has a special gravity. What in the world—itself not an altogether transparent idiom—can Schopenhauer have purposed when he affirmed that "were the universe to perish, music would endure"? And throughout, underwriting what I take to be the crucial common ground, Boccaccio in his *Life of Dante:* "I assert that theology and poetry can be said to be almost one and the same thing; indeed I say more: that theology is nothing more than a poem of/on God" (*che la teologia niuna altra cosa è che una poesia di Dio*). To which I would add that philosophic discourse is a music of thought.

3

The magnetic fields around "creation" are exceptionally charged and manifold. No religion lacks a creation-myth. Religion could be defined as a narrative reply to the question of "why there is not nothing," as a structured endeavour to demonstrate that this question cannot elude the contradictory presence within itself of the verb "to be." We have no stories of continuous creation, of undifferentiated eternity. There would, in a strict sense, be no story to be told. It is the postulate of a "singularity," of a beginning in and of time which necessitates the concept of creation. Is this postulate incised in human mentality? Is it impossible for us, at the level of intuitive immediacy, to imagine, to apprehend substantive meaning, existence without origination? Epistemology and the philosophy of mind have made of this a central crux. Thomist and Cartesian faith consider the availability to us of the bare notion of the infinite to be a proof of the presence of God. Subtly, however, these classical models of consciousness insist on the finitude of the infinite so far as we, with our limited reach, are able to reason. It is of our infirm ("fallen") nature that we cannot conceptualize on anything but a formal-mathematical plane, that which has no beginning. *Pace* the ironies of the cosmologist when, like Stephen Hawking, they invoke the nonexistent "mind of God," something at the very roots of our consciousness and of language continues to ask: "What of the hour before the big bang?" Out of which "illegitimate" or childish question—children and grammars of creation are intimately meshed—unfolds the compelling conceit of a first making. Of a first *fiat*. The algorithms of the computer can devise scenarios in which the universe is one of reversible time, of the "unbegun." In their natural state, in natural language, the human intellect and its psychological matrix, possibly to the deepest levels of the pre-conscious, will raise the matter of foundation. A child strains to uncover the facts or myths of birth.

We have no myths, no figurations, of a non-creating deity. As

we shall see, mystical and subversive experiments in thought
have, at certain moments in theology, ascribed to God regrets
over creation, withdrawals from it or the impulse towards annihilation (which is the sombre backdrop to numerous fables of flood
or universal fire). But our definitions of the divine are, not logically but tautologically, at one with the attribute of creativity. Numerous divines and metaphysicians have gone so far as to discern
in the absolute equivalence between God and the act of creation
the sole constraint on God's freedom. He cannot but create. He
is, by self-definition, *le Grand Commenceur* (René Char). A sterile God, one who would not, in Hegelian idiom, negate negation,
would be worse than a sinister absurdity: He would be a final
aporia, this is to say a non-sense, an irresolvable scandal in logic.
(The "tiredness" of the Prime Mover *after* the labours of creation
is another matter. Kafka felt it in his bones.)

Prior to Kant, the line between theological and philosophical
discourse is fluid.[1] Both these extravagantly human enterprises
have the same root. Human beings are persuaded that the totality
of sensory-empirical data such as observation, the sciences and
rational analysis which can assemble and order them, is not the
whole story. Or, in Wittgenstein's aphorism: that the facts of the
world are not, will never be, "the end of the matter." This persuasion, held at an intuitive core by, one suspects, the great majority
of mankind even in a scientific and technocratic age, is the begetter of our culture. It animates, literally, the fragile fabric of our
identity which, in other respects and, again literally, is bestial.

1. The Kantian demarcation may have prevailed only till Husserl. Consider
the two philosophic presences which were most marked in the mid-1990s: Heidegger's ontology is grounded in a constant "keeping at bay" of the theological.
Lévinas fuses both modes of discourse.

The intuition—is it something deeper than even that?—the conjecture, so strangely resistant to falsification, that there is "otherness" out of reach gives to our elemental existence its pulse of unfulfilment. We are the creatures of a great thirst. Bent on coming home to a place we have never known. The "irrationality" of the transcendental intuition dignifies reason. The will to ascension is founded not on any "because it is there" but on a "because it is not there." This pragmatic negation can be, has been read in many ways. "Because it is not *yet* there" has, as we have seen, been the postulate of the messianic and the utopian. "Because it is no longer there" serves as axiom for religious, historicist, and socio-psychological models of the human condition. The negation is brimful with different, sometimes antithetical allegories of time and of the sense of history. But it does not inhibit, let alone end-stop our unrest. More than *homo sapiens,* we are *homo quaerens,* the animal that asks and asks. This crowds the borders of language and of image (does music alone appear to cross these borders?) in the conviction, eloquent or inchoate, metaphysically arcane or as immediate as the cry of a child, that there is "the other," the "out there." The Latin adverbs *aliter* and *aliunde* help. As does the persona of "the Stranger" as we shall meet him in Scripture, in Plato, in the poets and painters. Prophets, epic singers, are blind, argues tradition, because they are so certain of the nearness of light.

Thus in philosophy, no less than in theology or poetics, the beginning of the story is also the story of the beginning. At its outset, a philosophy is an ontological narration, this is to say an account of how being originates. The pre-Socratic cosmologies are fables of reason. Illuminated by astonishment, the pre-Socratics—so vivid in twentieth-century thought—put forward disputatious myths of physics to account for the birth and architecture of reality ("fire," "water," the kneading of earth, the pregnant interplay of light and dark). But the metaphysical fascination with creation persists. The Platonic inquiry into man and the city of man has its foundations in his account of the making of the world as it is set out in the *Timaeus*. Even in its logic, Aristotelianism postulates a Prime Mover—one, himself motionless, who sets in movement the clock-work of being. It is this postulate which, decisively, reconciles Augustinian and Thomist Christianity to their pagan sources. Kant dwells on "first and last things." The *élan* of creativity is Bergson's main concern. In the Deism, more or less duplicitous and Aesopian, of the Enlightenment, the "architect" is reduced to being an "engineer." Frankly materialist-mechanistic cosmologies and biologies, after Comte and Darwin, would exorcise the spectre of creation altogether. We saw that it is now renascent from within these sciences themselves. They too ask: "What gives 'life' to life?" (as does Hofmannsthal in his *Death of Titian: "Indes er so dem Leben Leben gab?"*).

It may be that the arts, like theology and philosophy, are in essence an attempt at an answer.

In its aesthetic context, "creation" is under incessant pressure of neighbouring religious and philosophical values. The semantic fields overlap and interfere. A threefold etymological provenance complicates the lexicon. In the Torah, the vocabulary of creation, of shaping (on the potter's wheel), of causing to be, is obviously pivotal. In Greek, the denotative and connotative sphere of *poieō* and of its desiderate *poiēseō* is exceptionally dense. It embraces immediacies of action and complex causality, material fabrication, and poetic license. Much in this constellation remains to be fully understood. Latin *creatio* is grounded in biology and in politics: in the engendering of children and the appointment of magistrates. Among the thirty principal branches of meaning which the *Oxford Latin Dictionary* ascribes to *facio*, that of the poetic relates, strikingly, to the import of Greek literature (as in Terence's warning: *ex Graecis bonis Latinas fecit non bonas*, or in Cicero's tribute: *Sophocles ad summam senectutem tragoedias fecit*). *Invenio*, with *inventio* and *inventor*, "brush up" against the poetic as in Statius' *auctor et inventorque*, as does the rare *inceptor*. Characteristically, the Roman focus is on material, civic, legislative, architectural "finding" and "devising." Our concern will be *fingere*, that formidably polysemic verb, with its unsteady moral aura, which reaches English in the humble but highly suggestive form *dough*. The *fictor* is indeed an attendant on priestly rituals; he kneads the sacred offering. But he is also Daedalus, maker of images. In their self-sufficient strengths, Hebrew, Greek, and Latin at once defy and demand reciprocal transfer. An argument on grammars of creation originates, so far as our Western inheritance goes, in the intensities and inadequacies of linguistic-semantic exchange between the three tongues.

We shall see how naturally but how uncomfortably the makers of poetry and of art, but also of metaphysical systems, relate their making to the divine precedent. This presumption of affinity extends all the way from the sense of facsimile in the painter of icons to the "counter-creativity," to the "God-provocation" in the family of romantic and modern Prometheans. I hope to show correlations between the eclipse of the messianic and the "recession into empty phrasing" of "God" on the one hand and the evolution of non-representational and aleatory art forms on the other. Deconstruction, in today's critical theories of meaning, is exactly that: an "un-building" of those classical models of meaning which assumed the existence of a precedent *auctoritas,* of a master-builder. There are in Derridean deconstruction neither "fathers" nor beginnings.

Where aesthetic modes of making are at issue, the concept of creation is simultaneously unavoidable and vexatious. A rigorous understanding of *mimesis* (as in Plato's *Republic*), a strict reading of *imitatio* (as in certain Neo-classicists and extreme realists) knows only of "re-creation." Observe the pejorative inflection of this term towards playfulness, towards an interruption of serious activity. The artist "re-counts," he inventories the extant. Messiaen will insist that the dynamics of his music are a mere transcription of bird-song and of the "noises" put into physical nature by the Deity. Yet the counter-pulse of creation in the direct sense, of origination, is insistent. It is as old as the earliest epic singers and Pindar. The mirror held up to the world and to the life of human consciousness is a "making mirror." The paradox of creative reflexion could arise from distortion, from fertile optical "impurities" (on the physiological level, such claims are made to account for the "distortions" in El Greco). Art may be an incapacity to see the world as it is, an evasion sometimes pathological, sometimes merely infantile, of the "reality principle" (so Freud). Perhaps artistic fantasy only re-combines, makes a mosaic of, juxtaposes via montage and collage what is already there. A human head or trunk are set on a horse's body. Has any painter invented a new colour? Even the most anarchic (the word means "un-begun") of twentieth-century surrealist or non-objective artifacts re-combine, dis-order deliberately in space or in time, shapes, materials, acoustic elements selected from what is available to our sensory perception. No art form, it can be argued, comes out of nothing. Always, it comes *after.* Modernism can be defined as an exasperation with this cruel fact of posteriority. Ezra Pound bids poets and artists "make it new." An oedipal revolt against the "father"—in this case the given world—is as vital in aesthetic modernity as it is in psychoanalytic theory and deconstructive play.

Music is the problem. Above levels of rudimentary imitation and tone-painting—the song of the lark, the thunder of the sea—it denies similitude. It is "like nothing else." In what ways is the invention, if it is that, of a melody the "supreme mystery in the sciences of man" (Claude Lévi-Strauss)? But there are points at which the bearing of creation or invention on speech-acts, on literary language, is of comparable obscurity. There are poets (certain Dadaists and Russian futurists, for example) who have quite simply tried to fabricate new languages, only to find that the imagined syntax led back to established moulds. The great acts of metaphoric connection, of novel psychological insight, of seemingly unprecedented plots are, in some sense, original. They do alter what came before and what will follow. But are they creations in the radical meaning of the word? Science fiction plays with the notion of an ultimate computer which would contain within its programmes the combinatorial totalities of all subsequent making and finding. Such a computer would be another name for "God." The creation of the cosmos would be the only act, the absolute singularity, of authentic creativity. From God's point of view, human making and discoveries would be nothing more than re-cognitions and *déjà vu*. Tautologically, only God creates. But has He done so only once? The Kabbalah and today's astrophysics conjoin in speculating on a plurality of universes, either sequential or concurrent. Might He tire of this particular edifice in order either to construe another or to return to the inconceiv-

able unity within Himself pondered by mystics? Wherever it ob-
trudes, the verb "create" is uniquely resonant and unsettling:

> I will show you
> the underlying that takes no image to itself,
>   cannot be shown or said,
> but weaves in and out of moons and bladderweeds,
>   is all and
>   beyond destruction
>   because created fully in no
>   particular form . . .
>
> (A. R. AMMONS)

4

"Created fully in no particular form": the poet's wording recalls the "without form, and void" of the Authorized Version. The
thought of formless creation is as intractable to common sense
and natural language as are the special states outside the laws
of physics which mathematical theory posits in the interior of
a black hole. Nevertheless, it is as if this intractability mesmer-
izes. In theology, in philosophy, in the arts, and in recent science,
"nothing" and "nothingness"—words already personified in the
mid-sixteenth century—will not be denied.

Negative theology has always acted as a secret sharer. It dwells
on endeavours to conceptualize or, more exactly, to contemplate
unwaveringly, that quintessence of emptiness which results from,
which discloses a withdrawal or absence of God. The vacuum He
leaves behind, like a wake of ultimate non-existence, has a charge
of negativity comparable, in the guise of a naive imagining, to that
of certain "strange" particles energized without mass, in nuclear

physics. Oriental disciplines of meditation focus on absolute vacancy. Western masters of self-suspension, of total mental and psychic concentration have borne witness to touching the void, the "white light" of pure nullity. In the negative theology of Meister Eckhart, the divine abstention from presence, the "now much more in mine absence" of Tyndale's rendering of *Philippians* II,12, is central. Judaic mystical hermeneutics and esoteric traditions invoke the *tehom*, the "abyss of nothingness" which is the Creator's antinomian dwelling-place and the locus of His withdrawal (of His self-withdrawal?). In Judaism, what there is of post-Shoah theodicy, explicitly conjures up the possibility of an absence, of an absenteeism of the Deity so radical as to have "devoured," to have ingested into itself—again like the gravitational plunge into a black hole—the meaning, the legitimacy of life and the world. A ravening vacuum "nihilates" creation.

Early Greek philosophy and cosmology detest nothingness. Parmenides celebrates the identity of thought and being, the noontime of reason and of logic which makes it impossible to "think nothing." The horror of the vacuum is bequeathed by Aristotelian physics to Western science and, by constant simile, to our politics and models of the mind. It is precisely via the occult and mystical traditions, as these shadow orthodoxy and impinge upon it, in Pascal's obsession with the "abyss" for instance, that, long after Plato's *Sophist*, negativity and the problem of "the nothing" re-enter philosophy. Hegelian logic does more than domesticate das *Nichts*, das *Nichtsein*. It points out that the human capacity to predicate "nothing," that the apparent oxymoron in the proposition "there *is* nothing" are indispensable to serious epistemology and to our emancipation from the constraints of the innocently empirical. We will return to Hegel's seminal finding that "the beginning is not a pure nothing, but a non-being 'from which there will be.'" The *incipit*, for Hegel, is the unity of nothing and of being—precisely in that it *is*. Initiation therefore negates a particular negativity, a motion best translated by the French *anéantir, anéantissement* (where a hyphen after the initial 'a' would make emphatic sense). Being and nothingness, as in Sartre's *L'Etre et le néant*, are strictly indissoluble. There is a Hegelian sense, we will meet with it often in poetics, in which "becoming is also a process towards nothingness, towards extinction." *Enstehen* and *Vergehen* are inseparable in the dialectic of being. What defines a true beginning, is "an unfulfilled immediacy which cannot be analysed (*Nichtanalysierbar*)." We must take it to be *"das ganz Leere."* The phrase is elementary yet in some ways untranslatable: it signifies both that which is "wholly empty," and the "wholeness of this emptiness" (Hegel was at home in the legacy of Pietist mysticism).

But it is Heidegger who goes furthest in bending back the contours of ordinary language and rational syntax. In the historical context which is determinant for this study, in the time of the long eclipse of humane hopes and the dislocation of the future tense, Heidegger makes a verb of "nothing": *nichten,* "to nothing." This neologism goes much beyond *Vernichten,* meaning "to destroy." It adumbrates—notions of "shadow" are crucial here—the annihilation of the extant. Particle physics theorizes a nihilating collision between matter and symmetrical anti-matter. The Heideggerian transgression of language is, in some manner, analogous. It probes the abolition of the famous ontological difference between Being itself and that which is (the extant particular). If Being was to "in-gather itself" into a final unity, as in the *tsim-tsum* of the Kabbahlists, there would "be nothing, nothing." Heir to negative theology and exegete of Nietzsche's self-contradictory nihilism, Heidegger persistently circles around this vortex of "zeroness" (our dictionaries lag behind our needs; mathematicians are freer).

The arts glory in creation, in creativity. They would, in Shakespeare's sovereign phrase, "body forth" new, alternative worlds. Failing that, they strive to cram every rift of given reality with their performative means of re-creation and re-presentation. Yet they too have always known the provocation of non-being. "Nothing" and its temporal counterpart "never", thread terribly through *King Lear.* We can reasonably date the end of a classical aesthetics, of a bias towards plenitude, from Mallarmé's play with blankness, with white spaces in textuality (indirectly, Mallarmé drew on Hegel's intuitions of negation). The influence of this play on modernity has been extensive. Active silences are plotted in music. After Kandinsky, painting, often in an explicitly mystical-meditational idiom, seeks the purity of "absolute light."[2] The two virtuosos of abstention, Beckett and Giacometti, pare away towards a zero-point where substance is made shadow (place a Giacometti stick-man or woman against a lit surface) and language is modulated from articulacy to a naked cry, from that naked cry to silence. Minimalism asserts, with Heidegger, that "nothing is never nothing." It has found its theoretical discourse in the "breaks," "erasures," "cracks" (as in a wall) and "disseminations" of deconstruction.

But the underlying issue is there from the start. In the sciences, discovery, theoretical proposal, crucial experimentation are, to be sure, fuelled by individual talent or genius. But there

2. I have tried to show the strengths of this impulse in *Real Presences* (1989).

is in scientific developments an anonymous, collective inertial motion. Had this man or that team not "made the discovery" (a suggestive idiom), another scientist or team would have done so, possibly at almost the same moment. The invention of calculus, of the theory of natural selection, or of the structure of DNA are famous cases in point. Though material possibility, economic and social circumstance, historical openings bear on aesthetic creation, the making of the poem, of the painting, of the sonata remains contingent. In every case, it could *not have been* (we recall Leibniz's overwhelming question). The work of art, of poetics, carries within it, as it were, the scandal of its hazard, the perception of its ontological caprice. There is no logic to its necessity, however imperative the psychic, private motives for its genesis. Makers of art, of music, of literature have experienced this compelling needlessness either as a threat or a liberation. There are sensibilities and forms instinct with the "harsh desire to endure" (Paul Eluard's *dur désir de durer,* with its word-play on the talismanic name of Dürer). There are composers, writers, sculptors, architects maddened by the thought of the ephemeral, by the apprehension that their *opus* is destined for proximate or eventual oblivion. There are those, on the contrary, strangely comforted by the awareness that "it might not have been." Indeed, aesthetics knows of a sentiment of culpability, of radical unease, in the face of the finished product. It is not only that the poem or symphony or canvas might, need, not have been. There is a sense in which it *should* not have been, in which its composition and completion betray, fall desperately short of, the purposed truth or harmony or perfection. Even the most accomplished aesthetic object, it especially, is a derogation from greater potentiality, from an inward design. Virgil wished to destroy the *Aeneid* for its imperfections. Artists have obliterated their own works or found themselves perfectly incapable of looking back on them. Tinguely's "self-destructs," kinetic constructs which shake or incinerate themselves into dust, enact humourously a profound, complex dynamic of guilt and disillusion in serious creativity. The analogue is that of Anaximander's ruling on human existence: "it would be best not to be." Being is, inescapably, compromise.

Hence, as we shall often note, the affinities between the phenomenologies of art and those of the Western treatment of death. Perhaps it is not sleep, as the tag has it, which is brother to death, but art, and music in particular. Essentially expressive of vitality, of the life-force and wonder of creation, the work of art is attended by a twofold shadow: that of its own possible or preferrable inexistence, and that of its disappearance. Unlike science, art, and, I suspect, the metaphysical system with its claims to truth, are at the exact synapse where being at its most vivid—another adjective which incorporates "life"—joins with extinction. What appears to have been Leonardo's knowing choice of condemned techniques and material means for his "Last Supper," long in fact on the threshold of invisibility, exemplifies this juncture. Much in the music which moves us most seems to defy termination and to bring it nearer, to celebrate the inevitable. Kafka to Milena: "No one sings as purely as those who are in the deepest depths of hell: what we think is the song of angels is their song." Is this the only song which *must* be?

Our thoughts and feelings, however, find nothingness and the pressure of non-being difficult to sustain. The Malevich "White on White," the Ad Reinhardt "Black on Black" in our museums of modern art stifle myth. "Chaos Theory" is among the most prominent advances in late-twentieth-century mathematics and natural sciences. In ways utterly emblematic of our moral, political, psychological status at this moment in history, "chaos is come again." But it was there at creation time.

5

The imaging of chaos and of its surging out of nothingness, like a tornado gyrating around a dead stillness, is one of the notable acts of early Hebraic and Hellenic questioning. It will culminate in Book II of *Paradise Lost:*

> The secrets of the hoary deep, a dark
> Illimitable Ocean without bound,
> Without dimension, where length, breadth, and highth,
> And time and place are lost; where eldest Night
> And Chaos, Ancestors of Nature, hold
> Eternal Anarchy, amidst the noise
> Of endless wars, and by confusion stand.

Behind Milton's "Ten thousand fadom deep," behind Satan's quest for "the nearest coast of darkness . . . Bordering on light," lies a prodigal tradition.

In rabbinic exegesis, twenty-six aborted creations are said to precede the one recorded in *Genesis.* Twenty-six drafts, *maquettes,* or rough sketches. These ante-date language. Acceptable creation and its narration would be indivisible. Even further back is true nothingness. Contemplating this ultimate *incomunicado,* one Talmudist, Ben Zoma by name, is reputed to have gone mad. Does some far echo of the Hebrew *tohu-bohu,* meaning "chaos," sound in the name of Mahu, one of the daemonic deities invoked in madness in *Lear?* We have seen *tehom,* the abyss. And there is *hoshek,* the dark pit. What is arresting in Hebraic speculation, and intensely relevant to any philosophic and aesthetic analysis of creation, is the insistence on the agency, on the continuity of primal nothingness. It is not simply "pre-liminary." Its wild appetite for the generation of being and for the re-absorption of being into nullity, continues. The more dynamic the act of creation, the more insidious the "pull," the gravitational negativity of the bereft source. Now emptied, as are man and artist *post coitum,* as is God when He withdraws from His making. Which, we have seen, He can reclaim only by virtue of destruction. The mystical treatise *Zohar* dwells on a verbal ambiguity in the opening verse of Psalm 130. The evident sense, "I have called on You from the depths of the abyss (in which I find myself)" may be erroneous. We can read: "From the depths of the abyss (in which You are) I call on You." Though, strictly considered, unthinkable, the *En Sof* of the Kabbahlists, becomes the root of roots, the font of fonts. The mundane nihilist would forget, would suppress from preconscious witness, the infinite agency *in absentia* of the abyss of God, of that which irradiated the fruitful turbulence of chaos (the "clouds" from which galaxies condense).[3] Precisely as Heidegger posits, after Hegel, there cannot "be Being" without the eclipse, the inward contraction of non-being. But non-being which, according to the mystics, "is so that Being can be," presses on existence as does a vacuum on a membrane.

Art brings vehement confirmation. At the heart of form lies a sadness, a trace of loss. A carving is the death of a stone. More

3. Throughout the above, I am indebted to André Neher, *L'Exil de la parole* (1970); B. Rojtman, *Feu noir sur feu blanc* (1986); and M. Zarader, *La Dette impensée, Heidegger et l'héritage hébraique* (1990).

complexly: form has left a "rent" in the potential of non-being, it has diminished the reservoir of what might have been (truer, more exhaustive of its means). Concomitantly, in ways most difficult to articulate, major art and literature, music most readily, convey to us vestiges of the unformed, of the innocence of their source and raw material. The persistence of the abyss—French allows the epithet *abyssal* and it nominal use—is vitally ambiguous. There is the threat of deconstruction, but also the intimation of a great calm, of a tide whose return will cleanse matter of the separation, of the violence (I will come back to both these aspects) inherent in making. Michelangelo is almost obsessed by this nostalgia for the sleep in the marble prior to the chisel. These are no vaporous paradoxes, but stoic insights perennial to artists and thinkers. Rousseau's summation in *La Nouvelle Héloïse* is lapidary: "such is the nothingness of things human that, except for the Being which exists self-created, there is nothing beautiful except that which does not exist" (*"hors l'Etre existant par lui-même, il n'y a rien de beau que ce qui n'est pas"*). I find that a piercing sentence.

In the Hebraic perspective, creation is a rhetoric, a literal speech-act. As it is in the instauration of a philosophical argument, of a theological or revealed text and in all literature. The making of being is a saying. The *ruah Elohim*, the breath or *pneuma* of the Creator speaks the world. He might have thought it in a single instant (the lightning-flash immediacy of conception of which artists and mathematicians tell). But He spoke creation, and because discourse is sequential in time, the making took six days.[4] Nor does this seminal speech-act cease with the

4. Cf. P. Beauchamp, *Création et séparation* (1969).

first Sabbath. As Psalm 104 teaches, every living being derives its birth from its intake ("inspiration") of God's shaping breath. Why this insistence on the unison of divine creation and divine articulacy? The Judaic answer, today renewed in Lévinas's ethics, is profoundly suggestive. Speech demands a listener and, if possible, a respondent. To whom does God say, in *Genesis* I,26, *naasé adam*— "let us make man"? To His own solitude at the very hour in which that solitude is to be broken by the creation of man-the-listener, of man-the-respondent and gainsayer. In echoing turn, human speech declares its origins in transcendent dialogue. We speak because we were called upon to answer; language is, in the root sense, a "vocation." But again we perceive that it could have been, that it always can be, otherwise. The universe, like the poem or painting or metaphysical treatise, could have stayed pure, mute thought. It can be cancelled and reduced to trackless silence. Artists report works which they have chosen *not* to produce (Keats's "unheard melodies") or which they have destroyed for reasons we will look at later (Gogol burns the second and completing half of *Dead Souls*).

Expression, our "bodying forth" comports grave risks. Both preceding nothingness and internalized visions of perfection resist the violence done to them by the production of actual forms. Every piece of *kitsch*, every opportunistic banality or artistic, poetic failure is proof of the vengeance which intact perfection (in the mind's illumination) would inflict on matter. Are diabolical, in the authentic sense of that adjective, the abuses of poetic instruments for political-barbaric ends, for mere mundane profit, for the systematic vulgarisation of feeling. The violence, moreover, attaches to the separation between the maker and the made. There is, we have noted, a tearing away. Designation, as in Adam's naming of living things, isolates. It ruptures a primordial unity and cohesion. The strangely emphatic "very good" which God awards His making at the close of *Genesis* I—here the Authorized Version is faithful to the Hebrew—tells both of the artist's satisfaction and valediction. The thing made is no longer His. The further the artifact moves from the artist, in time, in the interpretations and uses others make of it, the less reparable it becomes, the less integral to its producer. The Flood stands for the menace of the Maker's second thoughts, for the palette-knife or whitewash in His *atelier*. So do de Chirico's feared visits to museums during which he was prone to pronounce his early canvasses or even recent works which he judged mediocre, to be fakes. The threefold interweaving of creation, of self-mutilation in the process of making, and of the begetter's exile from his works, already debated in the Lurianic Kabbalah, will colour not only Judaic attitudes towards secular arts to this day. It will take on a new fierceness in the late afternoon of certain elements in our culture. It will inform both prologue and afterword.

If the Hebraic reading of creation is a rhetoric, that of ancient Greek cosmogonies is "an erotic." Aetiology and process are, as in the psychoanalytic theory of the creative, libidinal. The etymology of Greek *chaos* is that of a "rent," of a violent "tear" as in a cloth. Of this brusque aperture—the *béance* in deconstruction—matter is born. Nothing "unborn" precedes it. It would seem that archaic Greek lacks any designation of an absolute *ex nihilo*. This lack points to the recurrent unease of Greek poetic and philosophic sensibility when confronting the irrational (also in mathematics) and the verbally unthinkable. Nothingness is, instinctively as it were, made figurative. It assumes the guise of personified Death, of Sleep, of insensate tumult. For Hesiod, existence stands at the threshold between inconceivable, inexpressible non-being and the created. In the Hebraic imagining there are enduring potentialities of "osmosis," of interaction at this boundary. For Hesiod, existence is immutable and *sui generis.* Chaos lies outside grammar and can, in consequence, never be elucidated. But of it are born Earth (*Gaia*) and Eros. Creation becomes procreation, it is the enactment of loving fecundity, of sexual commerce on the cosmic scale. In Aristophanes' *Birds,* teasing use is made of beliefs which seem to derive from Orphic mystery-cults. In black Tartarus, Chaos mates with Eros; from the cosmic egg laid by Chaos come the birds, first among living creatures. Suggestively, there are indications in Neo-Platonic cosmogony that Chaos is male. While remaining, at the same time, unknowable. Two contradictory lines of thought are operative in Greek traditions. The (rejected) intuition of a void prior to being, and the quest for a primal oneness, as in Parmenides, whose parthogenetic self-scission will release the creative powers of Eros. With uneasy tact, Hesiod twice relates the birth of the Muses. It is only through their gifts of remembrance and narration that mortal men can know something of the the birth of the world. But how can the Muses have been witnesses to their own creation? Hence Hesiod's far-reaching intimation that cosmological narratives deal with appearance, even if that appearance is held to be a truthful reflection of the facts. One cannot go back any further than inspiration. Creation and the poetic telling of the story are in some ultimate sense identical. "Where were you when I founded the earth?" asks God of Job. "Who can here declare whence it was born, from where it emanated?" challenges Book X of the *Rig-Veda.* So far as the mortal mind goes, the poem creates its cosmological content in the key of Eros "handsomest among immortal gods" (Hesiod).[5]

A third model is worth noting. Nietzsche cites Luther, inaccurately I suspect, to the effect that the Deity created our universe in a moment of inadvertence, of absent-mindedness. There are aesthetic analogies to this grim pleasantry. There can be suspensions of intentionality in the artistic process. The poet lapses into daydreams or is visited by dreams in sleep. He is "not himself" but entranced by ecstasy—Plato's Ion—or narcotics, as were Coleridge, Nerval, and representative Surrealists. The rhapsode does not will his finest songs: he is their inadvertent medium. In the practise of the *objet trouvé,* perceived, picked up at random—the patches on dank walls which inspire Leonardo, the ready-made, the piece of drift-wood, the suggestive pebble after Duchamp—purpose is absent. Unsolicited lineaments emerge from doodles; automatic writing goes its own way; in aleatory music intentionality is shifted to the executant or to randomness. Elements of pure chance have been included in finished art: the fly caught in the turpentine, the *métro* ticket-stub which peeled off Braque's brush and remained in the collage.

Theologically, the trope of inadvertence leads further. The insinuation of the monstrous into creation could point towards moments of distraction in the divine construction. Blackness would stem not from His absence but His absent-mindedness. Mytholo-

5. The literature is vast. C. Ramnoux's *La Nuit et les Enfants de la Nuit* (1959) and E. Fränkel's *Dichtung und Philosophies des Frühen Griechentums* remain indispensable. Cf. also R. Bragne, "Le récit du commencement" in J.-F. Mattéi ed., *La Naissance de la raison en Grèce* (1990), and B. Deforge, *Le commencement est un dieu* (1990).

gies abound in tales of a single but fatal inattention: eternal life is asked for, but the proviso of youth has been omitted; the child is bathed in magic waters of invulnerability, but the spot by which he is held is overlooked. The characters, the syllables dropped inadvertently by the "printer" of the world—Celan's *Leichenwörter* —are left scattered on the work-shop floor, marring, falsifying the intended sense. Jewish mysticism speculates that a second's lapse from concentration by the scribe to whom God dictated the Torah resulted in the omission of one accent, of one diacritical sign. Through which *erratum* evil seeped into creation. There is a touch not of negation but of divine largesse in Shakespeare's, in Proust's, occasional inattentions: a personage once eliminated reappears, a location is erroneously altered, a professed chronology goes awry. Distracted by something really important, God "lets drop out of His pocket" an unfinished cosmos. It may have been the Deuteronomist in his anxious piety who awarded that "very good" in *Genesis*. What distracted the Maker, who, in Coleridge's terms of enduring interruption, was God's "person from Porlock"?

Imaginings, conceptualizations of primal creation activate a wealth of theological, philosophical, and aesthetic energies. Around "creation" the three fields of discourse advance their overlapping or contrasting claims. In the Western tradition, the most famous of inceptions, that of the Hebrew text of *Genesis*, is fraught with theological, metaphysical, and grammatical uncertainty. Should we read: "When God began to create," or "At the beginning, when God created"? This indeterminacy is beautifully re-enacted in the untranslatability, but also within French, of the opening sentence in Proust's *Recherche*. Very early in our story of the story, theology, philosophical ethics, and aesthetics collide with a violence and depth of consequence as urgent, as unresolved today as they were more than two millennia ago.

6

Crippled by congenital disease, made blind or limbless by hereditary infirmity, begot in drunken rage or uncaring taedium, children have been known to ask their parents: "Why did you force me to be born?"[6] In times of massacre, of wilful torture and deprivation, such as the Shoah, the question pressed on children's lips. And there were, indeed, those who asked out loud. The bitter query came up again among those concerned with the possibility of thermonuclear or bacterial warfare. By what legitimacy do we procreate, do we sentence to a life-span of pain or victimization, beings who have not asked to be? Have they no right of reply? The interrogation of the ontological—"why is there not nothing?"—takes on a metaphysical and moral urgency perhaps new in Western perception. With their in-built focus on predication, on the unargued assertion of existence—almost all verbs and nouns contain the foundational "is" in a more or less manifest form—our grammars make it difficult, even unnatural, to phrase a radical existential negativity. But the reasoned eventuality of the failure of the human enterprise, of the prevalence of injustice, hatred, and violence in the "messianic eclipse," make the doubt inescapable. Would it have been better, as Anaximander states, if we had not been? Or to enlarge on the anthropomorphic, itself so minute in a universe in whose creation we had no

6. The question is put starkly in Yeats's *Purgatory.*

say: Would it have been preferrable if that universe had not come into being?

The issue is that of the nature of being. Normally envisaged as one of miraculous donation and opportunity or, at least, as one of open-ended ambiguities and complexities richly charged with positive consequence, being can also be conceived of as pure terror. Even where "beauty is born," it is, in Yeats's masterly insight, "terrible." Common sense cries out, moreover, that the birth of beauty is not the rule. Being overwhelms us with its blind, wasteful coercion. It is always "in excess." We are driven before it towards personal extinction. The word "Shoah" tells of a wind out of blackness (those "great winds from under the earth" heard by Kafka). We are blown to ash whatever the weight of our hopes or the dignity of our pains. Lévinas, in his unbroken dialogue with Heidegger's celebration of being, argues that only altruism, only the resolve to live for others, can validate and make acceptable the terror of existence. We must transcend being in order to "be with." A noble doctrine, but also an evasion. No self-sacrificial motion, no struggle for reparation, goes to the heart of the question. Is there in creation an enormity of irrelevance so far as human life is concerned? Have we no natural place, no at-homeness in the world, being instead unwelcome guests (as is proposed in Euripides' *Bacchae,* in Shakespeare's *King Lear* and *Timon,* or in the death-watch parables of Beckett)? In the "language-games" of religious faith the question becomes simply this: Does guilt, does some unimaginable irresponsibility attach to God's making? Picture to yourself the slow death of a tortured child.

The arts raise this question in a more modest and tractable way. What are the responsibilities of the maker towards his own product? Not much thought has been given to this topic. Does the artist or poet or composer have an absolute right to lay waste what he has wrought? Intuition suggests that we must discriminate between the destruction of the unfinished, of the rough, of the unpublished, as in the example of Gogol's novel, and that of a work already issued and presented (the de Chirico painting in the public gallery). Yet even here, there are nuances of uncertainty. The *Aeneid* manuscript was taken away from the poet lest he carry out his intention of effacing an imperfect opus. At what level did Kafka will or expect the burning of his unpublished fictions (the bulk of his work) by Max Brod—who decided otherwise? These are limit-cases. The root question is one of answerability, of the creator's obligations towards, responsibilities for, that which he has added to the sum of the world.

Working out of a Marxist-Leninist eschatology, Georg Lukács proclaimed that a thinker and an artist were responsible to the end of time not only for the use to which their compositions might be put, but for the abuse. Lukács had in accusing view both Nietzsche and Wagner. Concomittantly, he asserted that not a single bar in Mozart could ever be harnessed to inhuman purpose. (The point is finely taken: Is it true of the second aria of the Queen of the Night in *The Magic Flute*?) If, argued Lukács, a piece of literature or art or music, if a philosophic system, can be enlisted by political oppression, by commercial mendacity, there must be within the original form a germ of corruption, of untruth. There is in Lukács's edict a salutary exaggeration. The problem raised is real. Throughout history, the arts have been ornamental to barbarism. Plato in Sicily initiates flirtations between high philosophy and political despotism which extend to Sartre and to Heidegger. The commercialization of the aesthetic, its reduction to *kitsch* are among the determinant features of moneyed cultures. Citations from Shakespeare and from Immanuel Kant have been employed to sell soap-powder. A Haydn theme has been used to cadence the launching of a new line in hosiery. Did the text, did the music, in some sense, lend themselves to whoredom? The ironies run deep.

An artist may come to look with embarrassment on the success of work which he knows to be mediocre, whose crafting and making public has betrayed his own intentions or ideals. He may turn with distaste on productions which he has felt compelled to produce under political pressure, in economic need, or in irresistible hopes of mundane acceptance. The pot-boiler, the film-script, the erotic fiction, the official monument or mural, the birthday-ode to the leader, the didactic text at the master's service, may fill the author with revulsion. Frequently, an artist will look back with discomfort on early work; more bitterly, he may gauge, while denying this recognition to others and, in some measure, to himself, the enfeeblement of late inventions. Ibsen explores this dual anguish in *When We Dead Awaken*.

Do such feelings authorize destruction?

Consider the question of a playwright's, of a novelist's dominion over and answerability to the personae he has called into being. Is that dominion boundless or do the "creatures" have certain rights in respect of their creator? Asked in the idiom of positivist logic, the question sounds absurd. Even the most substantive of fictive presences—a Hamlet, a Madame Bovary—is, if you will, nothing more than the imagined consequence of semantic markers on a piece of paper. How can they have claims on their "onlie begetter"? Psychologically and, I believe, epistemologically, it is the positivist model which is deaf. Artists, writers have borne vehement witness to the autonomies, to the resistant substantiation taken on by the figures they are painting or carving, by the characters they are constructing. Pirandello's *Six Characters in Search of an Author* allegorizes this awareness. Tolstoy speaks for numerous writers when he tells his editor of the rebellious, unpredictable conduct of Anna Karenina as she threatens to break the mould of the novel or, at the least, to deflect it altogether from Tolstoy's announced design. Great portraits, those of Ingres, achieve a contradictory simultaneity (they are dialectical): something central about the sitter's inward being is laid bare, but no less vivid is the suggestion of inviolate inwardness, of that which the eye and empathy of the painter has not disclosed. The dramatist, the novelist who tells all communicates knowingness, not knowledge. He ruins in his creation the mystery of independent vitality.

This is especially the case in regard to sexuality. Adult drama or fiction does not lurch into the bedroom. They are not voyeuristic. They do not humiliate, and thus empty of integral life, the men and women they put before us. Their aesthetic ethic is contrary to that of *Romans* 9,20: "Shall the thing formed say to him that formed it, Why hast thou made me thus? Hath not the potter power over the clay, of the same lump to make one vessel unto honour, and another unto dishonour?" Dishonoured, "the thing formed" deadens. It becomes the frenetic "lump" of exhibited eroticism, of totally dissected animality, which populates late twentieth-century literature, theatre, and film. In precise contrast, observe Henry James in the atelier of his notebooks. Even at first, indistinct light, the nascent character, be he man, woman, or child, be he inarticulate or eloquent, is circumscribed by James's scruples, by provisionality, by a refusal to strip naked the buried lineaments of individuality. As he works his clay, James seems to augment, in an enigmatically compensatory technique, both the range of enacted, articulate consciousness in the person depicted, and the weight, the gravity of the opaque, of that which will elude him. In which elision resides the well-spring of the character's "animation" (the soul, *anima*, giving to form the breath of life).

Where this breath is made whirlwind, the relations of creator to created in theology, metaphysics, and the aesthetic are riven together.

Job the Edomite does not cry out for justice. Had he been a Jew, he would have done so. Job the Edomite cries out for sense. He demands that God *make sense* (one of the most unguardedly problematic phrases in the grammars of creation). He demands that God make sense of Himself. Refusing utterly the Augustinian "If you grasp it, it is not God," Job clamours to God to reveal Himself as other than insanely absurd. The unmerited horrors visited on Job open the possibility that the Creator is either feeble — the Satanic can prevail — or childishly capricious and sadistic. As one who does indeed "kill for his sport." That He is, as Karl Barth puts it in his commentary on *Job*, "a God without God." This eventuality, the dissolution into incomprehensible terror of the partner in Job's incessant dialogue, of the God with whom he has had a life-long discourse in the key of reason and of faith, is infinitely worse than Job's afflictions, dire as these are. If the Maker is such as his motiveless torment of his loving servant suggests, then creation itself is in question. Then God is guilty of having created.

In strict logic, Job would, at the start of chapter 3, undo Genesis. "Let the day perish wherein I was born, and the night in which it was said, There is a man child conceived." The *pereat* echoes exactly that in *Jeremiah* 20, 14–18: "Cursed be the day wherein I was born. . . . Cursed by the man who brought tidings to my father, saying, A man child is born unto thee." But in *Job* it is no individual, it is the cosmos which is cursed. The day is to be made darkness, "Let the stars of the twilight thereof be dark," let light go out undoing, un-creating God's primordial *fiat*. In concordance with the archaic Greek aphorism of self-malediction, Job asks why he was born. And having suffered this misfortune, "why did I not give up the ghost when I came out of the belly?" Blessed are "infants which never saw light." Extinction is hideous. Job declares its suffocating blackness. There is no compensation after death. But even nothingness is preferable to survivance in the hands of a meaningless or evil Deity.

Again, Job would deny what Augustine posits in his commentary on the *Psalms:* "I can only say of Him what He is not." Job the Edomite has held God to be not only glorious and merciful, but what matters far more to him: rational, susceptible of being questioned and understood. Now, in his lunatic suffering, Job demands to know the purpose of creation, the intention of the builder. The clay, made abject, turns on the potter. The ash, to invert one of René Char's luminous dicta, challenges the flame. An immense "Why?" surges out of Job. All the philosophical and aesthetic issues I have cited are in desperate play. The universe could not have been: a benediction in comparison with the world of injustice, of unendurable pain, of arbitrary homicide as Job experiences it. It could have been made just, rational, humane, by a supreme craftsman taking pride, bestowing lasting love on his product. By what histrionic vanity could God pronounce "very good" His artifact? When so many vessels "have been made unto dishonour," when the child and the innocent animal are tortured to leisurely death, when starvation rules at the threshold of plenty, when the foetus is blighted with incurable malady? But to repeat: though the complex of justice (theodicy) lies to hand, the Edomite asks first and foremost for a *rationale* of creation, for its reason (*ratio*). As if the piece of music played, simplified so as to mock or drown the cry of the tortured in the police cell or of the dying in the camps could turn on its composer and ask: Why did you make me?

God answers "out of the whirlwind" (I have alluded to the use of that image in the word *Shoah*). This answer takes the form, as we all know, of a barrage of questions. Jahve asks Job the Edomite where he was at the *incipit*, at the dawn-burst of creation. In these questions, the morning stars sing together—as they will in Goethe's transcription in the Prologue to *Faust*—doors are set against the hunger of the sea, the earth has been given measure and the seed made fruitful. Has Job given to the peacock its dazzling plumage, has he clothed the stallion's neck with thunder? "Canst thou draw out leviathan with an hook?" "Hath the rain a father?" The litany of asking deafens. A volcanic god has erupted into inhuman poetry. (I fully believe those who tell us that no translation or paraphrase, not that of Wyclif, of Tyndal, of the Jacobean virtuosos, not Dante's imitations or Goethe's, come anywhere near to the enormousness of the original Hebrew in this text of texts. A sustained magnitude and unparalleled linguistic inventiveness which do raise, at least for me, unsettling perplexities about the authorship. Can a man or woman in any dispensation rationally accessible to the rest of us, have "thought up," have found the language for, *Job*, 38–41, a language which empowers Job to *see* God through an act of hearing?)

All this is familiar terrain, crossed and re-crossed by later parts of Scripture, by exegetic and homiletic commentary, by theological hermeneutics, metaphysical-moral debate and literary study. Many have found Jahve's reply to be nothing of the kind. A "cosmological-zoological-mythological" (Karl Barth) farrago. Claudel rages: "What a disappointment! The Architect promenades us from one level to another of His constructions." In "complacent exhibitionism," God exhibits His successes and his *monstres*. What possible answer is this to the great cry out of "fundamental human innocence"? A racked human being begs for understanding and is processed instead around an art gallery crowded with the fabrications of a self-infatuated, even sarcastic Diaghilev. I use this comparison deliberately. At an immediate level, the speeches out of the whirlwind are an apologia—the most overwhelming that we have—for the doctrine known as "Art for Art." They thunder forth the vision of a cosmic Bayreuth, of life *per se* and of all living forms as parts of a Wagnerian *Gesamtkunstwerk*. This needs underlining.

Job's inquiry is ontological. Beyond Heidegger, it questions the being of Being (*das Sein des Seyns*). Formally, it is epistemological. The Edomite wants to know whether the universe makes sense, whether there is meaning to meaning. The framework of his questioning is explicitly theological. Each of these three categories of discourse has a rich vocabulary and semantic field. But God's answer will have none of them. His reply is that of a *Maître* brandishing the *catalogue raisonné* of his *oeuvre*. Its category is that of the aesthetic. It displays incommensurable design and beauty: the dawn, the stars at morning, the southward stretch of the hawk's wings, the grace of the unicorn. It exhibits shapes of sovereign force: the young lions in their den, the lightning bolt, the "strong place" of the eagle. The arch-craftsman hints at the secrets of his cunning: the springs of the sea, the treasures of the snow. And, most famously, God deploys in stupefying detail Behemoth and the Leviathan, *monstres* as mesmeric, as at home in our nightmares as are those set to roar and raven in the "Jurassic Parks" of our film industry. Like some ultimate Leonardo, the Deity in *Job* promenades us through a gallery of masterpieces, of rough sketches, of enigmatically encoded patterns, of grotesques and anatomies. In sequences and cross-echoes whose delicacy and numbing power, whose prodigality of significance and "indirect lighting" have defied millennia of explication and hermeneutic analysis, God's address to Job comes out of an artist's workshop. Prize exhibits, opus numbers.

Buber argues that creation itself is the only possible reply to Job. "The creation of the world is justice, not a recompensing and compensating justice, but a distributing, a giving justice. . . . The creation itself already means communication between creator and creature." God, so Buber, offers Himself to Job. He is the answer. In his study of *The Holy* (1917), Rudolf Otto comes nearer to the crux. He invokes the strangeness, the "weirdness" of creation, of the forms "made to be." Job's suffering is, on the level of theodicy, unanswerable. God, therefore, relies on something quite different from anything that can be exhaustively rendered in rational concepts, namely on the sheer absolute wondrousness that transcends thought, on the mysterium presented in its pure, non-rational form. What overwhelms the man from Edom is "the downright stupendousness, the wellnigh demonic and wholly incomprehensible character of the eternal creative power." We are meant to be convinced "by the intrinsic value of the incomprehensible—a value inexpressively positive and 'fascinating.' "

These are the tenets of the aesthetic. Of the anarchic, "Neronian" hypertrophy of aesthetic values. Beyond good and evil, beyond reason and social-ethical accountability, rages the drive to create, to engender form. Comeliness, proportionality are not essential criteria. Behemoth and Leviathan incarnate the naked pulse of creation even more faithfully than do the lilies of the field. In the aesthetics of God's non-answering answer to Job, "Art for Art" or, more exactly, "Creation for Creation" displays its enormity, its festive impertinence to humanity. The refusal of creation to justify or explain itself, the refusal of the potter to hold himself accountable to the clay, is implicit in the tautology of the Burning Bush: "I am what I am," or "I am/I am." It explodes in *Job*. God the artist could not contain even within His boundlessness the pressures of creativity. There "is" instead of there being nothing because He is in excess of His solitary being. Wonderfully, the Satan in *Job* suggests the figure of the critic. He is acidly intimate with the Deity as critics too often are with artists. His rôle may have been seminal: Satan may have provoked God into creating. "Show me," narks the critic-theoretician. Once creation lies before him, the Satan seeks out its flaws. He ironizes the Maker's self-satisfaction—that "very good." It is as if Satan sought to touch on some occult fibre of vainglory in Jahve. The best of those created in God's image, Job the true servant, will be tested to breaking-point and left broken. By allowing the Satan to proceed with his sadistic game, God comes close to risking the disclosure of some weakness within His creativity, within His craftsman's exuberance. Blake's engravings hint at such a reading when they match so visibly the features of Job with those of God.

For us, God's aesthetic riposte translates into the unrivalled fact of the text. On its own scale, the *Book of Job* mirrors and communicates to us the wild mystery of original creation, of being when it is made form. Because we have the poem, because it leaves us overwhelmed and mutinous, we are able to experience something of God's choice of the poetic in counter-blast to the challenges of the ontological, the ethical, and the religious. And in itself this experience exalts if it does not console. Nietzsche compacts this duality into a cryptic note set down in the spring of 1888: "Art affirms. Job affirms."

There is, in the genesis of great art and philosophic insight, something "other" or inhuman. The grammars of creation abide our question. Thus the iconoclasm and abstention from fiction which characterize an important part of the Judaic tradition, have their reasons. To make images of the Maker of all images is to touch on elemental forces at once too vast and too a-moral for man's understanding. Certain considered fears in Judaism, in Islam, and in Calvinism would leave the arts of begetting form to God. Platonism and Neo-Platonism are alert to such fears. But they labour to contain them, to humanize by the light of measured intelligibility the turbulence which sprang out of Chaos.

7

It is just because the chaotic and the demonic were so vivid to ancient Greek sensibility that such energies were invested in order. Madness and the legions of the night play a compelling role in Greek myths, in tragic drama, in the Greek view of women and barbarians. At no time is Attic rationalism and pride in mastered modes of personal and civic life imperceptive of the surrounding, always threatening sough of a primordial darkness. Hence the stress on instauration, on the founding of cities, of laws, of techniques, of artistic genres. Hence the Platonic equation, which I have cited, between the beginning and the optimal and that almost compulsive celebration in Greek discourse of daybreak, of the first light tiding towards the meridian. To found, to begin, is to act essentially. Yet even in the dawn of inception, the demonic is not absent.

It is a banality to say that the three semantic fields we are concerned with—the theological or "trans-rational," the philosophical, and the poetic—are conjoined in Plato. But it is this conjunction which affords his profoundly disquieted analyses of the creative their intellectual resonance and drama of feeling.

Scholars take the *Ion* to be early work, but it turns on a paradox which will vex Plato throughout. How can the aesthetic represent, call to persuasive life that of which it possesses no direct, existential knowledge? A painter, wholly ignorant of seamanship, can depict a vessel performing some expert manoeuvre in raging seas. An arrant coward can sing famously of battle. A playwright who has never held public office will put in the mouths of his characters searching perceptions of statecraft. The problem is not only one of illicit cognition, of an evident hiatus between performative competence and representation or mimicry (the crucial concept of *mimesis*). The dilemma is ethical. Enactments in the arts, in fiction, are not only factitious and, in a fundamental sense, illusory. They are irresponsible. Devoid of authentic knowledge of that which it re-creates, the aesthetic plays with reality. The botched painting, the failed drama are, in the strict sense of the word, inconsequential. The pilot who runs his craft onto the rocks, the loser in battle, are answerable even to the point of death. The artist proceeds, in more or less bruised vanity, to his next opus. But this "unknowing" and irresponsibility pertain even to the best, most convincing of poetic acts. The canonic uses of the Homeric epics in Attic schooling offend Plato's criteria of intellectual verity, of civic responsibility and of the transmission of *praxis* which is cardinal to education.

Faced with Socrates' teasing inquisition, Ion the rhapsode readily acknowledges that he is ingnorant, in any substantive way, of the high matters of state and of warfare which he recounts so fetchingly. But it is not his own consciousness which produces masterly rhetoric and pathos. It is the divinely inspired *afflatus*. It is the mantic voice of the Muses, of the *daimonion* which speaks through him. The epic singer is an instrument played on by supernatural forces. The *Ion* is among the earliest and most exemplary formulations of a poetics of inspired immediacy, of a theory of art founded on the notion of the artist as medium. The romantic and the twentieth-century idiom is that of visionary illumination, of formative dreams, of the sub-conscious. But the dynamics are identical: the poet, the composer, the painter are not primary creators. They are Aeolian harps—Coleridge's image—set into vibrant response by psychic impulses whose incipience, whose at first unperceived focus, lie outside conscience ordinance. Technique channels; it does not initiate. Ion's self-presentation, moreover, derives its special claims from the fact that the Greek rhapsode is both "author" and executant, both dramatist, as it were, and actor or mime.

Socrates elicits crucial attitudes. Ion feels himself to be a man "possessed." The eighteenth century will speak of "enthusiasm." Such possession is not gnosis or willed mastery. But it is ecstasy—a standing or being "beside oneself"—a self-surpassing and leap beyond the bounds of the empirical. Shakespeare never visited either Venice or Verona. Yet his "knowledge" of them is of such essence that it is made ours. "It is the god himself who says their saying," suggests Socrates at once ironically and concessively. The enigma of such knowing exasperates Plato who is himself so evidently a dramatist and maker of myths. To borrow from Slavonic reflections on the phenomenon of inspiration, of ignorant wisdom and clairvoyance, Ion may indeed be a "fool," but he is also a "holy fool." His testimony, precisely because ancient Greek epic and lyric poetry is sung, bears directly on the source of music. And it is, in the grammatology of creation, the birth of musical forms—complex musical figures can be "given" to the composer on the instant—which is the constant crux.

Ion is unquestionably demolished by Socrates, though he is scarcely aware of the process. The vanities, the mountebank inside artists and performing "stars" are shown naked. But not altogether. When Socrates makes of himself Ion's spokesman, when he articulates the magnetically transmitted energies of vision which seem to have their origins in the supernatural, a smiling seriousness is manifest. This seriousness will unfold in the *Phaedrus*. What is at stake is nothing less than the endeavour to reclaim for metaphysical inquiry and discourse, for the truth-functions of the dialectic, the status, that sanctity of an inspiration other than pragmatic, attributed to the rhapsode, to the blind seers who give us music and the landscapes of our imaginings. At the key moment in the *Phaedrus,* Socrates covers his head as do prophets and mantic celebrants. He invokes the Muses. He calls upon "that which has been poured into me, through my ears, as into a vessel, from some external source." He becomes as one truly possessed, and the style of whose philosophic address "is not far from the dithyrambic." Socrates knows that his mythopoetic disquisition on the true nature of love—the metaphysical *topos* in its purest form—has a "trans-rational" source and validation. He yields reluctantly to this insight. But if indeed the god has come to possess him, so be it: *tauta theō melései*. A man cannot accede "to the gates of poetry without the madness of the Muses." More disturbingly, access to certain orders of philosophic awareness, perhaps even of mathematical conception— the "flash" of the axiomatic—may also depend on some degree of possession. The theme is not one of irrationality. The lineaments of reasoned persuasion are sinewy in Socrates' argument on eros. Rather, what is at issue is the tempering of abstraction and dialectic through a moral vivacity whose voice is poetic, which, in its complex fusion, transcends analytic paraphrase. Commenting on the *Phaedrus,* Simone Weil speaks of God "seeking out man." This search, this pouring into the vessel, "is a downward movement that is weightless."

The doctrine of the immortality of the soul is central to the *Phaedrus.* It entails, in simple logic, the potential of inspiration from beyond the material or empirical circumstance. Authentic philosophic thought and responsible aesthetic production draw on sources not wholly under their command. Both are susceptible to seduction: trivial or inebriate art is sophistry. In Plato, morality and the ironies which it inhabits are the necessary insurance, always under pressure, against the corruption or desecration of the inspired. It is the contiguity between the acts of creating in philosophy and in the arts, their uncanny kinship, which makes Plato's quarrel with the poets so uneasy and which will determine in Neo-Platonism and in Neo-Platonic romanticism the attempt to equate truth with beauty, the highest poetry with the highest philosophy (an attempt never altogether convincing or free of rhetoric even in a Novalis or a Keats). No philosopher has been more vulnerably aware than Plato of the poet within himself. Does philosophy, where it is not formal logic, ever achieve real distance from its own performative style? From the insinuation of the "Muses"? Spinoza's meta-mathematical formulations represent the severest attempt we have at autonomy. But they too have their poetry.

Until the early nineteenth century, the *Timaeus* is the most influential and quarried of Platonic dialogues. It relates Hellenism and late antiquity to Islam; Islam to Christianity and Scholasticism. The *Timaeus* is the "Scripture" of Neo-Platonism in its renaissance and baroque versions. The branches of speculative imagining and doctrine centred on this text are manifold and diverse: mathematics, cosmology, astronomy, architecture, music, and the pursuit of harmonic ideals in the political. It is this shared pivot which connects the vision of the state and of universal order in Boethius to Kepler's study of planetary orbits. In the *Timaeus*, the three principal figurations of the unbounded—mathematics, music, and mysticism—are interactive. The strengths of suggestion in this triplicity are such as to make of the dialogue a presence in Western spiritual, intellectual history comparable to that of Holy Writ. Simone Weil's commentary is at once hyperbolic and traditional: the *Timaeus* "resembles no other Platonic dialogue, to so great a degree does it seem to come from 'another place'" (*tellement il semble venir d'ailleurs*). Its teaching is of such depth "that I cannot believe that it descended into human thought otherwise than by virtue of revelation."

Our persistent question, "Why is there not nothing?", takes the form: "Why is there not chaos?" In one sense this is a diminunendo of questioning, a weaker formulation. In another, it allows the analogy between divine creation and that of the artist-architect which is of the essence. The Kosmos of the *Timaeus* is "the fairest of all things." If creation out of the formless (chaos) is equivalent and expressive of causality at its best, it follows that its object is optimal beauty. The identification between that which is cause and that which begets creatively is the meeting point between the logic and the poetic of the creative act. Thus it is not only, as Vlastos emphasizes in his study of *Plato's Universe* (1975), that "the moral sense merges with the aesthetic" (*Kosmos/kosmeo* inhere in our "cosmetic"). It is that true logic is at one with beauty. The criterion is that of mathematics and of the "materialization" of mathematics in music. Though the concept of mathematical beauty, of the beauty which renders one theorem or proof deeper than another, is hardly accessible to the layman, it clearly plays a major part in mathematical thought. The Demiurge of the *Timaeus* is a supreme mathematician-architect who builds to the sound of music. Who sets into vibration that "harmony of the spheres" which will charm the philosophers, poets, and cosmologists from Pythagoras to Kepler and to Leibniz. But what of ugliness? Are we to understand it only as error or privation? In the struggle of the pre-Socratics and of Plato against unreason, against an unmastered universe threatened by distant but undeniable tidal waves of chaos, beauty, and its identification with ordered proportions, are guarantors, radiant and fragile, of man's stabilities of perception. *Ate*, signifying irrational rages, and the remembrance of the chaotic (at moments strangely seductive) always menace the polity of man, his place on the tonal scale of being. Ugliness is to be feared. Plato does not engage with its elemental vitality, with its possible legitimacy.

The Kosmos as we experience it is the Demiurge's "only creation." There is in the *Timaeus* no plurality of worlds as in Giordano Bruno's heresy or in the cosmography of the Enlightenment. The reason is that "the Ideal model is unique, and the world would be more like that model if it too were unique" (Vlastos). For Plato, perfection is oneness. There is no anti-matter on the other side of some black hole. In Hebraic and Christian-apocalyptic cosmogonies, God's omnipotence entails the possibility that He will destroy His creation altogether or start anew. Such an eventuality is alien to the *Timaeus*. The Platonic architect will neither demolish nor alter his design, which enacts the ideal of optimal comeliness. The Kosmos is in no way "work in progress." This counter-Darwinian model can stand for a definition of the classical, for a sensibility of the (immense, even unbounded) finite. A radical dissociation of temperament is at work here. There are minds, perhaps even communities of consciousness and belief, that glory in the limitless. There are, by contrast, those—Plato and Einstein among them—which recoil from the open-ended, from what Hegel calls "bad infinity."

The aesthetic parallel lies close. Art, music, literature know the conceit of the single masterpiece which will include within itself all other potentialities of informed beauty. Ideally, there is a *Gesamtkunstwerk* or the final Book which, in Mallarmé's programme and Borges's parable, contains, is homologous with, the universe. Mythologies of artistic purpose, notably in the romantic era, are obsessed by the theme of the *omnium* (Coleridge), of the *magnum opus* whose intended totality and perfection prove unattainable, in which defeat both the work and the maker are destroyed. Again, by contrast, there are aesthetics of variousness, of the fragmentary, of the deliberately provisional or incomplete (witness Leonardo). We have noted that modernity often prefers the sketch to the finished painting and prizes the draft, chaotic with corrections, to the public text. Such choices would seem to the Plato of the *Timaeus* absurd. Does a sane mind opt for a false algebraic solution when a true one has been found? The *Demiourgos*, the very word means "craftsman," moulds, cuts, splices, forges the raw material spilling out of chaos. He puts on it the stamp of pre-existing Ideal Form. He does not leave behind the litter, the discards of the workshop. As a result, the Platonic Kosmos is itself a clear image of the intelligible. It is, if you will, a god made visible. Its lineaments and articulations are mathematical, where this *mathesis* is simply the rational proposition of perfect beauty. Intelligibility is also made audible. Musical harmonies and the modulation of these harmonies into statecraft, into legislation, make primal creation resonant. Justice is like a musical echo to divine making. In the grammar of creation set out in the *Timaeus*, the word *kalos* signifies that which is beauteous in shape, harmonic when it enters relationships, and ethically admirable. Nowhere have the theological, the metaphysical, and the aesthetic been more intimately joined.

Physicists might call it a "cold fusion." A distinct chill emanates from the *Timaeus*. The Platonic architect is a cubist, a virtuoso of hard edges. His method is that of a Brancusi, without the smile, or of a Mondrian. But the spell of the mathematical, crucial to Plato, has been perennial in the arts. Music is most obviously at home with it. So are certain aesthetic programmes in language (Poe, Valéry). Theologically and philosophically, Spinoza elaborates an axiomatic, an algebraic expression of the transcendent. Beyond any particular instance, moreover, the *Timaeus* compels the question of whether there can be any worthwhile consideration of creation/invention which does not comprise, indeed centrally, the question of the genesis of a mathematical conjecture or proof. This question has been debated since antiquity.

Are the facts and truths of mathematics present in the world independent of human contrivance? Are they, as Plato would have it, eternally "out there"? Can, in Russell's *boutade,* only God have created prime numbers? Or is mathematics an axiomatic deductive system fabricated by the human intellect as is formal logic (of which it might be a branch)? In which case it could, as Goethe propounds, be nothing more than a sequence of tautologies:

> Mathematics has the completely false reputation of yielding infallible conclusions. Its infallibility is nothing but identity. Two times two is not four, but is just two times two, and that is what we call four for short. But four is nothing new at all. And this it goes on and on in its conclusions, except that in the higher formulas the identity fades out of sight.

Others, John Stuart Mill for example, have insisted on the observational, empirical source of mathematical practices and discoveries. However abstruse, mathematics is grounded in the measurement, in the timing, in the classification of natural data and human needs. Tautological, intuitionist, conventionalist, logicist positions have been argued with equal conviction by mathematicians and philosophers of mathematics. The development—a neutral term—of non-Euclidean geometries and of the mathematics of infinity after Cantor gave this debate new impetus. To the layman, it is all but inaccessible.

Yet it so clearly engages the issues of creativity. Of the solution after three centuries of Fermat's last theorem, a contemporary mathematician and philosopher of mathematics has exclaimed: "It is so beautiful that it must be true!" The question as to whether a topologist, a number-theorist, "invents" or "discovers" the next theorem, vividly suggests that of the origin of musical forms, of the inception of melody. Is there in both processes a necessary unfolding of logical postulates, a deployment made inevitable by its formal premisses? The geometry of Euclid, Bach's preludes and fugues communicate this sensation of the inevitable, of a seamless self-definition. At other points, mathematics no less than music conveys a sense of innovation, of the radical leap into the unexpected. The *terra incognita* was not, as it were, waiting to be found by virtue of formal or existential necessity. The object of discovery had to be imagined before it could be made real. As with music and certain kinds of non-representational art, however, the difficulty remains. How does this "making real" by the conceptual leap correspond (if it does) to the external world? Does it add to or, finally, derive from it? Why external reality should obey the rules of logic, why pure mathematics should, so very often, become applicable, is among the deepest of all metaphysical unknowns. We no longer share the certitude of the Neo-Platonists or of Kepler that the music of the spheres—the background radiation in current cosmology—is in the diatonic scale.

It is this uncertainty principle at the foundation of mathematics and of the possible correspondence between the mathematical and the empirical which allows deep-lying congruence between the mathematical and the aesthetic. Both are spaces of freedom, of disinterested play. Mathematics, wrote J. W. N. Sullivan in an admirable text of 1925, is just as 'subjective,' just as much a product of the free creative imagination" as is art. Its revelations of reality are also of a poetic order:

> The significance of mathematics resides precisely in the fact
> that it is an art; by informing us of the nature of our own

minds it informs us of much that depends on our minds.
It does not enable us to explore some remote region of the
eternally existent; it helps to show us how far what exists
depends on the way in which we exist. We are the law-givers
of the universe; it is even possible that we can experience
nothing but what we have created, and that the greatest of
our mathematical creations is the material universe itself.

This view would be wholly unacceptable to the Plato of the
Timaeus, or to Descartes when he postulates God's power to alter,
to invent anew the laws of algebraic geometry. Platonic mathematics is pre-eminent next to philosophy precisely because it invites man to "explore some remote region of the eternally existent." Only the unalterable Forms of the mathematical, which the
Timaeus articulates in essentially geometric-architectural terms,
can teach the human intellect that the divine order of the universe is at once bounded by its own completeness and infinite by
virtue of its everlastingness. If Anselm's proof of the existence
of God is founded on logic, that of the *Timaeus* is based on the
demonstrably mathematical structure and mathematically intelligible order of the world. I referred to a certain chill. But the
(white) light which streams from the mathematical poetics of the
Timaeus has seemed to many incomparable.

8

As always, comparison between Jerusalem and Athens is instructive. The range of Hebraic meditations on creation extends
from archaic, east-Mediterranean myths of an anthropomorphic
cast all the way to paradoxical speculations on inner divisions

within the Deity. The creation-question lies at the heart of kabbahlistic debates on the self-exile of the *En-Sof,* that inward absolute of God which itself is external to creation and to temporality.
An entire ontology of mirroring (the "speculative") and of imaging develops around attempts to articulate, even if only tengen-
tially, the unsayable. The narrative trope of the making of men
and women "in God's image," fundamental to Western aesthetic
theory, generates interpretations and symbolic-hermeneutic variants of the most dramatic and refined sort. But primary to the Old
Testament and Talmudic reading of the necessities and consequences of creation is the notion that God cannot, in some sense,
be Himself if He does not incur the perils of alienation, of contamination entailed by the making of matter and of man. In that
perspective, the answer to Leibniz would be: "there is not nothing because and only because there is God." And Satan's negation
would constitute an endeavour to render God infirm, incomplete
to Himself by corrupting, by making regrettable that which He
has had to create.

As Jewish scholars and thinkers, Lévinas eminently among
them, tirelessly point out, there is in the Torah a theme of inter-
dependence between God and man. Sacrifice is termed "the
bread of God." Anthropomorphic imaginings of a Deity literally
to be nourished shade into subtle hints at a spiritual "feeding of
God" in some sense necessary to Him. In turn, God's acknowledgement of this necessity would correspond to the Self-bestowal
of His presence, to the *kenosis* of His descent towards man (of
which the incarnation in Jesus is the logical extreme).

The Judaic God creates *ex nihilo.* No pre-existent materiality,
be it the wild vacancy of chaos, is conceivable. In another sense,
however, creation is not out of nothingness: it is a necessary ex-

tension of the nature of God which is the realisation of absolute being. That axiom must unfold. As we saw, a thorny conundrum persists: if He is indeed omnipotent, why must He create? Can He, without Self-impairment, abolish His creation or some parts thereof? Could it be that the overmastering impulse towards creativity in God energized negative forces—themselves latent, by definition, in totality? This will be the finding of Gnostic and Manichean representations of the duplicitous texture of the world. In the orthodox view, God within us brightens or fades as does a spinning star in accord with our conduct. The interrelation is exactly that. The creator's emanation into the dust and clay of the human person makes of that person a living soul, a witness to God's authorship (as the pot is witness to the potter). In some rudimentary sense, evil in man makes God "hold His breath." *Isaiah* 63,9 is simultaneously consoling and terrifying: "In all their afflictions He was afflicted." The made throws the shadow of its imperfection, of its corruptibility, on the maker. Thus a true prayer out of the pit of anguish is not so much a prayer *to* God as it is one *for* Him. So that His pain may be lessened (a number of Paul Celan's "counter-Psalms" turn on man's refusal to pray for God after the Shoah). Concomitantly, the torture of a child, of an animal, could unleash pain within God, a condition unfathomable to us but palpable, as are the climatic disorders caused on earth by the great flares that break from the interior of the sun.

Such suppositions take us far away from the master-builder of the *Timaeus*. From Hesiod's or Plato's assumption of a chaos pregnant with subsequent form. Nothing could be further from the mathematic idealism of the Platonic creation-myth than the thought of an ethical bonding between the Demiurge and man.

Availing themselves of the aleatory status of vowels in Hebrew, rabbis have played on *Isaiah* 51,16: "You are My people (*ami ata*)." They have read *imi ata:* "you are with Me" in the actual process of creation. Human thoughts, acts, even words have a continuing function in the quality and persistence of being. The exact aesthetic analogy is what is known today as "reception theory." The viewer, reader, listener is dynamically implicated in the realisation of the work of art. His response and interpretation are essential to its significations. In respect of the Demiurge, all this would strike Plato as obscurantist impertinence. As would Hebraic perceptions, later to be privileged by Slavonic Christendom, into the sacramental rôle of deformity. It is only at certain moments in Euripides that we find the suggestion that human morality and insight into reality principles have outgrown the horizon of the archaic divinities. It is Euripides who intimates the need for men and women to re-create *their* world—social, political, philosophic —not in the image of the ancient gods who sprang from the night, but in that of reasoned hopes and evolving ideals. *"Dieu a besoin des hommes,"* declared Sartre, the most Euripidean of modern writers. He may not have known how close he was to the Torah and how far from the *Timaeus*.

At no point in the development of grammars of creation will the tension between these two codes of vision diminish or prove other than fruitful.

II

Christianity and Islam transmute our terms of reference.

From the tenth to the close of the fifteenth century, Christendom in western Europe propounds, challenges, fine-tunes the two capital concepts of incarnation and of the eucharist.[1] After the Platonic-Aristotelian moment in Greek philosophy, after the Neo-Platonism and Gnosticism of late antiquity, it is the refinement into doctrine of the transubstantiation of the incarnate which marks the third main chapter in the disciplining of Western syntax and conceptualization. Every heading met with in a study of "creation," every nuance of analytic and figural discourse, can be related to arguments on the transubstantiation of remembered flesh and blood into the bread and wine of the sacrament. Incarnation and the eucharist, concepts utterly alien to either Judaic or Hellenic perspectives—though they did, in a sense, arise from the collisions and commerce between them— have distant roots which anthropology and psychoanalysis locate in blood-offerings and ritual cannibalism (the god or his surrogate is sacramentally devoured). At the opposite pole of the great trope, the incarnation of the Father in the Son and the transubstantiation of the body of the Son in the self-donation of the rites of *Corpus Christi* constitute a *mysterium,* an articulated, subtly innervated attempt to reason the irrational at the very highest levels of intellectual pressure. Uniquely, perhaps, the hammering out of the teaching of the eucharist compels Western thought to relate the depth of the unconscious and of pre-history with speculative abstractions at the boundaries of logic and of linguistic philosophy.

1. Cf. the authoritative study by Miri Rubin, *Corpus Christi: The Eucharist in Late Medieval Culture* (1991).

When we speak of analogy, of allegory, of symbolism, of formal and substantive transformations, when we invoke "translation" in the full sense, we adduce, consciously or not, the evolution of these key terms from within the patristic, early medieval and scholastic labours to define, to explain, the perpetually repeated miracle of Holy Communion. When Shakespeare finds "bodying forth" to image the generic presence of content within form, of meaning inside act, he is analogizing directly with (where "to analogize" is also a derivative from the theological) the "real presence" of the incarnate in the eucharist. At every significant point, Western philosophies of art and Western poetics draw their secular idiom from the substratum of Christological debate. Like no other event in our mental history, the postulate of God's *kenosis* through Jesus and of the never-ending availability of the Saviour in the wafer and wine of the eucharist, conditions not only the development of Western art and rhetoric itself, but at a much deeper level, that of our understanding and reception of the truth of art—a truth antithetical to the condemnation of the fictive in Plato.

We shall see that many thinkers and artists have sought to break free of this matrix. That they have found it to be dogmatic, impenetrable to critical intelligence and even repellent. On this latter point, Leopardi and Rimbaud are eloquent. But the very vocabulary of revolt—in the English lineage it goes back to the Lollards and to Wyclif—is knotted to Christian usages. A Lollard claim that Christ's body in the sacrament is nothing more than a "mirror-image of Christ's body in heaven," only displaces the dilemma. What "speculative" analogy, correspondence, dialectic underwrites the transfer? Almost scandalously, twentieth-century grammatologies and phenomenologies of aesthetic creation and of meaningful expression are enmeshed still in the idiom of scholasticism (to a Maritain, to a McLuhan, this meshing was a guarantor). There is little that would have startled Aquinas in the close-argued invocations of epiphany, of the light which shines through shaped matter, central to the theories and practices of Joyce or of Proust. It is the old heresies which revive in the models of absence, of negation or erasure, of the deferral of meaning in late twentieth-century deconstruction. The counter-semantics of the deconstructionist, his refusal to ascribe a stable significance to the sign, are moves familiar to negative theology. We will see that Martin Heidegger's poetics of pure immanence are yet one more attempt to liberate our experience of sense and of form from the grip of the theophanic. It may be that Lorenzo Lotto's "Annunciation" (now at Recanati), in which Mary is shown in bewildered flight from the divine messenger at her back, is the most incisive notation we have on the endeavours of the aesthetic to flee from incarnation. But two millennia are only a brief moment.

The non-specialist is aware only fitfully of the determinant rôle of Islam in the transfer to the West of ancient Greek thought and science. Most of us know even less of the creative pressures, at once collaborative and adversarial, which the spread of Islam brought to bear on medieval Christendom. Heir in a highly selective, combinatorial way to both Abrahamic-Mosaic Judaism and the teachings of Jesus, Islam develops its own philosophies and allegories of creation. These, in turn, connect with an aesthetics of intricate religious-philosophic tenor. The taboo, always only partial and often circumvented, on the representation of the human person attaches to a uniquely subtle aesthetic of the ornament, of the mathematical logic and beauty of the geomet-

ric. Persian and Arab calligraphy are more than suggestive of
algebra (itself, of course, partly of Islamic origin). Centrally, the
strain of iconoclasm in Islamic sensibility and architectural practice underlines the paradox latent in any serious aesthetics after
the Mosaic prohibition on the making of images and after the
Platonic critique of the mimetic. A *malaise* lies near the heart of
re-presentation. Why "double" the natural substance and beauty
of the given world? Why induce illusion in the place of truthful
vision (Freud's "reality principle")? Non-figurative, abstract art is
in no way a modern Western device. As ancillary to the reception
of the figural prodigality of the natural world, it has long been
crucial to Islam. In its formalized borrowings from the shape of
plants, from the geometries of live water, the Islamic ornamental
motif is simultaneously an aid to disciplined observation of the
created and an act of thanks. To borrow a key phrase: the aesthetics of Islam are indeed a "grammar of assent."

More particularly, Islamic mysticism is rich in creation-models
and in speculative presentments of the creative process at the
divine and the angelic levels. These make up one of the most
suggestive and complex theosophies ever thought or dreamt (the
visionary is inseparable from the analytic). In Sūfism, moreover,
the feminine components of the creative are perceived with a conviction only now visible in late twentieth-century Western sentiment. The *Sophia aeterna* revealed to Ibn 'Arabī as the source
of poetic inspiration and as the divine initiatrix of creative love,
takes the form of a young woman.[2] Creation is continuous. Living
beings, the manifold of the world, represent elements of the

2. In all this, I am simply following Henri Corbin, and more particularly his
L'Imagination créatrice dans le Soufisme d'Ibn 'Arabī (1958).

strictly infinite spectrum of possible "extants" in which the Divine Being manifests and essentializes His emanation. It follows that the "other world" already exists in ours (in a very different mode, certain Western and Neo-Platonic poetics will see the arts as embodying lineaments of a neighbouring eternity). In a sense, the formally abstract, recursive ornaments in Islamic art, those coolly interwoven spirals and branchings on the lintels of shrines and houses, signal the pure energy, the unison which, in theophanic exuberance assumes the countless outward guises of the inorganic and organic orders. As do certain kabbahlistic meditations, so Sūfism knows of a "sadness" at the secret source of creation, that of the unrevealed Maker experiencing His own hiddenness. There is prayer and consolation in art which is addressed to Him, however humbly ("If I could do so, I would dedicate this book to God," said Wittgenstein of his *Philosophical Investigations*). Islamic mysticism does not consider a *creatio ex nihilo*. Creation emanates from the potentialities inherent in God's being, a being which radiates "into" the coming into visibility and intelligibility (the epiphany) of all that surrounds us. So long as human productions do not take themselves to be rival to this "shining," let alone to excel it, they are condign responses to and reflections of the divine, primordial imagination. Symbols, which translate sensory data and rational concepts into something "beyond themselves" bridge the gap between creator and created, between the prime Mover and Maker and that which He has, in some sense, allowed to take on autonomous existence outside Himself. Coleridge was more of a Sūfi and disciple of Ibn 'Arabī than he knew.

No essay on the grammars of creation should leave out Islam. My ignorance compels me to do so.

2

We have seen that St. Augustine and today's cosmology rule out the notion of a time prior to creation. As in Heidegger, *Sein* and *Zeit*, are coterminous. Time comes into being. Other theologies and other metaphysics postulate an eternity in which creation occurs. Chaos would have its calendar and nothingness its history. In such a scheme, time would continue after being. In this debate, the temporalities of the work of art pose intriguing questions.

There is a common sense in which any human production, articulate concept, or aesthetic act takes place in time. This time has evident historical, social, and psychological components. Much of art demonstrably depends on contingent factors such as the availability of certain materials, of conventional codes of recognition, of a potential public itself involved in a context of timeliness. Even the most inward of lyric poems arises out of a complex matrix of temporal circumstances and social contours: first and foremost among them, the condition of the language which is always a result of diachronic and collective forces. The untimely, be it archaic or futuristic, plays necessarily against the historicity of the moment in which a thought is emitted or a work created. On the other hand, however, the philosophic construct, the work of art are, or aspire to be, timeless. They lay claim to a status other than that of common chronology. *Aere perennius:* the trope of immortality which has animated literature and art from the time of Pindar and of Horace almost to the present. Certain systematic philosophies have asserted not only the natural everlastingness of their postulates (Descartes) but, more provocatively, the finality of their truths, their capacity to end history. This is, famously, the case of Hegel and, more obliquely, that put in the introductory remarks to Wittgenstein's *Tractatus*. But the issue is not, principally, that of epistemological or rhetorical claims.

There is indeed a sense in which text and art engender a time particular to themselves. Even more than in philosophy, it is through poetics that human consciousness experiences free time. Syntax empowers a multitudinous range of "times." Remembrance, a frozen present, futurities (as in science fiction) are obvious examples of the free play with time without which the epic poem, the universe of narrative fiction or the film would be impossible. At the boundaries of the grammatical, which are always being tested by poetic needs and inventive transgression, time can be negated or held in immobility. Thus the Johannine pericope in which Jesus affirms: "Before Abraham was, I am." Or, on a humbler level, the surrealist and modernist experiments in narrative—analogous to those in particle physics—in which the reel runs backward, reversing time's arrow.

Certain paintings "temporize," generate their own time within time, even beyond the powers of language. Consider Giorgione's "Il Tramonto" or his "Tempest." Observe Watteau's "Le Bal champêtre" or "La Partie quarrée." Such paintings draw us into a time-grid integral wholly to themselves. To say that the landscapes, personae, or motions depicted in them transpire "outside time" is inaccurate. On the contrary: the sense of time's presence, of its *Da-sein*, in the Giorgione composition, in the Watteau grouping, is compelling. But the time shown is not that of the viewer. And the elusive wonder of such paintings stems from the instability they induce in our perceptions, from the need, never satisfied, to renegotiate at each moment the non-correspondence between time in the painting and in the museum hall. How this effect is achieved is a matter which, duly, defies words and analytic decomposition. It is as if, in the Giorgione landscape, time was somehow "spaced." In the Watteau pastorale, the time-sense seems to emerge from the lit air. Even the shadows in Watteau have a logic other than that of mundane sun-dials.

Both these artists often include musicians in their paintings. This component underlines the play with free time. It is a commonplace that the relations to time in music are not only of the essence, but autonomous as in no other human activity. Music has been defined as time organized. Each piece of serious music "takes time out" and makes of it an independent phenomenality. The capacity of music to operate simultaneously along horizontal and vertical axes, to proceed simultaneously in opposite directions (as in inverse canons) may well constitute the nearest that men and women can come to absolute freedom. Music does "keep time" for itself and for us. It sets the chronometer as it chooses. In ways which, again, elude verbal paraphrase, music which is chronometrically rapid can induce feelings of tranquillity, of open time, as it so often does in Mozart, whereas music which is formally slow (those Mahler largos) can build up a stressful thrust and sense of imminent urgency. The proposal that music will be even "after" our universe is effaced (Schopenhauer) may express the intuition that the temporalities within a musical act and structure are independent from those of the biological or the physical laws. We shall see that music appears to relate to death and to the refusal of death as does no other device. The arts, and music above all, give to man the freedom of his otherwise mortal city.

What has been less often thought about are the ways in which the paradox of "timeliness" in the coming and evolution of Christianity have altered the conditions of Western creativity. The paradox is, simply and unfathomably, the ministry and promise of Jesus in a certain moment of history. Why then? Why not before, or after? The Passion, Resurrection, and soteriological promise they entail (that of salvation) divide human time, i.e., history. They also set an end to time, a finite eschatology which is that of the apocalypse and of the entry of the human soul into authentic eternity. No parameter of the temporal is left untouched.

Why labour to produce art and artifacts when our world is nearing its end—an expectation central to early Christianity? Why, even as the Second Coming recedes from imminence, expend time and energy on *mimesis* when individual and collective salvation depends on *imitatio,* on striving to follow Christ and the saints on the road to blessedness? Long after their historical-theological context will have faded, these questions, eschatological and "Puritanical," will retain their resonance in our experiences of art. Even more important are the effects of positive analogy.

I have pointed to the revolutions of sensibility centred on the concepts of an incarnate "God-man" and on his transubstantiation in the mystery of the eucharist. After Christ, the Western perception of flesh and of the metamorphic spirituality of matter alter. The human face and body are seen less as created in God's image—an abstruse, formidably remote trope—than in that of the radiant or tortured Son. It is the cohabitation of radiance with torture, of resplendence with and within abjection, which distinguishes Western perception and representation after the life and Passion of Christ from that of antiquity. A profound revolution of visual and tactile values, of felt signification and nomination also in language, leads from the very earliest depictions of the Man of Sorrows or of compassionate light to the human body and visage in Rembrandt or Van Gogh. The "melting of flesh" both "solid" and "sullied," meaning "soiled"—magnificently, this textual crux in *Hamlet* enfolds an ontology of human presence after Golgotha—or the flaying naked of body and soul when Lear is reduced to a humanity at once minimal and essential, looks back to this same revolution. In Christian civilizations, the habitation of the self in its carnality has been made radical and paradoxical. In the consecration of the blood-wine, spirits are made spirit. The first-person singular, so far as it partakes in Holy Communion, is neither the "I" of Judaism nor the *ego* of classical and pagan antiquity. Today's deconstructions of this transcendent *persona* in the critiques of a Foucault and a Derrida are a logical consequence of the "mopping up" of Christianity.

Embodiment and transubstantiation "thicken" language. This is not a matter of conceptual depth or imaginative immediacy. No texts surpass the *Book of Job* or *Ecclesiastes* or the Prophets. None reach deeper than Aeschylus or Plato. The question is otherwise. Jesus' discourse in parables, his statements of withdrawal from statement—of which the episode in which he writes in the dust and effaces his writing is the emblematic instance—give to linguistic verticality, to the containment of silence in language, a particular impetus. As do the constantly polysemic, stratified techniques of semantic motions in the Pauline *Epistles*. It is these parables and indirect communications, at once more internalized and open-ended than are the codes of classical rhetoric, which beget the seeming contradiction of enigmatic clarity, the *"comprehendit incomprehensible esse"* celebrated in Anselm's *Proslogion*. In turn, from these dramatizations of manifold sense, evolve the instruments of allegory, of analogy, of simile, of tropes and concealments in Western literature (though here also there are obvious and indispensable classical sources). Specifically and, as we saw, counter-Platonically, the status of fictions is theorized and enacted. For Petrarch, it is legal fictions, essential to the discovery of truths in human conflicts and conduct, which validate the general use of the fictive, of the "feigned," in the communication of *veritas*. Aquinas reaches higher. By virtue of the "substantiation" of the supreme mystery of divine presence and agency in outward form (that of the eucharist) man can and must "make sense" of the sensory. The *ingenium* of the artist who shows us imagined and mimetic forms, who makes matter mean, the capacity of the arts and of literature to adduce symbols, renders fiction a *figura veritatis*, a figure and figuration of the truth. It is this semiotic of the symbol which, in Jacques Maritain's telling phrase, makes "realism surreal." It is this materiality of the immaterial argued in the wafer and wine, which endows the particulars of experience and of aesthetic re-presentation with their fictional truth-functions. Gerard Manley Hopkins's sermon of 20th August, 1880, reaches the "heart of the matter" (itself an idiom extraordinarily crowded):

> And when I ask where does all this throng and stack of being, so rich, so distinctive, so important, come from, nothing I can see can answer me . . . For human nature, being more highly pitched, selved, and distinctive from anything in the world, can have been developed, evolved, condensed, from the vastness of the world not anyhow or by the working of common powers but only by one of finer or higher pitch and determination than itself and certainly than any that elsewhere we see, for this power had to force forward the starting or stubborn elements to the one pitch required.

It is precisely this "forcing forward" which, from the early Middle Ages to the Enlightenment, makes Western art, architecture, music, and high literature religious in content and purpose. It is the "pitching" (no one excels Hopkins in evoking the sinewy structures of music) which is functional in our cathedrals, in the numberless medieval and renaissance paintings on holy subjects, in the music of Bach but also of Beethoven. It is this same "forcing forward" which makes secular poetry ambitious of revelation. Which makes Western arts fundamentally metaphoric and "symbolic of." "The achieve of, the mastery of the thing!" in Hopkins's most famous exclamation. Or to summarize: in Western poetics the relations between object and presentment, between "reality" and "fiction" after the Christian message and doctrine of sacramental transmutation, become *iconic.* The poem, the statue, the portrait (the self-portrait most searchingly), the nave tell of, provide lodging for, a real presence. The sentence or pigment or carved stone are shone through. The imagined is an icon, a true fiction. It is, in a definition which circumscribes everything I have been trying to say: a *"fictio rhetorica musicaque composita."*

3

This formulation is offered in the *De vulgari eloquentia.* It is in the spirit and intellect of Dante, more closely than in that of any other Western presence of whom we have certain record, that the three semantic fields of "creation" and "creativity"—the theological, the philosophical, and the poetic—are organically made one. Dante is our meridian. To turn to him is neither academic philology, nor literary criticism nor simple delight, legitimate and fertile as these are. It is to measure with the greatest possible precision the distance from the centre, the length of our current afternoon shadows—though, assuredly, these shadows announce a new and different day, what Dante himself would have called a *vita nuova*. To repeat about Dante what others may have said already, and said better, but in the context of my argument, is a necessity. His "triplicity" informs that argument. For he organizes, makes irreducibly vital, the reciprocities of religious, metaphysical, and aesthetic codes in respect of being and of generation. Dante's apprehension of theology is schooled and profound. No faith is more innervated by thought. He engages with philosophical issues at the highest level of general perception and technicality (Dante was a logician of the intuitive). There is—banality —no greater poet, none in whom the *summa* of knowledge, of imagining, of formal construction is made to reveal itself in language more commensurate to its purpose. Thus any reflection on the intersecting spheres of creation in the religious, metaphysical, and aesthetic senses, is, at one level, a re-reading of Dante.

Observe the creativity of the *Vita nuova* and of the *Commedia* "elementarily." The *Vita nuova* analyses the germination of that novel concept of love and of love's constraints on language which it enacts textually. The *Commedia* aims to encompass within the upwardly mobile potential of human understanding—the *moto spirituale*—the history of creation and the lineaments of the afterlife. The world after the world had been given mythical, which is to say erroneous though poetically inspired, visitation by fables of Olympus and the underworld in ancient literatures. It had, eschatologically, been visited by the risen Christ. But Dante's annexation to consciousness of the Inferno, of Purgatory (unknown to the ancients or to early Christianity) and of Paradise, his demonstration of the myriad connections between "here" and "there," constitutes an act of veritable creation. Compared to which the voyages of late medieval and renaissance navigators are almost promenades. Consider the crux of Dante's creation of that which he discovers: the terrain of Hell, of Purgatory, and of Heaven, so much of which he is the first secular traveller to report on, are also temporal. They are "time-spaces." It is the singular twist of intellectual power within the *Commedia* to map time inside space. The chronology made sensible by the Pilgrim's motion extends from the time before time when God was about to create our universe to that end of time marked by the Last Judgement. If ever there has been a palpably relativistic cosmology it is Dante's: in the three realms of ultra-mundane experience, space-times are bent out of or into meaningful shape by the gravity, literal, of evil or of grace. Time bends into bounded infinities of suffering in the places of damnation. It opens into an infinity of light, without conceivable tedium, in the spheres of blessedness. In Purgatory, the accelerations of time, the time-dimensions which are represented spatially, alter in accord with the progress of the soul towards everlastingness. Only Proust, who is at certain points Dante's heir, can comparably re-create and convey the pull of time on space.

The *Commedia*, manifestly a product of *poiesis* and of energized thought, is at the same time an extended reflection on creativity, on the analogies, fraught in the extreme, between the divine *fiat* and the *ingenium* of man. In its licensed audacity, the epic invents that which is already there. Dante's analytic awareness of the unresolved tensions between his fictive inventiveness and the axiom of revelation—he can only tell us what God and God via Beatrice have intended him to see—is crucial. Here, as in no other secular text, the fiction must be that of truth. This paradox is made

graphic by the early rumour according to which the author of the
Commedia carried on his skin the burn-marks of Hell.

The practice of creation in Dante is formally specific. In his
treatises on the vulgate, in his minutely calibrated explorations
of the limits of the communicable in the *Paradiso,* Dante is programmatically creating a new national language. His choice of
the vulgate for his *Commedia,* his combinatorial and innovative
uses of that as yet dispersed and hesitant tongue, is by itself an
eminent deed of begetting. We know little of the pre-history and
evolution of the special epic idiom in Homer. Dante's instauration of a "vulgar eloquence" and Luther's composition of German
in his Bible translations represent unique acts of linguistic creation, of the giving of speech to a nation and society. There is,
therefore, in Dante's prose and poetry a particular making. Here
the craftsman makes both the tools and matter of his making.

The contrast with Shakespeare is compelling. Yet, to my knowledge, and unsurprisingly, it has never been pressed home. Interpretation of the inmost is possible only among peers—Coleridge
on Wordsworth, Akhmatova on Pushkin, or Auden on Yeats.
There are magnitudes and complexities of vision before which
ordinary scholarship and criticism are lamed. Only the facts can
be made out. Via the organization of the plays themselves and
the pronouncements of certain characters, Shakespeare provides
a definition of the theatre, of the nature of acting and of the stage
which have become canonic (although the underlying trope of the
world being a stage and of life chronicled and compacted in the
mirrors of the theatrical had their long history already). Shakespeare affords unrivalled expression to the belief in the heal-
ing, mind-restoring powers of music and to the identifications of
musicality and eros. These also are traditional insights. The list-

ing of the poet with the lunatic and the lover by Theseus in the *Midsummer Night's Dream* is a long-established jest. We will see that Dante cites and meets with artists and writers intensely individualized. Most strikingly, these are all but non-existent in the teeming catholicity of Shakespeare's cast. The Poet and Painter in *Timon of Athens* are of no weight. I have always wondered whether it is not Feste, in *Twelfth Night*, who, although obliquely, embodies Shakespeare's closest approach to the persona of the artists, whose elusive sadness comes nearest to that which lies at the heart of the creative. Nor is there anywhere in Shakespeare a theorizing discourse on aesthetics, let alone any disclosure of his personal experience of creativity. Intuitively, one looks to the sonnets, the only work of Shakespeare which invites some provisional "nearing" to the compositions of Dante. If anywhere, it is in the sonnets that we would expect windows on the self. There may be in these inexhaustible texts, with their dynamics of a "perpetual in motion," of a grouping and re-grouping at each reading some private sub-text. Sonnet 38, "How can my Muse want subject to invent," teases expectation. The Horatian-Ovidian paraphrase in "Not marble, nor the guilded monument" of Sonnet 55 promises more than it allows. "Why is my verse so barren of new pride?" in 76 turns to a lover's hyperbolic compliment. Some sonnets tell of a "writer's block," others of a rival master. Nowhere is there any sustained reflection on what it is to be Shakespeare, on what it is to be a supreme maker. The constant invocations of the Muse are wholly conventional. There is, it may be, an irony which escapes us in "all my best is dressing old words new," in the admission in this same seventy-sixth sonnet "That every word almost doth tell my name." Is there not a closed world in that "almost"?

The utter contrast with Dante suggests evident reasons. Dante is a considerable figure in the history of Western philosophic theology. He remains a political theorist of the very first rank. We have noted that his explicit commentaries on language, on style, on rhetoric, on allegory represent criticism and semantics at their greatest strength. There are, in the *Paradiso,* sections in which the pressure of metaphysical and epistemological analyses or of a theory of history nearly deflect the lyric motion. Was there ever a consciousness less seduced by theory and by abstraction than Shakespeare's? Was there ever a sensibility more receptive of the manifold disorders and instabilities of human existence, of the energies of unmastered being as they spill over the confines of doctrine or of reason? The abstention from any definable theology in Shakespeare, from any systematic philosophy, has often been observed. It puts off a T. S. Eliot or a Wittgenstein. Every nerve in Dante comes alight when he grapples with a theological mystery, as it does in Marlowe when he dramatizes in *Doctor Faustus* man's limitation of God's capacity to forgive. These are impulses antithetical to Shakespeare's concrete universality, to his observant neutrality in the face of the extant. As in no other witness (Montaigne, perhaps, comes closest), the "I am" in Shakespeare accords with the "it is" of what we call reality.

But there may be in Shakespeare's discretion in respect of the grammars and phenomenology of creation, both religious-philosophical and aesthetic awareness. Imbued with a seemingly limitless gift of self-dissemination, with the power, as it has so often been summarized, of becoming both Iago and Cordelia, Ariel and Caliban, Shakespeare cannot (or is this too a naive misreading?) but have registered an analogy with God. Though we know nothing which would document this perception, it is difficult to believe that the creator of the third and fourth acts of *Lear* or of a substantive fiction such as *Hamlet* did not, be it fitfully, glance at the possible parallels between his own enterprise of "giving life" and that of the First Maker. Tolstoy, a not altogether disparate example, viewed his own shaping might with ambivalence. The begetter of Anna Karenina or of Ivan Ilyitch felt himself to be God's competitor. They were, as he put it, two bears wrestling in the forest. There was immense pride in this sentiment, but also dread.

Dante's creativity is self-enclosed in Christian doctrine. It is, even at its most exalted level, an *imitatio Dei* sanctioned by a Thomist faith in the divinely inspired and epiphanic legitimacy of the poetic imagination. The "true fiction" of the *Commedia* "*continues* creation, 'creates, so to speak, on a second level'" (Maritain). The mere ability of a craftsman to impose order on the recalcitrance of matter and of empirical events tells, as Saint Augustine taught, of the *ordo universi*. Aesthetic success, which is always in some sense "musical" (this is to say "harmonic") makes this "order" and "ordinance" perceptible to human feelings. Shakespeare is buttressed, so far as we can make out, by no such creed. He goes unarmed. Hence the danger to him of any scrutiny too acute, too self-conscious, of the rivalry with God inherent in *poiesis*. Later masters (Flaubert, for instance) are bitterly alert to the paradox of their own death in contrast with the triumphant survivance of their "puppets," of the Emma Bovary born of semantic markers on a page. It is doubtful whether so focused a cry of the ego was in reach of the sensibility of Shakespeare and of his time. Concomittantly, however, God was a formidable presence. Could one, without everlasting peril, match something of His rights and powers of conception, of calling into life? Could one—ultimate blasphemy—in some enigmatic sense surpass these powers? Are there very many living men or women as prodigally put together as are Hamlet or Lady Macbeth or Prospero? Are there very many whose lease of life comes anywhere near that of these "undying" presences? Shakespeare may, most wisely, have chosen not to put the question of creation to himself or to articulate it in his works. Augustinian-Aquinian Dante can and must do so.

Thus Dante provides privileged access to almost the entirety of our theme, whereas Shakespeare's absence from this theme— he is its *deus absconditus*—renders such access problematic. I turn to certain motifs in Dante in the guise of co-ordinates. They will help us locate concepts of creation now lost or forgotten as is Adamic speech. They serve to map what is fruitful still in the received tradition. Working "away from" Dante, we may see contours of the new stories which lie ahead and of the impatient narratives we call theories.

4

Harold Bloom has stressed the "anxiety of influence." He has shown how a creative motion in poetry (in all art) occurs under the instigating, distorting, reactive pressures of the works of predecessors and of contemporaries. Influence is inevitably context. Still to be explored are the ways in which "anxiety" projects forward. There is not only Stendhal's strategy when he postulates the evolution, a hundred years after his own death, of a public proper to his neglected novels (a projection which proved accurate almost to the year). There are the internalized images which writers, composers, or painters devise of those creators who will, in turn, be influenced by their works, for whom these works will be seminal. There are in Goethe, in Joyce numerous and distinctive "foreshadows" of those who will draw on *Faust* or *Ulysses* for their own substance, be it in imitation or counter-play. In rare instances, such as Tolstoy and possibly Kafka (at some moments), we find the projection of a negative futurity. May the time come when the work will *not* be read, because mankind will have left behind certain tragic absurdities or desires. This too is an "anxiety of influence."

Less noticed—and this difference is characteristic of our bleak climate—is the crucially collaborative nature of *poiesis*. It is not actual historical collaboration I have in mind, that between a Goethe and a Schiller, between a Brahms and a Schumann, between fellow-Impressionists, important as it is. Rather, I want to point to the elected presences which makers construe within themselves or within their works, to the "fellow-travellers," teachers, critics, dialectical partners, to those other voices within their own which can give to even the most complexly solitary and innovative of creative acts a shared, collective fabric. Elsewhere,[3] I have tried to draw attention to what remains a *terra incognita* in linguistics, in poetics, in epistemology (Husserl being the exception). It is that of inward speech, of the discourse we conduct incessantly with ourselves. This unvoiced soliloquy in fact contains the bulk of speech-acts; it far exceeds in volume language used for outward communication. It also, I suspect, is under formative or inhibiting pressures of historical-social circumstance, of the state of public vocabularies and grammars, though it may add to them elements of a private argot. It could well be that, in Western cul-

3. Cf. *On Difficulty* (1978).

tures until recently, soliloquy has been the unheard eloquence, vituperation, poetry of countless women. Our true familiars are the "selves" or fantom-auditors and respondents to whom we address the lexical-grammatical-semantic currents of silent speech. Our consciousness, even when our inward audition and notice are fitful, is a monologue of the many whose creative powers, whose capacity to generate terror or solace, illusion or inhibition, are as yet scarcely analysed.

The ontological aloneness of the creative moment, the "autism" of the poet and artist is, one suspects, populous. The "other" in whose presence the writer or composer works is, time and again, a more or less imaged God. He is the "onlie begetter" and patron of the work. He is, moreover, the only just judge: "The only just judge, the only just literary critic, is Christ, who prizes, is proud of, and admires, more than any man, more than the receiver himself can, the gifts of his own making" (Hopkins to R. W. Dixon on 13th June, 1878). He is also, as we already mentioned, the rival, the jealous archetype who does not wish to see His own virtuosity challenged, let alone excelled. Or the iconoclast, disfavourable to the very enterprise of mimesis and fiction. Van Gogh's letters tell of numbing encounters with a God inimical to the "luxury" ("luxuriousness" lies too close for comfort) of art. But the "other" can be less awesome. He or she will be the dead or the living master whom the artist has invited into his internal work-shop: the qualified witnesses to his own intent and craftsmanship, the creative critic of his project, the partisan of his aesthetic cause. If we recall its fictive, "dreamt" foundation, Courbet's great painting of his crowded *atelier*, with Baudelaire self-absorbed yet indispensably "there" at the edge, is allegoric of the necessary hospitality of art, of the silent crowd within its egotism.

Rivalry is a donation, a dialogue of generosity. Master artists and craftsmen pace one another as do great runners. Hence the constellations of creativity—in Periclean Athens, in Augustan Rome, in the England of Elizabeth, in neo-classical France, in the Vienna of Haydn, Mozart, Beethoven, and Schubert—which mark the history of the arts. Here influence is not primarily "anxiety" but collaboration. Fascinatingly, a poet or painter or composer can issue his invitations without regard to chronology. It is often earlier masters whom he makes his decisive inner contemporaries (as Borges says: Homer now comes after Joyce). Picasso harnesses Velásquez and Manet into intimate participation. And, as we saw, there are summonings out of the future. Seeking to break free of the conventions or material limitations of his own age, a creative artist will conjure up a successor, possibly distant in time, who will fulfil his purpose. Where it is most original, most complete to our understanding, art is alive with annunciation. There are stronger truths to come (the music of Liszt's final period forces into being that of Bartók and Boulez).

The Dante corpus contains early lyrics whose authorship remains uncertain. So seamless was the unison between Dante and fellow-practitioners of the "new style." In the *Vita nuova*, much of the poetry is in dialogue with, in challenge to other technicians of the sonnet or the satiric vignette. Actual lines and rhyme-patterns are exchanged. But it is the *Commedia* which sounds in depth the modulations of collaborative *poiesis*. The voyage is crowded with artists. There are musicians and painters such as Cimabue and Giotto. (A single contemporary artist is named in the whole of Shakespeare's writings: the oddly chosen Gulio Romano at the close of the *Winter's Tale*.) Above all, it is poets, epic, philosophic, lyric, whom Dante implicates directly in the introspective process of his own making. Only Proust will rival Dante in this confident enrollment of great writers, composers, and painters, "real" and fictive, in his *dramatis personae*. Such enrollment declares an impassioned prodigality of the self, a pulse of creativity so vehement that it requires the representation of echo, its mirroring in others comparably creative (the "other" can be the long sequence of self-portraits as in Rembrandt). Thus the Pilgrim's exchanges with the other masters whom Dante elicits, as it were, from the manifold of his choral monologue, dramatize, analyze in exact nuance, every mode of relationship to predecessors and contemporaries as these are gathered into the fact-fiction of the creative self.

There are, we will see, "anxieties" in this reticulation, in this shadow-theatre of encounters. But far more there are celebrations of the enigma of shared origination. Only the Aristotelian deity engenders alone. Only God's self-address is, *stricto sensu,* a monologue. That of even the most "original" artists, taking this word at full strength, is polyphonic. Other voices urge the disequilibrium, the loss of sterile poise, which triggers imagining into motion. By these voices, analytic thought is made homeless to itself. It seeks to inhabit alternative forms. Aquinas defined ghosts as energized particles that had broken loose from the governance of the ego. It is, I believe, only this polyphony which throws any light on the paradox of signed anonymity, of the collectivity of the singular in great art, music, and literature. This search for alternative incarnations, whatever the unease at its source, whatever the soul's errancy in that "dark wood," is one of love at high risk. The grammars of creation are, in the final analysis, those of the erotic, of the shaping intellect and psyche in a condition of eros (the *Logos* in the arms of love, as R. P. Blackmur said, modelling his insight on the name of an actual basilica in the Abruzzi, San Giovanni in Venere). This understanding is at least as ancient as Plato's *Symposium*. It is enacted in the matter of the Narrator and of Virgil in the *Commedia*.[4]

In most writers, Shakespeare representative among them, the compositional process seems to show no correlations with what we know of the methods of discovery in mathematics. But in some poets (Poe, Valéry, for example), as in musicians, painters, or architects, the affinity to mathematical means and ideals is significant. They feel, they construct *more geometrico*. They bring to bear on the incipience of imaginative forms the ordering of the numerical and the geometric. This division looks to be fundamental. It distinguishes non-mathematical tempers in Western philosophy—a Hegel, a Heidegger—from those the matrix of whose thought is clearly that of mathematical reasoning and proof (Spinoza, Husserl, Wittgenstein). In the mature Dante an arithmetic sensibility is crucial. This is not, primarily, a question of numerology, although numerology is as important in the *Commedia* as it is in much of medieval and renaissance epic verse. It is a way, at once instinctive and elaborately willed, of disposing argument and narrative along numerical axes and in measured proportions. Inverse proportions govern the number of citations from Scripture and from Virgil. The holy word is quoted twice only in *Inferno*, eight times in the *Purgatorio*, and twelve times in the sanctified ambience of the *Paradiso*. Here a direct translation from the now absent Virgil occurs once only, as contrasted with seven such translations in Hell and five in Purgatory. A simi-

---

4. The literature is voluminous. For a recent study, cf. R. Jacoff and J. T. Schnapp, eds., *The Poetry of Allusion: Virgil and Ovid in Dante's "Commedia"* (1991).

larly graduated *diminuendo* organizes the one hundred and forty echoes of, derivations from, Virgil's works in the *Commedia*. These decrease as the Pilgrim ascends. But in an ultimate *ricorso,* as we shall see, the final canto of the *Paradiso* contains three explicit allusions to Virgil, where this threefold recall takes its august place within the trinitarian algorithm, within the sacred triplicities of the formal-theological design. (There is, of course, a trinitarian "phonetic" in the very name of Bea*tri*ce.)

Homer figures fleetingly as the blind street-singer whom Leopold Bloom hears when he leaves the Sirens in Joyce's *Ulysses*. In *Lotte in Weimar,* Thomas Mann re-creates the Goethe on whom he so consciously modelled his own development as writer and "Olympian" sage. Echoing Joyce's echoing, Derek Walcott meets with the Omeros of his saga, with the blind beggar and his dog out of a Caribbean Ithaka. Dante's relation to the Virgil of the *Commedia* is of an altogether different order of density and necessity. One says "Dante," forgetting the live intricacy of the triangulation which connects Dante Alighieri—the actual name "Dante" is used only once in the entire epic—with the narrating "I" and with the *persona* of the Pilgrim, speaking, feeling in his own substance and seen, as it were, as a third-person singular from without. Yet again, I see a veritable analogy only in the inwoven spiral which relates Proust to the *je* of the narrator. Dante chooses Virgil, but the Pilgrim is chosen by the author of the *Aeneid* at Beatrice's behest. Ordinarily, we speak language, though it is, neurophysiologically and historical-socially given to us. The true poet is spoken by language. He is its medium, elected, so to speak, for his osmotic, permeable nature, for what Keats called his "negative capability." Before being ours, the act of reception is that of the artist-maker. Supernatural dictation, which defines the biblical claim to a revealed authority, and invocations of the Muse in Western art, music, and literature, are encodings of this receptivity. Though crude, the symbolic polarization into a primary feminity of reception, of vulnerability to radiant dominance, followed by a masculine process of appropriation and voluntary shaping and mastery, is suggestive. The roots of *poiesis* reach deep into the androgynous, into the lost unison of male and female in Plato's anthropology. Together with numerous other levels—technical perfection and apprenticeship, safeguard and submission thereto, age and relative youth, the classical and the modern, the pagan and the Christian—the interplay between masculine rivalry and alliance on the one hand and feminine donation or need on the other, colours the relations between Guide and Pilgrim. As it does those between the creative self and its inward familiars in the act of art. And, as so often, the tensions to come are latent in the instant of the *incipit*, in the first light of the creative happening and naming of names.

Dante's recourse to Virgil was, in modern jargon, overdetermined. Virgil had been present to the Church Fathers. An aura of magic and of prophecy surrounded his name in the early Middle Ages. Two texts above all, the Fourth Eclogue and Anchises' oration in Book VI of the *Aeneid*, exercised Christian thought. They were read to be an actual prevision of the birth of Christ and of a renovation of human history towards its eschatological culmination.[5] St. Jerome had warned against such wishful interpretation. But from Augustine to Abelard, the prevailing view had been one of affirmative wonder. Touched by premonitory grace, by some

5. Cf. Pierre Courcelle, "Les Exégèses Chrétiennes de la Quatrième Églogue" in *Opuscula Selecta* (1984).

auroral intimation, Virgil had, together with a handful of other pagan spirits, the Sybil at Cumae among them, foreseen the rebirth of time via the miraculous birth of the Child. Countless homilies and sermons paraphrased, cited, embroidered on the annunciation in the Eclogue (often interweaving Virgil's words with those of Isaiah on "virgin"-birth): *"Multis enim ante nuntiabatur nova coelo uentura progenies."* In consequence, Virgil was not only to Dante the supreme master of epic verse and begetter of a truly national, foundational text, but a sage mysteriously illumined. His was the touchstone for the congruence of the poetic and the philosophic disciplines of creation with the theological. Hence the emphasis on symbiosis in the Pilgrim's salutation to his guide at the end of the second canto of the *Inferno:*

> "Or va, ch'un sol volere è d'ambedue:
> tu duca, tu segnore e tu maestro."

The poet's consciousness strives to achieve perfect unison with that of the predecessor elect who is both historically autonomous and, now, reborn from within. A "renascence" which Virgil's bucolic poetry, itself engendered by Greek pastorale but leaping forward towards a stage of blessed clairvoyance, precisely exemplifies.

Yet how incisively Virgil's status is qualified when the Pilgrim turns to him at their very first meeting in canto one: *"per quello Dio che tu non conoscesti,* "by that God whom you did not know" — a line prepared for by Virgil's own bitter admission that he will not enter God's realm, having lived outside its law. These initial equivocations set in motion one of the most moving, complex enactments of relationship, technical, philosophical, theological in literature. Every nuance tells of the ambiguity within concord

(*ambedue*), of the inescapable struggle arising from apprenticeship as it modulates into rivalry and surpassing. Over and again,
the "I" of the journey turns for rescue and enlightenment to "the
sea of all wisdom." The "gentle sage who knows all" must shel-
ter him from the horrors of Hell. However, already at the dramatic finale of the ninth canto, it is an Angel, one *da ciel messo*,"
dispatched from Heaven, who must intercede to keep the dae-
mons at bay. With that intercession begins a delicately probing
deconstruction of Virgil's authority. The *Aeneid* bears witness to
Virgil's visionary, in some degree preternatural, knowledge of the
underworld. But this knowledge pre-dates, is uninstructed by,
Christ's Harrowing of Hell which "breaks" history and time. The
imagined Virgil of the *Commedia*, the respondent to creative immediacy in the monologue of two, acknowledges that when he,
Virgil, came *"nel basso inferno,"* "this rock had not yet fallen." The
author of the *Aeneid* saw Hades before the descent of the Saviour
who, in *Inferno*, is never named directly. His understanding is
uncertain (*se ben discerno*).

We proceed towards a semiotic *dénouement* which has, so far as
I am aware, no matching counterpart in philosophy or literature.
Identifying himself with the Narrator, a concession charged with
psychological risk, with an apparent denial and self-denial of the
poetic, Dante vows to the reader that he is reporting verity. He
swears it (*"ti giuro"*) by that which is most precious to him, namely
the *Commedia* itself. A supreme truth-function authorizes the
poem. This paradox of true invention is intimately grounded in
the transmutation of the nature of truth through divine incarnation in Jesus. The "fabled verities" of the ancients, however excellent in form, are, in the last analysis, mendacious. Or, as in
the exceptional instance of Virgil, only fitfully veritable. The for-

midable crux comes in Canto XX. Pagan seers and mantics, the soothsayers, necromancers and black magicians in Christendom, are consigned to damnation. The *Aeneid* had offered a mythical account of the origins of Virgil's native Mantua. Now, in the deeps of Hell, but under the influence of Beatrice's far nearness, and in a time of truth A.D., Virgil corrects his own epic. The city was not, as he had taught, founded by Ocnus, son of the river Tiber and of Manto the prophetess. It was indeed begun by Manto herself, daughter of Tiresias. "I charge you, therefore, if you ever hear of any other origin ascribed to my city, let not falsehood defraud the truth" (XX, 97–99). The terms chosen by Virgil are of utmost weight: *"che . . . la verità nulla menzogna frodi."* The artist unmasks, corrects his own masterpiece in the name of a subsequent truth. (A similar but essentially ironic move is made in Gide's *Counterfieters.*) This retraction, bearing with such controlled exactitude on the interactive agencies of poetic truth, of prophetic or sibylline prevision and of revealed fact, carries Virgil to the threshold of grace. No pagan intellect, no soul prior to Christ's coming, came closer. Dante has committed to memory the whole of the *Aeneid* (*"la sài tutta quanta"*). He ingests it into every sinew of his own shaping process. He addresses himself through the beloved master. But Scripture bids him transgress the bounds of prophecy even in the *Aeneid* and the Fourth Eclogue. Such transgressions, with all that they imply of parricide (psychoanalysis would say, of the oedipal) mark the ripening of an artist or thinker, his "becoming what he is." A ripening made culpable but also enriched by repudiation. The step-by-step renunciation of Virgil's guidance is the axis of the *Purgatorio.* In some sense, I take the decay of the Narrator's relation to Saint-Loup to represent Proust's exegesis on this theme.

It is Virgil himself who adduces Beatrice's superior wisdom, her perception of truths from which he is barred. It is she who justly amends (in an "erasure" whose audacity surpasses that of late twentieth-century deconstruction) the celebrated *"desine fata deum flecti sperare precando"* (*Aeneid*, VI, 376) by invoking the efficacious and free tenor of Christian prayer. Virgil knows how to "make light" (*facere luce*), by virtue of poetic genius and philosophic sagacity. But Beatrice *is* light. Ineluctably, the modulations of adicu gather towards the strictly incomparable thirtieth canto of the *Purgatorio*. Trembling at the approach of Beatrice, the Pilgrim cites in Latin the original line 883 of the sixth book of the *Aeneid*. With this one exception, only God is quoted in the revealed original. *"Manibus, o, date lilia plenis"* refers unforcedly to the virginal flowers with which angels will salute Beatrice. But simultaneously, this quotation from Anchises' prophecy of the tragic death of the imperial youth Marcellus—these being the last words spoken in *Aeneid* VI—direct us to the constellation of themes paramount in Virgil: the elegiac, the imperial prophecies, the *tu Marcellus eris!* which echoes so closely the advent in the Fourth Eclogue. But Virgil's flowers do not tell of resurrection. His remains the principality of heroic but lesser death. Now melody and counterpoint unfold. Glimpsing Beatrice, the Pilgrim *"conosco i segni dell' antica fiamma."* These signs and signals of undying love flash literally out of Dido's remembrance, at the sight of Aeneas, of her former love for Sicheo: *"adgnosco veteris vestigia flammae."* Dante's translation is supreme homage, momentarily making of Dido a prefiguration of Beatrice. But even direct quotation is set alight by context (e.g., when St. Paul cites Euripides).

Farewell is at hand. Throughout, Virgil has been referred to as a father-figure to Dante and the Pilgrim. He will, one last time, be *"dolcissime patre"* at the moment of separation. But in a muddle of fearful love he becomes, in v. 44 a mother: *"corre a la mamma."* The femininity of the creative is inferred. Again, as commentators have long pointed out, a trinitarian algorithm organizes the gradual recession of Virgil's name. Named only once in v.46, he is present (after his actual departure) three times in the tercet 49–51, then once more in line 55. This ultimate nomination follows algebraically, as it were, on Beatrice's first word to the Pilgrim, on the one and only "Dante" in the *Commedia*. The actual valediction is an explicit recall of the Fourth Book of the *Georgics* which recounts Orpheus' farewell to Eurydice (scholars now incline to the view that Dante had direct knowledge of that text). The Orpheus and Eurydice motif is talismanic in the Western observance of the nature of poetry, of music, and of death. From earliest antiquity to Rilke and Auden, it crystallizes the intuition of a numinous potential in human language, in the *pneuma* or inspiration through spirit of the human voice, and of the voice of the poet in particular. At the threshold of rebirth, Eurydice, like Virgil, is ebbing into darkness. Virgil has foreseen this relegation *"ne l'etterno esilio."* In Limbo, amid the Parnassus of pagan singers, Orpheus stands next to Virgil. All the threads of poetics mesh towards a pivotal meditation on the meaning of meaning in literature, in secular art. The Pilgrim weeps after his father/mother, after Orpheus' desolation. There is medieval authority for the notion that Virgil was saved. The *Commedia* accords salvation to four pagan souls. Why the hopelessness of this adieu?

The maker of the *Aeneid* confesses that he acquired faith only after death. Even this faith knows a momentary lapse amid the terrors of *Inferno* IX. But the *erratum* seems to lie deeper. Virgil remains among *"le genti antiche ne l'antico errore"* because he will not trust his own inspired recognitions. He sets to sublime verse but does not act upon the revelations of the Sibyl in his Fourth Eclogue. At the close of the *Paradiso*, Anchises' prevision of the Augustan golden age translates into Beatrice's prediction of life everlasting. At some level, the actual writer of this Roman prophecy failed his own clairvoyance. He did not hear the Verb in the verb, and is doomed for having come so near.[6] Now the Pilgrim turns from the *Bucolics*, the *Georgics*, and the *Aeneid*, whose company has been the indispensable sharer of his own creative being, to another book. It is the Holy Bible, already present in the allegoric pageant which heralds the Garden of Eden in *Purgatorio* XXIX. A greater "Muse" (*"nostra maggior musa"*), one beyond even the most inventive poet's internalization, calls out. It is that which made possible the art of the Book of Job and of the Psalmist. It is that in which the fictive and the symbolic are perfectly at one, are tautologies of, the truths which they incarnate. At the highest level, *technē*, craft, intellection fall short: *"ben far non basta."* Only faith can substantiate. But although it is a prelude to truer glory, Virgil's *fallimento* leaves a bitter taste. Loving parricide is a twilit act.

There is a snapshot, taken on some country outing and under an indifferent tree, of Husserl and Heidegger in conversation. The older master bends towards his disciple in palpable hope of fulfilment, of enduring fidelity even where he himself will be excelled. Martin Heidegger, whose rustic "marching" outfit contrasts starkly with Husserl's, seems to be looking away from the eyes of his teacher and promoter. The two men stand very close,

6. Cf. the insightful reading in R. Hollander, "Tragedia nella 'Commedia'" in *Il Virgilio Dantesco* (1983).

but Heidegger's *Gestalt* prefigures the abyss to come, the necessary betrayal and supersession. An illustration to *Purgatorio* XXX?

Who, today, reads Statius? To medieval poets and mythogra-
phers he was invaluable. His Silver Latin *Thebaid* and fragmentary *Achilleid* had transmitted the matter of Thebes and of Troy
as yet inaccessible in their Greek original. But Dante goes further. Statius figures in thirteen cantos of the *Commedia;* only
Beatrice and Virgil play a greater rôle. Playing on an obscure supposition whereby Statius had converted to Christianity when he
composed the final books of his Theban epic, Dante makes of
him a "secret" Christian (*chiuso*) who, under Domitian's persecutions, chose not to profess his faith openly. So far as is known,
this episode is of Dante's invention. It is, moreover, Virgil who
draws Statius towards baptism by virtue of the annunciation in
the Fourth Eclogue. But Virgil's part is even greater: it is two lines
in the *Aeneid* (III, 56–7), denouncing avarice and opulent greed,
which alert Statius to his own impure life and prepare him for
virtuous conversion. Yet problems of understanding persist. The
beginning of *Purgatorio* XXI show Virgil and the Pilgrim in the
contours of Apostles on their journey to Emmaus. When they encounter Statius, his shade takes on more than a suggestion of
the risen Christ. His salutation is liturgical: *"O frati miei, Dio vi
dea pace."* With a courtesy inspired by desolation, Virgil, in his
response, identifies himself as the one "relegated" and unworthy
to share in that peace "which passes human comprehension."
In turn, Statius addresses the creator of the *Aeneid* with exalted
humility. His discourse is crowded with scarcely disguised Vir-
gilian citations. Dante clearly regards his own composition as
no less derivative from Virgil than was that of Statius. And in a
motion of consummate fusion, Statius defines the art of Virgil

in words which, more exactly than any commentary since, also define the genius of the *Commedia: "trattando l'ombre comme cosa salda"* ("treating shade[s] as solid things"). Thus, although Virgil is doomed to transcendent exile, the exchanges with Statius, at the limits of parting, celebrate his poetic-prophetic indispensability. *"Per te poeta fui, per te cristiano,"* confesses Statius. Pagan Virgil leads others towards Grace; Christian Statius cannot do so. Once more, a threefold logic operates: the three parts of the *Divine Comedy* can be seen to correspond to Virgil's pagan epic, to Statius' epics which are pagan in content but written by a convert, and to Dante's supremely Christian poem. Of which progression the subtle shifts in the order of march of the three poets as they approach and pass through the wall of purgatorial fire would be a representation. A seminal reversal impends. At the end of his *Thebaid,* Statius declares himself to be everlastingly inferior to Virgil. He can, at best, follow in Virgil's footsteps, "adoring" their spoor: *"sed longe sequere et vestigia sempre adora."* But now the "sequence," in the full sense, is inverted. It is Statius who precedes and calls himself *poeta.* This high term has been invoked only twice before: Virgil applies it to himself at the outset of the journey, and Homer, of whom Dante lacked direct knowledge, is referred to as *"poeta sovrano"*.[7] Much the lesser man, Statius now excels Virgil as does any soul in Christ.

I take Dante's prodigal invention with regard to Statius to be a vital component in his exploration of the reciprocities of influence. The intricate "trialogue" between Virgil, Statius, and the

7. Cf. A. Ronconi, "L'incontro di Stazio e Virgilio" in *Cultura e scuola,* 14 (1965) and J. H. Whitfield, "Dante and Statius: *Purgatorio* XXI–XXII" in D. Nolan, ed., *Dante Soundings* (1981). But much remains unclear.

Pilgrim communicates new aspects of the *communitas,* of the inwardly discursive plurality of the genetic process. It signals, as well, the key presence of the critical and the interpretative within the poetic. When the maker is in performative exchange with himself, this exchange is compellingly self-critical and hermeneutic. The serious artist is his own most searching critic and analyst. Via Statius, as we have seen, Dante not only re-thinks the eminent limitations to Virgil—limitations that empower his own transgression—but provides a lapidary definition of his own purpose: "to make shadow substance," to "incarnate" and "body forth" the truth of fiction. We shall see that this purpose can be realised integrally only by the *verace autore* who is God (*Paradiso* XXVI, 40). We shall learn that *autore* entails values far surpassing those of *poeta.* Even inspired art is not the authorship of final truth. Its "authority" is imperfect, even ambiguous. In Statius, this imperfection and ambiguity are made visible, albeit with that *cortesia* so characteristic of Dante.

Other masters and craftsmen people Dante's *Commedia.* Three times, in the narration of his narrated self—how else are we to put it?—the maker of the *Commedia* quotes his own earlier works. Twice in the *Purgatorio,* once in the *Paradiso.* The self-quotations are the opening lines of three of Dante's *canzoni.* The first tells of a music so soothing that it can calm the longings of the living and the dead. The second, from the first song in the *Vita nuova,* recalls the poet's discovery of a new idiom, of a new apprehension of love in the light of his encounter with Beatrice. Almost archly, the opening of the first *canzone* in his *Convivio,* as Dante cites it in *Paradiso* VIII,37, suggests that his earlier insights into the Angelic hierarchies are now confirmed. Whenever a painter, composer, writer quotes his or her earlier work (the example of

Mozart's *Figaro*-citation towards the close of *Don Giovanni* is canonic), the new context qualifies or expands or ironizes or corrects the source. These metamorphic movements are among the most revealing in the lives of the past tense in grammars of creation. Much about them remains to be studied.

Purgatory is the natural locus of the arts. Aristotelian *katharsis* bears on purgation through aesthetic empathy and response. Aesthetics, furthermore, are closely knit to temporality, to the compulsion in the human creator to outstrip time and the erasure through death. The ardent vanity of this aspiration is refuted in the eleventh canto, when Oderisi da Gubbio, an illuminist and miniature painter—a craft of condign scale and *humilitas*—warns the Pilgrim of the ephemerality of artistic and poetic renown. The lines are decisive:

> La vostra nominanza è color d'erba,
> che viene e va, e quei la discolora
> per cui ella esce de la terra acerba.

Fame (that nomination to glory) is as the hue of grass, transitory. The sun which makes it grow then bleaches it. Appositely, it is in this same canto that we meet with Cimabue and Giotto and that Dante sketches his ambivalent intimacy with the work of his immediate contemporaries: Guinizzelli and Cavalcanti. Cavalcanti haunts the *Commedia*. It is from one of his most celebrated sonnets that Dante takes the fierce image of the rain of fire in *Inferno* XIV. Now the mentor is slighted, in order, speculate scholars, to provide a materialist and heretical foil to Dante's eros of immaterial beatitude.

After Virgil, it is Sordello, the finest of the Italian poets who chose to write in Provençal, who adorns Mantua. Having put his gifts to "honest" use (*onesto* is no less a crowded word here than it is in *Othello*), Sordello is, for a spell, privileged to guide Virgil and the Pilgrim. Bertran de Born may well have been a more inspired troubadour than Sordello. But having, according to Dante, acted traitorously in his political career, Bertran is hideously damned. We see him swinging his own severed head by the hair "like a lantern" in the pit of Hell. As the soul ascends through Purgatory, the ethical prevails more and more incisively over the aesthetic.

So many poets, artists, thinkers, in radical contrast to Shakespeare. Each meeting, each dialogue, explores aspects of the contextual and communal fabric of poetics, of the internalized polyphony of executive forms. The last example in the *Commedia* is also the most puzzling. Paradise has need of doctors and saints to celebrate God's presence according to intellect and faith. It does not require artists or poets. In the *Paradiso* being is itself perpetual creation. The symbol is consumed in the reality. The grammars of generative imagining and fiction fall away as the word is made light. Yet one poet *does* appear in the realm of the blessed: Folquet de Marseille. Already in Purgatory, the master of Provençal, Arnaut Daniel, had referred to Folquet's *"folle amor,"* to his infatuation with the wife of a great lord. Though in Paradise, Folquet recalls his wild love. He claims that his adoration of Venus was indeed a sublimation of carnal desire, but incomplete. Eros remained in immanence. Renouncing mundanity, Folquet became a Cistercian, a bishop of Toulouse and the scourge of the Albigensians. Now he speaks in two registers: that of the rhetorician and singer of eros and that of the servant-lover of God. At one level, Folquet appears to provide a final focus for the seminal part of the Provençal legacy throughout the *Commedia:* Arnaut prefigures his art, Bertran was his friend, Sordello had predicted his ascent to ecclesiastical eminence. At another level, this sanguinary personage acts out a relegation of poetry in the name of moral-theological primacies as drastic as any since Plato.[8] The election of Folquet strikes us as strange; but the logic of Paradise is other. The true masters are those who relinquish their vocation. Tolstoy would have had his rank in the *Paradiso*. Would Rimbaud?

5

I have suggested that Dante's works can be experienced as an unbroken meditation on creation, seen poetically, metaphysically, and theologically. Dante's concept of the created extends to the foundation of civil-political society, to that of language and of a new aesthetics. He is, in the image of the Psalmist, filled with, quickened by, the wonder of the fact of coming into being. Wittgenstein's well-known remark on the boundless amazement which should reflect the existence of the world could have been Dante's. They share also a sense of the incommensurability of that existence. It and its bounds of meaning are, as modern logical theory would express it, "non-computable" to human reason, to its linguistic means and scientific investigations. The *Paradiso* is the *summa* of Dante's systematic wonder. One comes to hear it as a dialectical hymn—verse and antiphon—on the blinding evidence and incommensurability of the verb "to be." Its sources are *Genesis*, the *Timaeus*, Aristotelian physics of causation and, above all, the trope of divine light already argued by Neo-Platonists and Duns Scotus. Both genesis and consequent existentiality are direct emanations of the divine *viva luce*. Like Saint Bonaventura

8. Much of the material is reviewed by T. Bartolini, *Dante's Poets* (1984).

before him, the Pilgrim conceives of God as light *proprissime*. This light takes on a "liquid" tenor. God is *eterno fonte*. Hence the image in the address to Piccarda Donati (*Paradiso* III, 85–7) in which God's "peace in motion" is described as oceanic. In turn, the rays of light are arrows actually "shooting forth" created beings (a scriptural conceit which Aquinas commented on in his *De caelo*). The Prime Archer never misses. Each shot is perfectly intentional and intentionally perfect.

For our purpose, the essential is Dante's rendition of God as artist and craftsman-artificer (*artista* or *artefice*).[9] He creates, so Aquinas, as does the craftsman, *sicut artifex rerum artifiatarum*. He so cherishes His creations that He does not leave them out of His sight. In analogue, *intelletto* and *arte* are the tools of the mortal maker. On a lesser plane, the Platonic-Augustinian "forms contained in the Divine intelligence" are given material, verbal embodiment. Their variety is prodigal, yet concordant with a unified transcendent source. Even miracles accord with this ordering: they are products "where Nature never heated the iron nor beat the anvil" (surely, Blake knew this definition out of *Paradiso* XXIV). Matter, however, can resist the governance of informing. It can be "deaf" to the artist-craftman's design: *"la materia è sorda."* It does not answer to *"l'intenzione de l'arte."* Following on the *Timaeus,* both Aquinas and Dante find in Nature the "unsteady hand" of a secondary making. Whence imperfections and the ways in which the empirical can falsify, can betray the inner blueprint of its begetter.

Tensions between the model in *Genesis* and the Aristotelian

9. I follow the lucid guidance of P. Boyde, *Dante Philomythes and Philosopher* (1981).

postulate of the eternity of the cosmos, tax Dante as they did the whole of medieval cosmology. The *credo* in the twenty-fourth canto substitutes for "Maker of heaven and earth," Aristotle's unmoved Prime Mover *"che tutto il ciel muove, non moto."* In *Paradiso* XXIX, it is Beatrice who explains the true nature of creation in terms which (uneasily) combine mythology, mathematics, astronomy and all manner of prudent circumlocutions. Time has been made out of eternity, matter out of light (a strangely Einsteinian thought). The universe is temporal, God is not: *"in sua eternità di tempo fore."* Space is bounded, but not the "beyondness" which is God. God has created in an act of pure freedom, of ontological liberality so that His "ideas" could take on autonomous substance. This concept of a supreme gratuity will inspire the aesthetics and theory of the world of German idealism, and of Schelling in particular. As in the human artist, creation is the genesis of absolute freedom. Its liberality of donation, of exit from the inward of the self, is a manifest of love. Dante's or Schelling's paradigm raises the question of whether aesthetic creation can be, at any lasting level, the product of hatred. In the final analysis, are Juvenal or Swift or Thomas Bernhard, those virtuosos of loathing, inventors rather than creators?

In *Paradiso* XXV, Dante Alighieri envisions himself returning to Florence to be crowned poet. When writing this canto, he must have been perfectly aware of its cruel implausibility. Thus he crowns himself and, once more, distinguishes the *Commedia* from its antecedents in Homer, Virgil, and Statius. One last time, he claims its eminence in respect of medieval epic and romance. King David appears, representing, validating, the mission of sacred literature (ll.73–4 translate from the ninth Psalm). At its most elevated, the making of the poet is indeed sacred and immediate to the summons of true imagining which are those of revelation. The long pilgrimage ends in Dante's homecoming to a poetic-revelatory achievement which no outward banishment can negate.

We have proceeded from Virgil to the ancient masters of song in Limbo; from Orpheus to Statius. The journey has led to the minute analysis of poetic influence, inheritance, and rivalry as Dante calls to witness the troubadours and his Tuscan and Neapolitan contemporaries. David climaxes the logic of the voyage. He rounds in glory the investigation of creativity and creation, of divine authorship and human *poiesis,* of the concentric spheres of the aesthetic, the philosophical, and the theological. Now truth and fiction are made one, now imagination is prayer and Plato's exile of the poets refuted.

The centrality of Dante's poetics of the transcendent and of its unfolding in language have not occurred again.

III

That perfect triplicity of inquiries into creation, theological, meta-physical, and poetic enacted in the *Commedia,* is unrecapturable. But the argument has persisted. As have the complex relations of the semantic fields of "invention" and "creation." The Latin *invenire* would appear to pre-suppose that which is to be "found," to be "come upon." As if, to invoke the question underlying this study, the universe had already been "there," had been extant for the Deity to find, perhaps to stumble upon. Turned to haughty paradox, this *invenire* is implicit in Picasso's: "I do not search, I only find." The tenor of discovery attaches to the Latinate verb when it first enters the English language towards the close of the fifteenth century (*invention* is thus a late-comer). Yet very quickly, the overlap between "finding" and "producing" or "contriving" becomes evident. After the 1540s, *invenire* can pertain to the com-position, to the production of a work of art or of literature. In a usage charged with complication and suggestion, John Oldham will admonish the poet to "take a known subject and invent it well." Here the motion is one of re-creation, of the novel vari-ant on a theme or matter pre-existent (normally that of classic mythology and classic genres). For Dryden, on the other hand, "invention" clearly signifies "a making," an act of *poiesis.* The dis-tinction from "creation" is rhetorically effaced.

But the spaces of meaning and connotation around "invention" are, almost from the outset, disturbing. The aura of "feigning," of "fabrication"—itself a term in the highest degree ambiguous—of "contrivance," modulating into falsehood, is audible after the early 1530s. As the term ripens into currency, both spheres are present: that of origination, production and first devising on the one hand, that of possible mendacity and fiction on the other. No look at these intimately cognate dualities can be exhaustive.

As I noted, something within the deep structures of our sensibility balks at the phrasing and concept: "God invented the universe." We speak of a major artist as a "creator," not as an "inventor." Yet "inventiveness" may figure eminently among his virtues. Is there an analogy with those seminal differentiations between "fancy" and "imagination" in Coleridge and German idealism? Do we attach to "creation" the notion of the primary, where "invention" would indeed be secondary in respect of prior constituents, of elements waiting to be assembled, conjoined, or found? Yet is Marcel Duchamp, whom I take to be the key figure in the aesthetics of modernism, creating or inventing or *neither* when he offers his *objet trouvé* to our startled amusement and discomfort?

There seems to be—every step here is of the most tentative, provisional order—an absence from "creation" of precisely the penumbra of falsehood, of contrivance inseparable from the linguistics and speech-acts of "invention." Said to a child (or even an adult): *n'invente pas* signifies "do not lie, don't tell fibs." To enjoin: *ne crée pas,* would, in every respect, be a nonsense phrase. In another register, however, that of the iconoclastic, prohibitions on "creation" can be cardinal. I have already cited the taboo on the "making of images" in Judaism and Islam. To create such images is to "invent," it is to "fictionalize" in the cause of a virtual reality, scenes, real presences beyond human perception or rivalry ("I know not 'seeming,'" says Hamlet in his rage for truth). Time and again, we will meet up with the artist's sense of himself as "counter-creator," as competing with the primal *fiat* or "let there be" on ground at once exultant and blasphemous. Is the lack of humour, so marked in the Hebraic-Christian delineations of a revealed God, instinct with the seriousness of creation? Invention is often thoroughly humorous. It surprises. Whereas creation, in the sense of the Greek term which generates all philosophy, *thau-mazein*, amazes, astonishes us as does thunder or the blaze of northern lights.

Do any of these compelling dichotomies and contiguities between "creation" and "invention" apply to the exact and the natural sciences? On a naively positivistic basis, sciences seeks to find, to locate, to elucidate theoretically and empirically what is already "there." But we know how misleading such a narrative would be. It is not only, as Kant argues, the fact that human mentality and logical procedures are, as it were, anchored in the consciousness of the subject, that we read the world and all phenomenal experiences by the determining light of certain specific cognitive and innate categories. It is that the process of scientific hypotheses and and verification can be, normally are, radically inventive and innovative. Science construes changing worlds, inevitably tailored to its own investigative means and conventions of rational admissibility. It is where the sciences translate into application, into technologies of every kind, that the notion of "invention" becomes at once manifest and elusive. It seems difficult to deny that Thomas Edison "invented" the lightbulb, that he did not simply stumble upon that which was already "there." On the other hand, a deep-reaching uneasiness or sense of magnification does attach to the statement that Edison "created" this useful object. Definitions blur.

The layman has little access to the centrality and epistemological entailments of the debate over creation and discovery, over construction and finding, at the heart of mathematical thought. The controversy obtains to this day; indeed modern mathematics has given it a particular edge. Are numbers Platonic realities, pre-existent to the human intellect, whose deployment is, ultimately, a universal necessity of reason? Or are they a human contrivance, a code whose seemingly unbounded progress and ramifications are an invention of mortal cerebration, of man's instinct for play at the highest pitch? What ambiguities of cognitive proposal inhere in the concept and verbal designation of "real numbers"? No human exercise seems richer in edification (in "building") than pure mathematics, in none are truth and beauty more dynamically allied. None the less, numerous mathematicians have regarded themselves as discoverers, as explorers of units and relations integral to the fabric of phenomenal nature. It is as if prime numbers, like the galaxies revealed to the astronomer or astrophysicist, had a substantive reality and rule-bound function waiting to be come upon and understood. In which sense, the matter of, say, elliptical functions or transfinite numbers will outlast the human minds who have been its guests.

Close to intractable are the associations we make—subconsciously, it may be—as between invention and form and creation and content. A new metrical or stanzaic pattern, the use of new materials in art or architecture, the "two-part inventions" in Bach's compositions for harpsichord, strike us as undeniably that. The artist invents, as does the engineer or designer. The "invention of content," on the other hand, would seem to be a perplexing, awkward rubric. Content declares an attachment to creativity, to generative acts that go beyond the performative. The musical content of the Bach-invention, resistant as it is to any verbal re-statement or paraphrase other than intuitively metaphoric, solicits the concept of eminent creativity, of a be-getting informing its particular executive, technical form which may, indeed, have been invented for the occasion.

Yet the entire distinction is suspect. It is, very precisely, the nature of any serious art, of any literary or philosophic text, to render inseparable the categories of "form" and of "content." The content of the painting is, at every point of execution and perception, that of its formal means. The sense of the fugue or sonata is exactly that. Above fairly rudimentary semantic levels, paraphrase and translation are condemned to distortion or incompletion just because the significance of the original is wholly embedded in its lexical, grammatical, conceptual specificity. An ode or epigram speak its worlds as a sonnet does not. Content forms; forms substantiate. Thus the discriminations between the invented and the created, however instinctive to our usage and unexamined reference, breaks down decisively across the range of the aesthetic and the semiotic.

Nevertheless, we sense "creation" to be fundamentally above "invention." Whatever the complex speech-nodes and blurred demarcations, the "creator" exceeds the "inventor" in the hierarchies of valuation. Reflection tells us that even the greatest of poets works in and with the pre-existent means of languages; that the most original composer will subvert the conventions he has inherited from musical history; Picasso's *Demoiselles d'Avignon* not only depends on oil, canvas, and modes of brush-work already long-established, but cites and implies the past which it is seeking to overthrow. We know all this, but insist on the attribute of creation, on the simultaneously obvious and undefinable analogy with creation itself, this is to say with the theological or cosmological narrative of that which is made, which is called into being.

In classical and medieval Western sensibility, in Plato as in Dante, this attribution of analogy was explicit and ubiquitous. The mathematicians's, the thinker's, the artist's creations are enacted in the image of the prime Maker. We will observe the extent to which this mirroring retains its force in music, that it is dynamic not only in the aesthetics of Bach but in those of, say, Mahler and Bruckner. But secularization, the metamorphic changes in the "telling of the story" which largely define modernity and the imposition of a post-Cartesian, post-Galilean rationale, debilitates the derivation of, the analogue with, of aesthetic-philosophic creation from that of cosmic origination. The epiphanic dimension modulates into metaphor and image, into a bright ghostliness wonderfully exploited by, for example, James Joyce.

The inquiries into "creation" (Kant's *Schaffung*) and "invention," on origins and originality in German idealism and German romantic theory are of particular strength. They document a period of transition whose consequences are vital still.

2

German mentality is fascinated, dare one say obsessed, by the turbulent dark of inception and initiation. "Genealogy," the invocation of the untranslatable monosyllable of the primal, *Ur*, are as instrumental in the romantic anthropology of Hamann and Herder as they are in the morals of Nietzsche and the depth psychology of Freud. The ontology of Heidegger can be read as one of pre-existentiality, of an intimation of primordial being anterior to the particularities of the phenomenal. According to Heidegger it is precisely in language and in art that this "precedence" has left enigmatic but luminous spoors. Why this obsessive recursion to sources, to time before time (whose canonic episode in German sensibility is that of the descent to the "Mothers" in Goethe's *Faust*)? The German language meshes late; in Luther and his successors. The German nation even later. A thirst for legitimacy of foundation, for empowering ancestry inspires German thought and politics. Creation, be it mythical and mythopoetic in the most evident degree, must be established as against assemblage, contingent fabrication or invention. A twofold manoeuvre is at work: the claim to Nordic-Teutonic daybreak—so eloquent in Wagner; and the appropriation of both classical and archaic Hellas. In the latter move, the archaic is endowed with a seminal aura. Martin Heidegger's exaltation of the pre-Socratics is the logical climax to a claim of affinity with the very prologue to Western thought and consciousness. It is the fragmentary darkness in Heraclitus, in Anaximander which points, paradoxically to first light. Whatever the motives (and the political-psychological dangers), it is in German metaphysics and aesthetics that an inquiry into *schaffen* and *erfinden,* into the creator and the inventor, will find a singular intensity of insight.

Hegel historicizes concept and consciousness. The act of thought is strictly inseparable from temporality. The Hegelian model posits time as integral to being (whence Heidegger's *Sein und Zeit*). To be is to be "in time," within horizons of perception and *Begriff* ("grasp," "internalization") which are totally historical. It is this historicity of human consciousness, this ascription of process and "kinetics"—of being in motion—to every intelligible phenomenality, which makes the Hegelian system so representative of its own age. Hegel himself insists on the seminal rôle of the French Revolution and the Napoleonic saga in the genesis and articulation of his phenomenology and of his logic. The pressure of motion on and within even the most abstract of experienced and realised consciousness is formidable. Thought is history unfolding in the radical climate of accelerated time created by revolution and world-empire. Platonic-Kantian postulates of stable eternity yield to the "calculus," if one can put it that way, and thermodynamics of man's voyage through historicity (the image of an Odyssey of the human spirit is Schelling's, but it derives closely from Hegel). Even death has its history.

Debate, at once epistemological and political, has focused on Hegel's often opaque proclamation of finality. The Napoleonic possibility, taken in its broadest theoretical and empirical sense, marks the fulfilment of man's historical destiny. It is emblematic, though that notion is itself inadequate, of the self-realisation of *Geist*, of man's self-conception (where "conceiving" carries the full meanings both of procreation and of the immediacies of intellection and understanding). Famously, the passage of Napoleon under Hegel's window on his way to the battle of Jena in the precise moment in which the preface to the *Phenomenology* was being completed, serves as an iconic coincidence. Philosophy achieves its long journey—for Hegel the history of philosophy *is* philosophy—at the hour in which history itself draws to its ineluctable "end." Just what this finality signifies remains a vexed issue. One of Hegel's most impassioned modern exegetes, Alexandre Kojève, saw the fulfilment and termination of the historical process not in Napoleon but in Stalin. The "totalitarian" or "totalized" configurations of society under twentieth-century despotism and technocracy can be taken as relevant to Hegel's imperative of closure. More recently, the collapse of Marxist-Leninist societies has been read as "the end of history" in a Hegelian, though "liberalist" and free-market, sense.

This fascination which Hegel's systematic sense of an ending has diverted notice from his inquiries into inception, into "beginnings." In any totalization of temporality, the question of genesis is no less indispensable than that of the coda. Here, as in the mystical tradition or in poetry, the end is truly in the beginning. The logical, the cognitive problems which this necessity raises concern Hegel no less than they did St. Augustine. However, even in respect of the difficulties inherent in Hegel's idiom and arguments, the considerations in the "Wissenchaft der Logik" on the *Anfang*, on the beginning, are among the most recalcitrant. It is (fascinatingly) evident that Hegel wrestles with intractability.

"*Moderne Verlegenheit um den Anfang*" (modern embarrassment about/uneasiness with the beginning): Hegel's remark could almost be self-irony. He asks—the question is not often put so starkly—"How can there be a beginning to knowledge, to *Wissenschaft?*" The observations which follow circle around this dilemma; they can best be read as a series of "stabs" or aphorisms rather than of rigorously sequential discourse in the customary Hegelian mode.

The concept of the "principle" contains etymologically and conceptually that of inception. The "form of the beginning" is its principle. The first thought, an arrestingly Hegelian notion, is an act of "thinking that which comes first." On any positivist or neurophysiological plane, this suggestion of a primal thought, like that of an *Ur-wort*, defies plausibility. But it is vital to Hegel's historicity of human inwardness. An absolute immediacy—perhaps something like Husserl's radical intuition—characterizes this initiation of all logic, this primal "thinking of thought." Being made self-aware "*ist das Anfangende*," "is the process of beginning." Hegel also designates it as "pure presence," an aspect which may be intensely pertinent to the theme of aesthetic creation and the achievement of principality through form.

For us, for any human mind, to "think beginning" is to return to the source, it is to "proceed backward" in the most urgent and engaged sense. We touch here on a motif which is instrumental in numerous metaphysical and aesthetic constructs. It is that of Platonic reminiscence, of Plato's striving to elucidate the transcendentally pre-existent without which there could be no ascertainable knowledge. Here also are the Wordsworthian-romantic intimation of seminal insight in the child and Bergson's dynamic attachment of matter to memory. The *ricorso*, the oceanic moving, as it were up-stream, presides over the homeward voyage of Odysseus, over the return of the Pilgrim to the primal font—to the "baptism" of being—in the *Commedia*. It is the inward spiral at the substantive and formal heart of Proust's *Recherche*. Or, as Hegel puts it, the *Anfangende,* the "nascent," never absents itself from the *Fortgang,* the progress, the march forward (*Gang,* "walking," being in movement, inheres in both terms) of consciousness or the work being pursued. The phrasing is almost kabbahlistic: *Geist* "resolving, deciding itself to the creation of a world" ("*zu Schöpfung einer Welt sich entschliessend*"), must return, in perfect circularity to "*unmittelbaren Sein,*" to unmediated being. Almost certainly, this formulation lies behind the trope, itself laden with aesthetic implications, of Nietzsche's doctrine of "eternal return."

But what is this *das Anfangende?*

Der Anfang ist noch Nichts, und es soll etwas werden. Der Anfang ist nicht das reine Nichts, sondern ein Nichts, von dem etwas ausgehen soll; das Sein ist also auch schon im Anfang enthalten. Der Anfang enthält also beides, Sein und Nichts; ist die Einheit von Sein und Nichts, —oder ist Nichtsein, das zugleich Sein, und Sein, das zugleich Nichtsein ist.

A "nothingness" which, being "impure," is the matrix from which something is to emerge. Existentiality is a compelling potential in the singular energies and inherence of a nothingness (*Nichtsein*) which is simultaneously a *Sein* or being-there. The crucial ambiguity which, for Hegel, is not a contingency or defect of grammar, lies in the *ist*: "the beginning *is* as yet nothing." That *is* signals and determines its seminal presence. The void, as it were, is active.

It is endemic in the Anglo-Saxon liturgy of common sense, of pragmatic doubt, to regard propositions of this kind as verbiage, as characteristically teutonic instances of philosophic muddle. In arresting fact, Hegel's *Nichts* on the way to becoming *Etwas* is closely analogous to the premises which authorize today's astrophysics and the theories of "the beginning" in late twentieth-century cosmology. Often, science will mask, by mathematical formalization, the verbal, the metaphoric suggestions of a prior epistemology.

The *Anfang,* says Hegel, proceeds towards being, in that it distances itself from or "sublates" (*aufhebt*) non-being. This is the key move in the dialectic: the negation of negation, the annihilation of nothingness (*néantissement du néant* in Sartre's rendering) in any initiatory, which is to say authentically creative act. This annihilation or "subsumption"—the problems we have in finding clear verbal expressions for these concepts is of itself like a radioactive emission in a cloud chamber, confirming high but immaterial energies—preserves nothingness within the deployment of being. We will find this paradox, if it is that, to be of exceeding significance in any attempt to categorize, to discriminate between creation and invention.

Again, Hegel circles around the core of "primacy": that which constitutes and energizes the inception is *"ein Nichtanalysier-bares"* (it cannot be analysed). This concession is of the essence. Much that it fundamental in theological, philosophic, aesthetic discourse is "non-analysable" or analytic. But that is no refutation of its truth-values, of its indispensable function in the generative priority of intuition. On the contrary. Analysis may come late in the history of consciousness, and there may be a perspective, though one to be argued with scrupulous hesitation, in which the "analysable" is also the (ultimately) trivial.

We can think of this *Nichtanalysierbares,* "in its unfulfilled immediacy" as pure being, as "total emptiness" *(das ganz Leere).* (Particle physics now postulates elementary units with neither mass nor dimension.) As we shall see, Hegelian emptiness will beget a deciding legacy in modernism: Mallarmé will derive from it his *blanc,* his "white blanks"; non-objective and minimalist painting will dwell on emptiness; an Hegelian inference of generative "absence" underlies the rhetoric of deconstruction. There is even in the Derridean postulate, meant ironically, that language would have stable sense only if its markers were "turned towards God," like an echo of Hegel's haunting observation: *"das unbestrittentste Recht hätte Gott, dass mit ihm der Anfang gemacht werde"* ("God would have the most indisputable right to be the one with whom a start, a beginning is made").

The absolute fusion of nothingness and being via the process of becoming entails an intimate contiguity between genesis and extinction, between *Enstehen* and *Vergehen.* In an ontological sense, even the most manifest and awesome creation is ephemeral. It is, if you will, a "self-destruct" whose history, like history itself, has its ending. To enter into being is to take a first step towards nothingness, exactly in the manner in which the newborn is on the way to death (Montaigne). Concomitantly, annihilation is an "*Uebergang ins Sein*", "a transit, a modulation towards being." Here also, an everyday experience is being abstracted: the abolition of the generative moment in music and the return of music to "fulfilled disappearance," are a familiar, although perennially challenging, fact.

Thus there are in the *arcana* of Hegel's meditation on beginning suggestions and figurations which we can verify both in the "unanalysable" matter of common experience, and which were to prove fertile throughout modern art and literature. A second fundamental text is Hölderlin's "Ueber die Verfahrungsweise des poetischen Geistes" "Concerning the modes, the means of proceeding of the poetic spirit". There are points both of contact with and difference from Hegel; as there were in the relations, initially almost symbiotic but subsequently alien, between the two men. And perhaps it is worth stressing that even if Hölderlin's incomparable poetry was lost to us, his contributions to the philosophy of literary forms, to hermeneutics, would remain of the very first significance. (Hegel, unless I am mistaken, wrote only one poem he judged worth preserving: it was addressed to Hölderlin.)

The very opening, where "opening" is at stake, of Hölderlin's reflections is a sentence whose involuted length matches that of Broch's *Death of Virgil* or of certain leviathan bubblings in *Finnegans Wake*. Paraphrase is inevitable albeit reductive. What Hölderlin, no less than Hegel, is grappling with is the defining articulation of the creative moment, of the time-context and point in time in which the poet, the *Dichter*, will be ready for the reception of his "matter" (where *Stoff* carries more distinct connotations of "aesthetic subject," of "poetic raw material"). Are we in the world of Keats's letters, a witness contemporary with that of Hölderlin? Yes and no. Also Keats is intent on identifying the moment, the concentrated circumstance of the surge and budding of creation. But Keats's testimony is narrative; it images and acts out; its introspection is that of a metaphoric psychology. Hölderlin, in a strategy characteristic of German aesthetic investigation after Kant's *Kritik der Urteilskraft,* aims for systematic generalization, for experience made theory.

The human spirit, rules Hölderlin, is both common to all and specific or singular to each individual (such dualities or seeming contradictions will organize Hölderlin's argument in a cadence readily Hegelian and dialectical). The spirit is empowered to (*bemächtigt*) reproduce itself in its own, personal incarnation and in that of others. The poetic irradiates inward and outward. The problem is that throughout this dynamic of internalization and externalization *"die Form des Stoffes identisch bleibe."* I read this to mean that in the dialectical relations between creation and reception, the generative form, that which "informs" the content, must retain its integral and originating identity. But this "conservation of perfect energy" is unrealisable. Or rather, the artist, the poet will perceive a fundamental conflict (*Widerstreit*) between the work's identity to itself and its transformations in the process of expression and reception. Unison and change (like Hegel's being and non-being) are not fused. But it is when, at the highest pitch of percipient imbalance, the poet or artist feels this conflict, when it becomes wholly "sensible" (*fühlbar*) to him, that the moment of creativity comes upon him. It is then, and only then, that the *Dichter* is ready for, is open to, the *"Rezeptivität des Stoffes"* ("the reception of the content or matter"). It is, strictly understood, this condition of irreconcilable tension which informs, which is the form of, the aesthetic. Most strikingly, Hölderlin's model anticipates precisely on Roger Sessions's location of the source of musical composition in a composer's experienced immediacy of "irreconcilable levels of energy."

What, according to Hölderlin, are the threefold sources of content in, never to be wholly assuaged, search of executive form? The reply is one familiar to eighteenth-century theories of mind and representation. There are "events, perceptions, realities"; there is thought, passion, and the imaginary; there are "fantasies" attached more or less cogently to the realm of "possibilities" (*Möglichkeiten*). Neither Locke nor Kant would have found this proposal novel. Now, however, Hölderlin ventures into deeper waters.

The "matter arising" may lead the poet into error, into "erring." Drawn from the totality and interrelations of the "living world", the *Stoff*—perceptual, cognitive, imaginary, "surreal"— resists the limitations enforced on it by aesthetic form. The manifold vitality of content, essentially incommensurable, essentially uncircumscribed in its density, does not wish to "serve" the artist or poet as a mere "vehicle" (one thinks of the desertion of the circus-animals in Yeats's poetics). It is this resistance which animates, which gives soul and spirit to, the actual form of the work, engendering within that form an imperfect but vital "*Ruhepunkt*" ("a fulcrum," "a point at rest," as in the tranquil eye of the storm). By means of metaphor—the privileged mystery—or "hyperbole," signifying the extreme stress of formal means, the artist separates representation from the living, unconfined source. This dissociation, however inescapable, however resplendent in its *Darstellung*, which is the poem, work of art, composition, or, indeed, philosophic system, comports an element of both violence and diminution. In the deepest sense, art is also artifice. The creation of individual works is at once a process of fulfilment and and an abstraction (a word whose etymology speaks of a "severing," of a "pulling apart"). This abstraction leaves behind it—carries within it?—an organic whole which, in the moment of aesthetic expression, is rent and diminished. The creator seeks to make reparation by virtue of a "poetic life," a life lived at high risk and in uncompromising commitment to the ideals of his calling. In this poetic existence, "material," "form," and "purity" interact at the most intense level, yet their meshing is also conflictual. At this point, Hölderlin's account of the generative and transformational "kinetics" of the poetic is almost uncannily consonant with the notations in Keats's letters.

If the creative *Geist* is boundless (*unendlich*), what relates it to the necessary limitations of all articulate and performative signs? How can it enter the constricting lineaments of genre (for even language is limited in regard to the unfolding infinities of the perceived and imagined world)? Hölderlin defines the function and aim of art as "*die Vergegenwärtung des Unendlichen*" (the making present, the making contemporary of the unbounded). How, he asks, can that which is in incessant motion, as are thought and all vital processes, be made "punctual" (again, *Punkt* is a key-term)? The agency is one of creative contrariety, of *Entgegensetzung*. The poet, the artist chooses freely to set himself or herself in opposition to the claims of the non-finite. He seeks mediation between a child's indiscriminate identification with the wholeness of the world—the Wordsworthian intimations of unboundedness—and the willed abstraction which, ineluctably, chooses an expressive but bounded form. Thus there is in mature poetics an understanding, a comprehension (in both senses of the word) of irreconcilable contradiction. Motion is at rest, communicating the paradox of the "momentarily lasting." Of twentieth-century poets, it is, I think, René Char who comes nearest to finding metaphoric equivalence to this guarded but compelling notion.

Hölderlin's next move is, in a way characteristic of the Hegelian climate, a dialectical reversal. The infinity of potential content has been trapped, as it were, in the limited configurations of conceptual and aesthetic statement. But language generalizes, universalizes, negates individuation. The poet strives to be understood by others, to achieve a *Wiederklang* or echoing resonance. In a subtle but also radical dialectical movement, that which executive form had made bounded and momentary now radiates towards its own kind of open-ended universality (*Allgemeinheit*). By virtue of a "magic stroke," *Zauberschlag*, poetry restores to life, to the incommensurability of "the lived," that which abstraction and reduction to local,temporal form had taken from it. Supreme art or philosophic argument is, according to Hölderlin, "re-flection" in the most manifold sense and connotation. Motion and counter-motion achieve, though this is manifestly rare and more of an ideal than an actuality, an equation in which *"Geist und Leben auf beiden Seiten gleich ist"* ("spirit and life are equivalent"). This equality resolves, sublates, the primordial conflict between spirit and matter, between reality and the conceptual or imaginary appropriations and negations of such reality, between the absence of existential reality from all linguistic and symbolic designations and the real presence which must nevertheless "inhabit" the sign (Hölderlin's formulation rigorously prefigures the semantics of negation and erasure in theories of deconstruction). These resolutions, which are fundamentally one, would abolish the duality, the well-spring of gnosticism, at work in Western philosophy and aesthetics after Plato. The spirit is made immanent in poetic form, but the impulse towards communicative universality and "untimeliness" in language "transcendentalizes" this immanence. The poet's language directly embodies the ebb and tide of "re-flection." It is at once ineradicably his or her own and universal. It demonstrates the apparent contradiction of "limitless singularity." Its determinant elements, clarity and opaqueness, swiftness and retardation, abstraction and concreteness, conjoin in that *"Stillstand der Bewegung"* (that "standing still of motion") which matches the universal to the particular.

That music makes this model lucid, indeed palpable, seems evident. Whether words and syntax, even at Hölderlin's level, can fully do so is another matter. But why should quantum physics have a monopoly on contradiction and difficulty?

3

Preliminary findings as to certain differences between creation and invention now suggest themselves. The proviso is that such discriminations cannot be absolute. The formal and existential reach of the two concepts and of their semantic-conceptual fields overlap. There are impurities of invention in acts of creation; there are vestiges or foreshadowings of authentic creativity in invention. The zones in which the differentiations are the most difficult to enforce, in which there is a more or less intractable blurring of demarcations, are also among the most philosophically and pragmatically informative. As throughout, any final attribution to the created or the invented realm may be provisional and intuitive.

Being is axiomatically twinned with non-being. To be is "not

not to be." All phenomenality is alternative: to other possibilities of substantiation and, more radically, to "insubstantiality," which is to say to inexistence. This universal obtains at the most obvious level, where "obviousness" precisely enacts its all-embracing truth. The dichotomies which determine the human condition, such as life and death, such as light and dark, can be understood as specialized, though pervasive, enactments of the totally welded duality of presence and absence. To be present is not to be absent. The seeming vacancy of absence entails, in ways which will be crucial to our argument, the fulness of presence. This twinning is enunciated by each and every linguistic proposition, by each mental and articulate act of predication. A statement, a definition, a nomination are positive negations: "this is not that." The status of "that which is not" will, first, imply the un-predicated, the un-named incommensurability of alternatives. When I say "this is this and not that," I am also postulating that this "not that" could, virtually without limit, be other. Every proposition sets other worlds to one side (as, for example, did Euclidean geometry prior to the advent of non-Euclidean geometries and spaces). It is at once the enviable strength and inherent weakness of all mathematical, logical, and scientific systems, in so far as they are axiomatic, to make of that "which is not," of that which is irreconcilable with the axiomatic set, an error. "Natural thought," if such an expression is allowed, natural language do not necessarily relegate the negated, the "not that" to the category of error. Definitions, nominations, perceptions, demarcations are perpetually re-visited. They are incessantly metamorphic. The "this is" of today will become the "this is not" or "this is also that" of tomorrow. Perceived and spoken being always keeps non-being and alternatives in reserve, as it were, for new mappings.

Negation is the vast storehouse of as yet unperceived, un-needed or undeclared possibility (we shall see that there are links between "invention" and "inventory"). It is the vital privilege of non-formal, non-mathematical, or meta-mathematical awareness and discourse to keep the "not that," the negated, within reach, to preserve "otherness" for future reference and use. As Hegel insists, human thought itself proceeds via the negation of negations when it seeks a creative grasp of being.

I have cited already some of the theophanic and polytheistic creation-narratives which arise from the almost tautological relationship between being and non-being, from the inherence of absence in any figuration of presence. The underlying logic is one of freedom. The Maker, the Demiurge was "at liberty" not to create. This postulate can and has been disputed. There have been theodicies and cosmologies in which the nature of the divine, its manifest justification have been identified with the imperative of creation. To be "God" is to acquiesce in a necessity of self-deployment, of universal generation. The notion of sterility and solipsistic solitude has been held to be alien to the ontology of the divine, of the First Mover. Indeed, as we noted, kabbalistic and theosophic speculation has advanced the conjecture that necessary emanation into other modes of being, into "worldliness" and substance, has led to a scattering or dissemination of the divine unity. In some metaphoric way, the God of the "broken vessels" has been "lamed." This would account for His withdrawal from our imperfect universe.

The more confident view, however, has been that of a primordial freedom. The supreme being could have chosen to dwell in the uncreated infinity of the void. Creation is, in the strict sense, optional. It enters freely into a diacritical relation with, abstention from non-being or nullity. All religion, all theology could be defined as an endeavour to grasp, to offer thanks for, the gratuitous miracle of creation. It celebrates or, in the case of negative theology, questions the unfathomable choice whereby "there is not nothing." This other option, although we cannot conceive of it or attach to it even the most spectral of images, can be supposed to have had its own exceeding logic and plausibility. Only nothingness is at perfect rest. There were, moreover (there are) other possible choices. I have referred to the idea of numerous preceding creations, of "rough drafts" from the Maker's atelier. Aristotelian-Thomist cosmology insists on a single universe, modelling the will and perfection of its architect. Other hypotheses, long judged heretical, invoke a plurality, indeed an infinity of other worlds, of "universes" either analogous to or radically different from our own (*la pluralité des mondes*, intimated by Giordano Bruno and argued by the Enlightenment). Creating freely, the Deity or first principle can re-create in corrective or playful prodigality. An obvious menace attaches to this liberty: that of subsequent unmaking, or God as Tinguely trashing His own artifact. The Noah-legend, so widespread in diverse mythologies and cultures, is a weak version of such possibility. It is not merely human and animal forms which can be returned to non-being; it is the cosmos itself. There is no guaranteed tenure in the fact of existence. Stars burn out. Hence the anxiety of the major theological and metaphysical doctrines in regard to time. As Plato's *Timaeus* seeks to make plain, once created, once in being, the cosmos is everlasting. For Aristotle it is eternal (a rather different concept). Judaeo-Christian perceptions of God look to the rainbow, to the celestial promise that annihilation will not be visited on created being. Does this pious hope not abrogate God's absolute freedom?

The intuition that being could not be, that creation could be undone—anti-matter annihilating matter either in passing or finality—should breed terror. That *Angst* and sudden brush against nothingness does at moments arise in us as from atavistic and distant depths. But the fascination with non-being has been more vivid than the fear. We saw how it has been recurrent not only in theological mysticism but in Western philosophy from Parmenides to Plato's *Sophist*, from the *Sophist* to a culminating rôle in Heidegger. Every degree of existence, of substantiality has had its mirror in annulment or cancellation. Each has been dwelt on by speculative and grammatological conjecture: *annullatio, abnegatio, exinanitio*, increasing, as would negative numbers, to *annihilatio*. As Italian free-thinkers and libertines of the spirit proclaimed in the early seventeenth century[1]:

Nulla, Nulla è perciò più efficace della divina Sapienza, Nulla più nobile delle virtù celeste, Nulla più glorioso e desiderabile della beatitudine eterna.

Nullity, le *néant* is more efficacious than divine wisdom; it is the noblest of heavenly virtues, more resplendent and desirable than everlasting bliss. Il *Niente* is the source and destination of the universe. All created matter is constituted of nothingness: "*Non era il fuoco: chiamo Iddio il Niente ed ecco che, convertito in fiamma, s'immnalzò nel più alto seggio sopra tutti gli elementi*" ('fire was not;

---

1. Cf. the fascinating documents in *Le Antiche Memorie del Nulla*, ed. by Carlo Ossola (1997).

God summoned it from nothingness; transmuted into flame it rose to predominance over all other elements). Even at its most concentrated, "*Materia sia quasi Nulla.*" Or includes, causally and ineradicably, an origination, a bias towards nothingness and nullification.

We are now, I believe, in a position to suggest a preliminary definition of "creation." The creative act and that which it engenders is characterised by two primary attributes. It is an enactment of freedom. It is integrally at liberty. Its existence comports implicitly and explicitly the alternative of non-existence. It could not have been. The numerous instances in which artists or thinkers proclaim that they "had no choice," that they were compelled by over-mastering necessity to create this or that work, to develop this or that train and construct of thought, are rhetoric. This rhetoric may have absolutely legitimate psychological motives; it may arise from a valid strategy of empowering introspection. But it remains, at best, an apologetic flourish. Any authentic mode and consequence of creation arises from the concomitant freedom not to be, not to have come into being. (Or, as we shall see, to have been altogether otherwise, something else in every degree.) This is why "creation," properly understood and experienced, is another word for "freedom," for that *fiat* or "let there be" which has meaning only in its virtually tautological relation to "let there not be." It is solely in this gratuity towards being— being is always a gift—that the artist, the poet, the composer can be thought "god-like," that their practice can be termed analogous to that of the First Maker.

The second cardinal attribute in creation is one of apparently paradoxical inclusion: the work created carries within it, declares to us, with greater or lesser evidence, the fact that it could not have been or could have been otherwise. Formed being houses the remembrance, the always attendant possibility of the un-created (the "unborn"). The outward marker of this essential co-habitation (*quasi Nulla*) is the presence in even the most accomplished of aesthetic realisations of imperfection. A more or less subtle breach is inwoven into the patterns of the carpet; architects violate the formal canon of the Greek temple, allowing error in the volume or placement of their columns. Perfection, even if it could be achieved, carries death. It is the precedence and constant potentiality of non-being which affords creation its wonder of "givenness" and its vulnerable truth. "Creation," therefore, offers itself for definition as *that which is enacted freedom and which includes and expresses in its incarnation the presence of what is absent from it or of what could be radically other*. Abstraction makes this postulate obscure. Clarity and familiar recognition lie in its application.

4

Music is silence interrupted. As each note emerges and as it dies away, it remains in dialogue with silence. This dialogue is formalized by virtue of the intervals and pauses between musical units—between notes, bars, movements—without which there could be no musical organization. But silence is not the only un-declared agent in music. The physics of the audible sound, the physiology of its reception entail the emission and audition of overtones and undertones around each note or chord. No natural musical moment is pure unison. Such unison would be a sterile artifice or "white noise." The unstated ambience of extended tonality surrounds, prolongs, tempers each musical fact and form with a sustaining, literally vibrant context. Seas, heard only liminally or sub-liminally, sound in even the smallest of musical "shells."

The unstated or discarded is present in a second mode. Musicology, musical analysis such as we find in Allen Tyson's Beethoven-studies or in Richard Taruskin's monumental investigations of Stravinsky, abound in examples. The finished composition, the score internalizes, in ways as diverse and complex as is music itself, prior or alternative motifs, tone-clustres, thematic material. Beethoven's Triple Concerto incorporates discarded fragments of what was to be its first exposition. Expansiveness grows directly out of the compression and transformation of prior trials and possibilities. Throughout the drafts of the C Sharp Minor Quartet, two fundamentally divergent plans are retained. The options chosen by Beethoven enlist the ideas held, as it were, in abstention. Some six hundred pages of sketches underlie this opus. Nothing goes wholly lost. As Robert Winter puts it: "the traces of Beethoven's most serious affair with the subdominant have left their impact on virtually every phase of the quartet." The composer excises, in his drafts, the transition passages between the second and third opening subjects in the *Eroica*. But these reappear "as a component of the vast motion towards E minor . . . beginning at bar 284" (Lewis Lockwood). In the F Major Quartet, the master hesitates over the retention or omission of repeat-signs. In Beethoven's characteristic economy of immensity, there is a constant pressure of reluctance to leave relegated ideas unused or, at least, un-cited, be it in metamorphic guise. For their part, students and performers of Liszt have pointed out in how many works the tensions arises from an avoidance of the dominant but the dominant's implied presence.

No less than in art or literature, a body of musical work can be haunted and informed by an "unrealised." The most "likely," consequential of operas is Verdi's *King Lear*. The project occupied Verdi's sensibility and ambitions from his early discovery of Shakespeare to the very last days of his long life. From decade to decade, the *aggiornamento,* the postponement of *Lear* intervened more urgently in the operas Verdi was actually producing. Over and over, the crux is that of fathers and daughters, or, as in the case of *Traviata,* of would-be daughters-in-law. *Simon Boccanegra, Rigoletto, Aida* centre on the theme. It is present, obliquely, in half a dozen other Verdi operas. The absence of *Lear* is formidably "there."

The rôle of creation in the origins of art is pivotal to this entire study. I will return to it in the context of Heidegger. At present, I am trying to elucidate in what ways the freedom, the gratuity of aesthetic creation, and the constancy within such creation of absent and alternative forms may discriminate between the concept of creation itself and that of invention. In what ways are the freedom not to be or to be otherwise instrumental in the creative process?

There are far more sketches and maquettes than there are works; the discarded is, immensely, in excess of the retained and realised. I have alluded to the artist's reiterated sense of frustration, of sorrow in respect of the finished or published *oeuvre;* each of whose components is an inevitably reductive, diminished articulation of far richer and more inward possibilities. To the artist each masterpiece communicates a recurrent defeat. It atrophies in seeming but fundamentally spurious perfection, leaving behind and unfulfilled the unbounded intuitions of the work-shop. In creation, *and this may indeed be a cardinal difference from invention*, solutions are beggars compared to the riches of the problem.

The diminutions, the abstentions and "paring away" which generate executive forms—the painting, the statue the edifice —are functional in the palimpsest of preceding and alternative versions which underlie the finished product (where "finished" carries ominous overtones). Especially in regard to painting, modern techniques of radiography have made available the successive layers, the archaeology in motion which inhabit the canvas. The successive alterations in gesture and placement, the limbs re-drawn or omitted, the shifts of focus and lighting which are the strata of sequent possibilities beneath, say, the surface of a Titian, of a Rembrandt, or a Manet, are now accessible to view and genetic re-construction. Let it be said in passing that this scholarly-critical indiscretion, like that which bears on the drafts and cancelled states of a literary text, raises problems of legitimacy, of tact of spirit. Are we altogether licensed to penetrate, to bring back to interpretative light, those stages of creative monologue within the painter, of compositional rejection which he chose to cover over (literally), to obliterate from himself and the viewer? How far voyeurism? None the less, the investigation of the stratigraphy of a major painting, of the maquettes or clay fragments of a major sculpture (where these are extant), of the early trials, often scratched out, of a master-engraver such as Rembrandt or Goya, is not only informative as to genesis and intentionality. It confirms a decisive aspect of creation: the retention of the rejected, of the alternate, in the "completed" work.

At levels of which Freud's problematic but acutely suggestive examination of Michelangelo's *Moses* is a celebrated example, the prior visions—the original torsion of Moses's arm and body, the cancellation and addition of figures in Titian's *Marsyas*—continue at work in the statue and narrative painting as we have them. The exact tenor of that *modus operandi*, of that absence in action, is difficult to verbalize. It can be a degree of tension between surface and "undercoat." Time and again, the muscular flourish in a Rubens, the rhetoric of mastering pose and gesture, are in a relation of tension inward. They leap from, they hint at the volcanic though formally invisible forces of alternative design and configuration which now lie underneath or "inside." In the drawings and "stick-men" or women of the later Giacometti, the volume rubbed or stripped away, the densities flayed from the portrait or persona, are of the essence. Their missing but inferred "circumstance"—"that which stands, surrounding"—is vividly substantive. Hence the enigmatic but wholly persuasive sense (it presses on us like incarnate wind) of minimal vastness in Giacometti's *reductio*. Or consider some of the ways in which earlier designs, suppressed or amended structural elements in a building, deploy their thrust, their concealed demands in the Cathedral of Chartres as we now read it. Again, the voice of the buried roots can be made out in the far branches. Creation is also utmost conservation of energy.

Art has other ways of making ostensible the undeclared. Vermeer, Chardin paint silence. Their silences tide through the lit or shadowed air as does the translucent wash in Chinese paintings, themselves virtuoso presentments of silence. In Redon's *Rue de village à Samois* (in the Van Gogh Museum in Amsterdam), the pressure of silence is such as to have emptied the street and bent the light. Quite properly, it is not in reach of language to translate or paraphrase these renditions of charged absence, but they are evident. So, perhaps even more undefinably, is the capacity of painting to exhibit the passage of time. The landscapes which inform, which are figurations of the "foreground" myth and narrative in Poussin tell of impassive sovereignties of time. It is this temporality, inwoven in the motions of light and cloud-shadows across the pastoral depths, which makes the mythology both archaic and timeless. Poussin's great successor, Cézanne, articulates the flow of time over mass, the constructive and erosive shaping by time of rocks and trees. The Mont Sainte-Victoire series is a matchless enactment of chronology. There is an almost tactile sense in which certain Annunciations—that of Fra Angelico in San Marco, that of Lorenzo Lotto with its bristling cat—paint the future tense. Again, this fact is susceptible to neither verbal metaphrase nor technical analysis. But it is both sensorily and cognitively manifest. The ability of painting, perhaps of certain sculptures, to express musical sounds, is a major chapter in itself. Vermeer again, but also Giorgione and the sounding of jazz in Mondrian's New York-period. This "sonority" need not arise, although it often will, from the depiction of actual instruments or performance. An unmistakable sound-world—a singing voice, a street-organ, a band in the garden—comes at us, as it were, through the windows flung open to summer in Matisse or across the sparkling waters of Dufy.

In all these cases, creation affirms its intimate contiguities with absence; with being which remains unused but whose "background radiation" empowers the claims of art to represent, but also to rival and, in certain regards, to exceed life. Remember Guardi's talismanic gondola on the green lagoon: silence past silence, time ebbing, an incipient music which is also the bone-white shadow of the city on the far horizon. All absence is in play.

Most radical are those aesthetic traditions and artists who negotiate nothingness. This is to say, those who would include in their works the performative presence of non-being. By so doing, these modes of art and strategies of space direct perception back both to their origins in nothingness and to their freedom not to have been. I am arguing that this freedom of non-being and its phenomenality within the painting or sculpture or architectural design are defining of creation. Not surprisingly, the aesthetics of energized vacancy relate to those movements of theological-metaphysical meditation on the absolute, on the mystery of white light and total blackness which I have referred to previously. Such immersions in the void are practiced in Zen Buddhism, in Neo-Platonic and Plotinian figurations of eternity, in kabbalistic tropes of divine withdrawal and negativity. However different their context, such doctrines are the kindred background to the aesthetics and poetics of the minimal, where "minimal" signifies the plenitude of an incommensurable freedom and potentiality.

It is a calculated emptiness, the blanks between shaped solitudes—the single vase, the rock—which generate the tranquil tautness of Japanese interiors and temple-gardens. There is an enigmatic concordance here with the emptiness, already noted, of the Holy of Holies in ancient Judaism. In the most convincing of Japanese architectural lineaments and archipelagos of sand and stone (the actual scale can be unsettlingly restricted), silence is lit and light made silent. An analogous striving to touch the void has inspired commanding movements and theories in modern art. We now know how manifold and historically rooted were the impulses behind the minimalist paintings of Malevich, of Lissitzky, of Rodchenko, of the "white on white" and "black on black" produced shortly before, during, and after the First World War.

The Theosophic concepts, the light-mystique, ultimately Neo-Platonic or Pseudo-Dionysian, which prepare and accompany these minimalist totalities, will extend all the way to the practise of Ad Reinhardt, Elsworth Kelly, and the school of American "illuminates of the void" associated with the Pacific north-west.

The process of evacuation towards fulness can, perhaps, be followed with the greatest degree of logic and deliberation in the works of Mondrian (himself marked by Theosophy). Mondrian's initial picturality or realism yields step by step, via more and more abstracted horizontalities of sea and dune, to a pure linearity. In a well-known sequence, the densely rendred tree becomes, first, the minimal linearity of its structure, and then a set of markers in a space still animate with the absence of trunk and branch. But it is a series of seven canvases dated between 1931 and 1938–9 which allows us to follow Mondrian's increasingly confident, which is to say abstemious, mastery over the dynamics of emptiness. There is the *Composition with Red* of 1931, followed, a year later, by that *With Yellow and Double Line* (where the spaced between the lines takes on its seminal force). The *Composition Blue White* (1935), *White and Red* (1936), and that *Composition with Blue* (1937) seem to constitute a "triad," moving towards the two dominants. There are the masterpieces of 1938: *Lozenge with Eight Lines and Red* and *Composition with Red*. Almost nullified, compelled to formal marginality, the touch or passage of primary colour declares the whiteness, the blankness of the central areas. In Mondrian's best work, that "which is not" informs the mastered but profoundly generative freedom of the centre. Out of that expectant emptiness will surge the algebraically representational versions of Broadway and boogie-woogie in Mondrian's final works. These are, however, a lesser delight and a compromise. The eloquence, the descent into and homecoming from the calm vertigo of "being as yet to be," are affirmed in the 1931–38/39 modulations.

Arguably, therefore, it is non-objective and minimalist art forms which take us nearest to the fabric of creation. Abstract art, most especially where it incorporates, where it relates immediately to, emptiness in action or the absolutes of light and dark, communicates, so far as such communication is feasible, intentionality at liberty. It enacts what Aristotle called *entelechy*: the pure deployment of potential form. It maintains seminal contact with generative forces, be they "without form and void," from which art arises and whose unlimited modes of being, of coming into shape, it pre-figures. Non-representational, minimal art is always pre-figuration. It implies, it is an annunciation of, unbounded possibilities of representations in advent; possibilities, suggestions of nominal substance and mimetic objectivity for which the blanks (*blancs*) at the centre of a Mondrian or the "galactic dust" gathering towards compaction in a Reinhardt "black on black" keep, as it were, "open house." Precisely as the "composed," programmed silences in the music which leads from Webern to John Cage and Morton Feldman—Keats's "unheard melodies"—adduce the non- or pre-being, this is to say the primal silence, from which all music emanates and into which it ebbs.

Thus the abstract and the minimalist arts recuperate that which was prior to the local, and presumably ephemeral, options which inform our particular universe. They infer that infinity of the possible, of the alternative—an infinity which crucially comprises that of not being at all—from which our world is anthologized. Representation necessarily bears witness to the mosaic of the actual, a mosaic formally and existentially reductive and beggarly, whatever our everyday impressions of its prodigality. Representation is an inventory of the choices made, whereas abstraction narrates the abyss of total freedom which preceded and contained these choices.

The mathematical elements in much of non-objective and minimalist aesthetics are of tantalizing significance. They hint at the notion that pure mathematics, with its zero at the source, has a place in the originating vortex of pre-being; that its *principia* are functional prior to the confined intellect of man. Plato, Descartes, and Leibniz seem to have intuited this paradox. Pure mathematics would pertain to the realm of creation as do applied mathematics to that of invention.

Again, absolute polarities are probably fictions. The gradations between naked abstraction and photographic realism, between emptiness and thronged assemblages, are multitudinous. There are frequent uses of willed abstraction or counter-realism within classical representation: Mondrian-like squares and lozenges give to Uccello's battle-pieces their lifeless intensity. There are, on the other hand, compelling suggestions of reproduction in non-objective paintings: certain Jackson Pollocks strongly invite the reading of aerial mappings of megalopolis and spaghetti-junctions. Of great interest are works in which these duplicities, these transitions from representational narrative to abstraction and vacancy are themselves the theme. Consider Turner's studies of tempestuous light and his late aquarelles of Venice—the city dissolving into the sea from whence it implausibly arose. Or the break-down of legible form in the final stages of Monet. In such instances, mimesis deconstructs itself back into "informal" creation. Arrestingly, such dissolution towards the source of being is realisable in event the most insistently material and present of media: witness the passage from the literal to the abstract in certain Brancusis. But ontologically, the difference remains.

Where the medium is language, relations to non-being and to genesis, which I take to be integral to creation, raise problems that are virtually intractable.

5

All human constructs are combinatorial. Which is simply to say that they are *arte-facts* made up of a selection and combination of pre-existent elements. We have seen how vexed is the question of divine or astro-physical creation "out of nothing" (*ex nihilo*). That option is not open to human beings. Combinations can be novel and without strict precedent. The yoking together of the disparate, the generation of the androgynous or the hermaphroditic, can assume and beget limitless guises. But even the most revolutionary of designs, of chromatic assemblages, of new tints, makes inevitable use of extant material, which is itself circumscribed by the limitations of our optical nerves. The most "futuristic" of musical compositions, the most emancipated of atonalities, enlist prior sounds, and these also are constrained by our means of acoustic reception. Performative novelties—acrylic paint, the neon-tube, the saxophone in its time, electronic music today—obscure this fundamental truth. What they "make new" is the old re-combined, differently hybrid. What they exploit and generate metamorphically are given raw materials, themselves almost dismayingly confined to the narrow bands, to the spectroscopy as it were, of our physiology. So far as we know, evolution has not added to that reach (in the case of olfactory awareness, there may have been disuse). Always, reality is already there "for the ask-ing." Thought and the arts are, no less than the sciences, its ques-tioners.

Colours do carry with them associative and symbolic signals. The semiotic fields of white and black seem to comport values, discriminations, emblematic hierarchies which *may* reach into the recesses of the human psyche. When the orthodox Jew adopts white for his mourning and the anarchist black for his hopes, they are putting forward "counter-allegories" to the overwhelm-ing norm. The red/green cut appears to straddle both instinctual, possibly pre-conscious recognitions—red forbids, green licenses—and cultural-historical conventions. The lunatic logic whereby the Red Guards in Beijing strove to invert all traffic-lights, so as to make of red the colour of victorious forward motion, failed. In Christian Mariolatry, blue stands for a specific liturgical-allegori-cal blessing. There are traditions in which yellow, being solar, pro-claims, is reserved for the imperial.

Tactile implications attach to materials. The differing signs emitted by, say, the use of gold, of bronze, of granite, of alabaster, of glass in sculpture, in architecture, in the decorative arts, re-late both to aesthetic codes in a particular society and to visceral reflexes, to the "feel" of hand and body in contact with the object.

But significant and, it may be, deep-structured as these asso-ciations are, they remain of great generality. Their relative status, their indeterminacy afford and almost unbounded spectrum of combination and re-combination. The artist plays freely against the cultural-physiological norm. He can make bronze or marble torrential, undulant as does Bernini. Wood can be made lapidary by Brancusi or turned to burnished metal by the lime-tree carvers of the German baroque. There are in El Greco, in Soutine, greens which smoulder with despair. In short: the elements, the composites of all artistic making are indeed pre-existent; they do, in certain cases, bring with them a determinant surcharge (*surdétermination*). But the spaces for innovative transmutations are vast and open-ended.

What of music? Again, the demarcations between the neurophysiological and the cultural-conventional are exceedingly difficult to draw. It *may* be the case that tonality, the resolution of discords or a return to the dominant do satisfy expectations of a psycho-somatic origin. Experiments with mammalian responses to tonality and atonality suggest this. But not very much is mapped as yet of the relations between physiology and musical consciousness, between the inner ear and the psyche. By far the greater proportion of our identifying responses seems to be culturally programmed. The emotive aura ascribed by composers and listeners to certain keys, to certain chords and cadences, would appear to be historical and only conventionally prescriptive. They differ markedly as between European, Indian, and African musical systems.

What is even more telling is the fact that musical sounds and the notes which transcribe them are in essence first-hand. They may have been used innumerable times in previous compositions; they may have been sounded since the inception of man. But they are of the "new present"; they are freehold. It can happen that composers of exceptional power and persona appropriate certain tone-colours, modulations, or instrumental effects (as did Wagner, Mahler, Stravinsky). For a spell, those who use this material will, by design or not, be quoting or imitating or parodying (Shostakovich is a virtuoso of these secondary uses). But the spell dissipates. New signatures emerge. Thus musical notes, to an even more radical degree than colours, do not entail lexical and syntactic pre-determinants. They allow their user the almost naked freedom of the arbitrary. *Pace* Mozart, G-minor can, today or tomorrow, be made to laugh. And E-major will recover from the *Ring*.

Language is not like that. Language is its own past. The meanings of a word are its history, recorded and unrecorded. They are its usage. Prior usage does not, or only very exceptionally, attach to any colour or musical sound a specificity of meaning. Words mean. In the most rigorous sense, meaning is etymology. Each word comes to us, as we learn and use a language, with a more or less measureless freight of precedent. It will, where it pertains to common speech, have been thought, spoken, written million-fold. This priority and circulation determines, over-determines its meaning and meanings. The "total" dictionary, the dictionary which comprises all dictionaries, contains and defines the atomic particles of all meaning. These particles orbit the often unrecapturable nucleus of their origin—what were the first words, how did metaphor begin?—along paths drawn by grammar. Grammar does change, but very slowly, and only at the surface, as if its foundations were indeed innate. Thus the infinite library, that of Borges's fable, in which are shelved all past, present, and future books, is simply the ultimate lexicon and grammar of all grammars. In whose words are latent all sentences, which is to say all conceivable, though formally infinite, combinatorial possibilities and eventualities.

But none of these possibilities, with the arguable exception of nonsense-rhymes or Dada vocalizations, can be newborn. The *a priori* of its antecedents, what the word and syntactic mode have meant, mean now as products of past meaning, is the condition of its intelligibility. Communication is historical through and through. Understanding is the yield of previous definition and placement. We cannot "look up" a colour or musical note in order to identify a specific, singular meaning. We can, we often must do so, when meeting with or making use of a word. The house of meaning is always already furnished to (sometimes suffocating) excess. It is a seemingly infinite prison of combinatorial potentialities whose building-blocks, whose content and executive means are prior to us. They are already extant both phonetically—the speech-sounds available to the human larynx—and in semantic substance, in inherited sense. Even the most prodigal of wordsmiths, a Rabelais, a Shakespeare, a Joyce, adds only infinitesimally to the inherited stock. Neologisms are melded, though usually in analogy to or extension of the available; words and turns of phrases are coined; the dictionary grows by millimetres. It can also thin out. Obsolescence causes seepage. Particles and orbits of a given vocabulary and grammar are, as it were, extinguished, lost from visible and colliding energies (though they may, and frequently do, re-emerge when a speaker or writer quickens the dormant and the archaic into new luminosity). But across the sum of natural language such addition or wastage is virtually marginal.

The means of all meaning, if communication is to be intelligible, are a *prescriptive legacy*. They are cumulative out of time past. A "new language" generated *de novo* by some science-fiction edict or word-processer would be strictly meaningless (and how can there be language without meaning?). Solely a translation into a tongue accessible to us, only a bi-lingual lexicon and relational grammar would give it sense, which is to say a binding historicity. I want to come back to the reticulations of time and

of meaning. But let me say at once that there is a perfectly pragmatic, verifiable (indeed axiomatic) truth to the rhapsodic and
Heideggerian assertion that "we do not speak language; language
speaks us."

How little attention we give to the organic servitude of meaning, to the prescriptive nature of its articulation. How rarely we
attend to the compelling fact that words are a currency endlessly
shopworn, soiled, pre-empted by immemorial circulation; that
the newest, brightest minting is usable only in relation to preceding denominations ("definitions") and rules of exchange. There
are in everyday life and sentiment occasions, motions of mood
and apprehension, when words "fail us." When, physically as it
were, we run up against the walls of language as these encompass
and limit meaning. But even this experience is voiced by us in
terms necessarily pre-packaged; it is in expressions worn to their
bone that we seek to define our constraints or that brightness and
abyss of required articulacy somehow out of reach. Our erotic,
our sexual discourse, be it of the most intimate, be it "baby-talk"
made personal by private and clandestine fantasies, is pitifully
public. Millions have been exactly there before us. The whispers
of shared ecstasy are choral.

The serious writer, the poet above all, is a man or woman in
an utterly paradoxical language-situation. He or she will be exceptionally attuned to the history of words and to grammatical
resources. He will hear in the word the remote echoes, the soundings in depth, of its origins. But he or she will be auditive of and
able to register the overtones, undertones, connotations, family
kinships which vibrate around the word (Shakespeare's "perfect
pitch" and audition of the totality of a semantic field remain in-

comparable). Yet at precisely the same moment, the poet will be conscious, almost to despair, of the normative dictates of the lexical grammatical code, of the ways in which the coin in his or her hand has been rubbed flat, devalued, or altogether debased (clichés) by universal usage. Sometimes, frustration, the compulsion to "make it new," will initiate experiments in the invention of unprecedented words and even syntax. There are instances in Russian futurism and in surrealist poetics. But success is, at its rare best, only momentary (the two verses of invented, infernal discourse in Dante's *Commedia*). To communicate, even at the high vibrancy of the lyric poem, is to offer access via equivalence, via paraphrase (albeit partial), as does a dictionary. In the act of utterance, if this act is intended to be intelligible, "private language" becomes lexical and shared (hence Wittgenstein's refusal of the very concept of linguistic privacy). What the poet aims for, as we shall see, is that novelty of combinations which will suggest to the listener, to the reader, a corona, a new-lit sphere of perceptible meanings, of radiant energy, at once understandable and adding to (transcending) what is already to hand. It is in that deep-lying and generative sense that achieved poetry, always rare and somehow "counter-factual," is metaphoric.

How, then, is it possible to think new? How can new thoughts be crafted or cobbled out of material—words, sentences—itself "pre-stressed" and irreparably second-hand (we think in words). How is any new philosophy conceivable when its only executive form is that of linguistic discourse, shuffling counters which have served already a billionfold? It is only the non- or meta-linguistic medium of algebraic and symbolic notations which empowers formal or mathematical logic, which allows discovery within the axiomatic system. Again, it does seem to me that this dilemma, one of the most challenging in epistemology, has received only transient, often conventional notice.

A first distinction needs to be made. Self-evidently, a pre-Socratic or Scholastic thinker cannot make his point on, say, the nature of the *Logos* and of propositions by adducing the telephone. Fundamental to Descartes's model of cognition were certain developments in the science of optics. Where it refers, where it images and exemplifies, human language evolves and changes with the matter of the world, itself subject to incessant novelty. (Strikingly, however, so very many of the new nominations— "telephone," "television," "atomic," "biogenetic"—are hewn out of the most ancient, etymological wood. Modes of intelligibility are radically conservative; they enlist the roots.) Where it narrates, inventories, classifies, and analyses the realities of the human context, their altering furnishings and phenomenality, language makes fresh moves. It speaks, and speaks of new things incomprehensible to previous cultures and habits of recognition.

On the face of it, this seems to be a mere banality. But is it? Though the components of the word are as ancient as classical Greek, any sentence which contains the word "telephone" innovates on *all* sentences prior to Alexander Graham Bell. But is that innovation, is that addendum to the dictionary of the verbally definable, fundamental? Or is it, rigorously considered, trivial? In these deep waters, one gropes. What I am asking is this: In what measure, if at all, does reference to a telephone in an inquiry into the communicability of "truth," or into the central problem in epistemology of one's knowledge of other minds, alter, let alone resolve, the question? Knowledge of sound-waves, of electro-magnetic functions, of metals and plastics associated with the invention and perfection of the telephone has increased dramatically. Language is enriched by and accountable to this increase. But what of the substantive questioning of the issue—the emission and reception of sense, the accessibility of minds outside(?) or own? Are we saying anything ontologically *new*? Are we articulating solutions which improve on Plato or on Kant? Are their questions made obsolete? Might it not be—"there is nothing new under the sun"—that we are putting on offer semantic units, constituted of old words and inherited grammars, assembled in more or less novel combinations? Are we attempting to do no more than to re-arrange into alternative patterns the stones in the mosaic—a mosaic of meanings, associations, paradigms, and figurations inherited, re-composed across the millennia?

An even more perplexing uncertainty arises. How can even the most "revolutionary" and inspired of thinkers be at all confident that he or she is thinking new? Recorded utterances are the microscopic tip of an unfathomably massive ice-berg below the surface. For each and every voiced and recorded (remembered) act of speech, of statement, there are, in the past and simultaneously, unrecorded, unvoiced uses of language immeasurably more numerous (for example, in the mute soliloquies which generate the stream of consciousness in every human psyche). How can anyone know whether or not that which he or she is thinking has not been thought innumerable times already, quite possibly in the very same words and/or syntactical fabric, or in words and grammars closely analogous? What, fundamentally, is a "new thought" (in old words and on semantic ground infinitely common)? I repeat the distinction: it is that between a thought authentically new and a thought whose terms of reference are only materially-historically new. Yet I am fully aware of the fragility of this distinction, of the extreme difficulty of setting out, of making plausible the intuition that in new words the thoughts that matter are as old, as circumscribed by the legacy of available sense, as is language *per se*.

Not all philosophies engage this crux. It is paramount in Spinoza. Spinoza was acutely distrustful not only of the vagueness, of the polysemic indeterminacies in natural language, but of the inherent metaphysical pre-suppositions and self-deceptions which the vocabulary and the grammar of theological, of philosophic texts bring with them. Hence his resolve to purge his own Latin of its inherited accretions, of its misleading echoes and precedent. To do so, Spinoza incorporates an explicit lexicon, an explicit set of rigorous definitions, one might almost say a code of syntax made transparent (his polishing of lenses), into his treatises. But even this cleansing is only preliminary. Spinoza's propositional construct comes as near as it can to the mathematical. The underlying matrix is that of Euclid. Throughout Spinoza's *Ethics*, the argument by means of axiom, theorem, lemma, and proof aims to leave language behind. The formulations, expositions, and demonstrations are algebraic. Spinoza's is a heroic endeavour to think new, to render thought and truth tautological, by surmounting language.

This labour to break free of the bonds of inherited discourse so as to reveal truly creative, unprecedented insights, is strenuous in Nietzsche. He both gloried in and feared his mastery of rhetoric and the philological wealth and intimacies with etymology which inspired it. Nietzsche's philosophic writings hover incessantly on the edge of poetry as does a hummingbird when it feeds. They reach for a lyric-epigrammatic genre and are haunted by the limitations of the prosaic. Thus a continuity of transgression, of the leaps across the language-frontier, leads from the *Phaedo* to *Zarathustra*. When his death is imminent, Socrates composes and sings lyric verse. Scholars puzzle over this manoeuvre. But it not poignantly clear? Even the most suggestive of merely spoken or written myths no longer satisfies Socrates's impulses towards the unveiling of new truths, of the new light out of death. At the very noon of his mission, of his bestowal on the world of the "never-before-thought," Zarathustra rebels against the prison-house of language, against the soul-gagging weight of its lexical-grammatical past. Even song, "surpassing" as it is, will not suffice. Zarathustra (Nietzsche after him) must "danse his vision." Ultimate philosophic renovation can only be dansed.

Yet are the steps themselves not ancient and worn as is man? And is one major element in Nietzsche's doctrine of eternal return not his acknowledgement of the recursiveness, of the stasis in even the most ecstatic of thoughts?

Famously, the early Wittgenstein finds language to be generically inadequate to the philosophic enterprise. Whatever is primary for the understanding and needs of the human condition, in both ethics and metaphysics, lies beyond verbal or written expression. The truly important half of his *Tractatus,* rules Wittgenstein, was the unwritten. Unfortunately, he offers no account, however oblique, of what processes of insight, of communicable advance into essential issues, are to be found on the "other side of speech." In his last, incomplete treatise on the visible and the invisible, Merleau-Ponty does seek to go further. He hints tenaciously at mute encounters between the human body and the pre-linguistic facticity of the world. These encounters would discard the eroded assumptions, the circularities built into language as we have inherited it. But again, no examples of this creative muteness are (can be?) forthcoming.

In the history of Western philosophy, Heidegger's is the most consequent subversion of language short of silence. The "lightning flash" of symbiosis between human saying and the originating truth of being has been cancelled out by ultimately sterile modes of articulation. The false Platonic and Cartesian programmes of transcendent logic and rationality hold language and, therefore, potential insight, in thrall. To break out of these millennial confines, a new language is needed, a language linguistically antinomian to all that has been ossified after the pre-Socratics. Though there are precedents in the Rhineland mystical schools, notably in Meister Eckhart, and in the parataxical usages of Hölderlin, Heidegger's speech is at many points *sui generis*. His neologisms, his lapidary re-definitions ("un-definitions") of known terms, his violences of syntax, his deliberately irresponsible strategies of translation, engender a sometimes mesmeric, sometimes repellent idiolect. Almost brutally, Heidegger invites the question as to how this new idiom can be understood by those trapped in the dim places of wornout misprision. As early as in his lectures on the phenomenology of religious experience in 1919–1920, Heidegger proclaims that his teaching will have been fruitful only if his audience has *not* understood him or has understood him amiss. The risks are evident. With time, it may be that a considerable portion of Martin Heidegger's immensely influential works will turn out to have been more or less private soliloquy (though one uniquely resonant and sonorous).

It is a poet-novelist who may have come closest to rendering conceptually sensible the problem of philosophic innovation.

How can the mere re-combination of established, already bound-lessly associate and connotative markers (*ego* after Descartes, after Rousseau, after Freud) be made to yield new understanding? Hermann Hesse's *Glass Bead Game,* or *Magister Ludi,* comes near to conveying figuratively its "passing beyond" language, its aban-donment of a medium irreparably soiled and emptied by politi-cal inhumanity and mass-market circulation. The language of the game is that of a Pythagorean ideal of music and of mathematics, in whose combinatorial interplay truths, both new and genuine, mappings hitherto unperceived, are liberated. But this entranc-ing fiction is itself, to be sure, only a metaphor.

Thus the whole question of creativity, of creation in thought seems to me to remain elusive. Being rooted in language, it resists clarification from within. There is no leaping over the shadow. Is there in poetry?

6

An *ars combinatoria* points to invention and re-invention. It does not entail creation as I am trying to define it. Yet it is to creation that literature, and poetry above all, lay insistent claim. We recall Paul Celan's: "I have never invented." Where are the sources and evidence for creation in texts, oral and written, which are assembled, almost entirely, out of words and grammars ready-made (a fact which generalizes the fundamental challenge posed by Duchamp's *objet trouvé*)?

The sovereignty of the pre-fabricated extends far beyond dic-tionaries and rules of syntax, potent as these are. Our existence, our consciousness of self are thrown into language. We have not chosen that language. Only the enigma of the deaf-mute may provide a sanctuary, an "outside." We can strive to alter our language(s). We can deliberately renounce our native tongue. But this is merely to enter another room in the furnished house. From infancy—perhaps, according to certain theories of neuro-embryology, even earlier—we translate being and the world into speech-elements, into grammatical constraints and sequences, already extant and imposed on us. This translation may be empowered by innate perceptions of rules and rule-bound transformations (the Chomskyan model). In which case the imposition and constraint are even more binding. The world translates itself to and for us in pre-set lexical-grammatical ordinances. Attempts to break the contract between word and world, to re-negotiate it because none of us was party to its signature, lead either to autism and the silence of unreason or, as we shall see, to poetry. But they are *attempts* only, condemned to more or less palpable failure by the very fact that they too are organized linguistically, that they can be narrated only to the self and to others. Quite precisely, the autistic child sees through the trap and refuses such narration.

In natural language, however, verbal-grammatical means of meaning are never entirely pure. It is just this which demarcates natural language from symbolic logic, from computer-codes and the formulation of mathematics. Each word, indeed each articulate sound and its potential of significance, has its non-linguistic context. "Body-language" is a short-hand whereby to circumscribe the multitudinous components of physical stance, gesture, motion which accompany, qualify, often undermine or contradict utterance. Inflection, stress, accentuation, pace, volume are integral to any message. Locale, the historical-social setting, gender, conventions of implication or exclusion, are instrumental in signification. Together with "physique" in the most circumstantial sense, they can make formally identical pronouncements entirely different and even reversed (the boundlessly complex sphere of circumstance surrounding "Yes" and "No" in different cultures and erotic conventions).

Language is, therefore, both embedded in its cumulative past and in a manifold present, with its physiological, temporal, and social modifiers. Even at its most casual, sub-literate levels, an act and deed of human saying are, to some degree, *rhetorical*. They aspire to being heard, to persuade, by enlisting, consciously or not, instruments attached to word and sentence but not, strictly considered, linguistic. The purely semantic leads into the semiotic, into the surrounding phenomenology of making and communicating sense. Thus well before it leaves itself behind in order to "danse its meaning," language is radically choreographic and "multi-media."

Yet here also, our bodily range, the pressure on us of ambient and established signal-codes, renders creativity questionable. How many fundamentally new, unprecedented enactments, motions of intelligible meaning, have we added to the repertoire? Excluding—an immense exclusion, to be sure—the referential, that "telephone" inaccessible to Socrates, how much is there in our modes of discourse and communicative functions which would have struck an ancient Sumerian or Greek as utterly alien? This is why hermeneutic transfer, the interpretation of intended meaning and translation are possible, though always imperfectly, across millennia. What have we added to, what have we "created new" in respect to Hector's sorrow over Andromache, to the rage of Moses or David's stricken love for Jonathan? The "background-noise" of intelligible presence in even the most archaic signals remain as vivid as the flash of the light-house on a far horizon.

At some absolutely formative level, we conduct our lives from the cliché of birth to that of death. We vary innumerably, but very rarely in essence, on themes pre-set and always re-stated by the pre-established facticity of language. How, as the American poet Amy Clampitt asks, are we

> to realign
> the warp of history by
>
> more than a snippet, or
> forestall, when the wailing
> stops, the looming torpor—
>
> except from, just possibly,
> inside the fragile
> ambush of being funny.

How can re-combination, unlimited as its play may be, satisfy Osip Mandelstam's lapidary image of creation, that "thirst for the virgin soil of time"?

The perception of recursiveness, of an "eternal return" of themes, motifs, narrative, and dramatic situations presented in analogous executant forms, has bred intriguing conjectures.

Robert Graves's deliberately pointed axiom that "there is one story and one story only" (that of the Muse, that of every poet's submission to the "eternal feminine") finds its counterpart in structural anthropology and formalist narratology. Analysts of myths and folk-tales argue that the originating cells of all such tales, by they those of oral epic, of drama, of subsequent prose fiction, are identifiable and restricted in number. The Quest, the Lost or Rejected Child, the Descent into the Underworld are seminal core-units on which subsequent poetics embroiders and varies endlessly, but according to deep-seated formal and structural principles. Even as a strictly limited set of phonetic markers generates an infinity of possible verbal and written combinations, so all literature, all telling of tales and of the world, arises from a set of archetypal *données*. "Theme and variation" is not only a musical device, but the linguistically ordained dynamic of literature *in toto*. Once again, the suggestive analogue would be that of the universe according to relativity theory: a time-space unbounded but finite.

The questions are: What is the source of these primal *figurae*, how are they transmitted across time? Structural anthropology, notably with Lévi-Strauss, seeks to establish a logic of myths (a *mytho-logique*). The tales told and re-told throughout the planet, albeit with local *variora*, mirror the biological-social constants of the human species. They externalize and image instinctual and cerebral processes common to mankind. More specifically, they enable the mortal psyche to live with, to respond to insoluble provocations and contradictions such as those posed by incest-taboos, by our ambiguous relations to the natural and animal environment, or by the ineluctability of death. Neuro-physiological evolution, if it has indeed taken place at all since the nascence of human self-definition and articulacy, is essentially unperceived. The modern body, the modern nervous system continue to inhabit and encounter primordial imperatives. Science does tell new stories—those altering "paradigms"—but does not reach very deep into such primal determinants as love or hatred or death. These remain the object of incessant recursion, of tales told before. The shock of great literature is that of the *déjà-vu*.

Psychoanalysis would go even deeper. Its archaeology seeks to excavate the strata of consciousness, to find bed-rock. A number of canonic myths and their literary variants and metamorphoses have proved enduring, have been perpetually repeated, because they exhibit to the light of rational imagining, of controlled expressive forms, the needs, the volcanic thrust of pre- and sub-conscious material otherwise suppressed. These key stories are the dream-truths of individuation, of our infantile and sexual being. The triplicities in *King Lear* or in *The Brothers Karamazov* are typological variants on the universal folk-tale of Cinderella. Hamlet simply returns to the nightmares of Oedipus.

Pace his embarrassed acolytes, Freud came to intuit in both *Totem and Taboo* and in *Moses and Monotheism*, some mode of bio-somatic transmission, some mechanism in a collective unconscious. He knew that there was no possible physiological explanation for any such transmission. But the overwhelming spell of the primal stories, their universality, their recognition far beyond the individual psyche, seemed to Freud compelling. Jung categorically postulated a collective inheritance of archetypes, of foundational images and narrative patterns. Our art, literature, religious beliefs, and dreams are a legacy. They draw on an inventory of primordial icons older than reason and incised, as it were, in the colletive soul (there is more of Jung in Chomskyan transformational-generative grammar than might seem). Thus the cognizant imagination comes home, via art or literature or dream-situations, to a common ground, to a shared nativity, though it may, in any analytic-positivist light, believe that it has never been there. A thousand times-over, blinded, aged fathers will cross waste places leaning on young, talismanic daughters. Once the child is called Antigone, another time, Cordelia. Identical storms thunder over their wretched heads. A thousand times-over, two men will fight from dawn to dusk or through the night by a narrow ford or bridge and, after the struggle, bestow names on one another: be these Jacob/Israel and the Angel, Roland and Oliver, Robin Hood and Little John. Again, there is not a shred of scientific evidence for any such Lamarckian transmission of *Ur*-memories. The (racial) undertones can be dubious. None the less, what poet, what alert reader of literature will be altogether insensible to the (literal) depths of Jung's suggestion?

Literature is language, whether oral or written. It is, as Mallarmé reminded Degas, made of nothing but words. Its components are arbitrary phonetic units pre- and over-determined by consensual usage, by precedent meanings and connotations. Its major themes appear to conform to that law of *ricorso,* of the "riverrun" upstream invoked by Vico and by Joyce. Originality would, indeed, signify a return to origins. Could it be, therefore, that literature is the most inventive but least creative of artifacts? Could it be that the principal congruence is that between fiction, which is the substance of literature, and invention (we have, already, noted the crucial affinities between the fictive and the invented)?

This paradox merits closer study.

7

In the arts of language, the concept of "creation" attaches most directly to that of character or *persona*. It is exemplified, principally, by the making present in fiction, be it that of poetry, of drama, or of the novel, of men and women, of children, and, indeed, of animals. This presentment persuades us of their vital substance, of their existential weight, even where the genre is that of fantasy or the surreal. There is a palpable weight, an organic roundedness to the *personae* among Dante's dead or in Milton's celestial orders. The cognitive riddles, the unknown dynamics of narrative method which generate the life-force of the fictive character press on us with their evidence, but deny us any finality of explanation. Odysseus first took shape in a rhapsode's voice; his native substance was that of the vibrant air and of the human ear. Joyce's Ulysses first arose as a sequence of alphabetic markers on a piece of paper. Materially considered, the man from Ithaka and Leopold Bloom are nothing more than a combination, an encoding of oral and written signs, symbols, lexical-grammatical units arranged and disseminated via sound-waves or script. Emma Bovary is the resultant of so and so much ink expended on so and so much paper.

Yet the utter insufficiency of any such definition is inversely proportional to the shock of being which it seeks to situate and account for. A scandal (authentically theological and epistemological), both overpowering and everyday, informs the "life"—the word begs every question—of Penelope or Ophelia or Don Juan. This life, within the respondent listener, spectator, and reader, as well as in history and society at large, may, rather brutally, exceed and surpass our own. It does so in time. Our earthly existence is brief and terminal. The *persona* engendered by a writer (or painter, or sculptor, or composer in harness with language) can persist across millennia. No temporality dims the high rages of Moses, the urgent unclarities of Hamlet, the mien of Don Quixote. La Fontaine's *monsieur* fox brushes past centuries. The author can be nameless; the *Da-sein*, the "being-there" of the character he has sent into the world may endure not only long past his begetter's life, but beyond that of the locale and culture in which she or he was begot and, most unnervingly, via translation, long past the language of its birth. Neither Homeric Greek nor Aramaic are still much with us. Agamemnon and the guests at the Last Supper enforce their unquenchable presence.

To the author—witness Flaubert moribund—such perennity is at once glory and outrage. To those of us into whose little lives a Dido of Carthage, a Mr. Pickwick or Hans Castorp out of *The Magic Mountain* demand access, the obvious contrast between the two relevant categories of existence can be only a recurrent, perhaps rueful wonder. But not only chronology is at issue. The epic, scenic, or fictional agent, the *dramatis persona* in the inclusive sense, possesses a vitality, a density often surpassing that of any living being. There is, in ways both obvious and inexplicable, so very much more to the Wife of Bath, to Molière's Tartuffe, to Proust's Albertine, than there is to the vast majority of us. So much more immediacy of voice and of gesture, of psychological suggestion, of variousness and adaptability via translation, imitation, parody, re-enactment and graphic illustration (Cleopatra's "infinite variety"). The "Hamlets" bred out of Shakespeare's template defy enumeration. They are animate in theatre, in opera, in ballet, in film, in lyric verse, in painting and the plastic arts. They will quicken semantic and semiotic events and media still to come. The meanings of Don Juan, from Tirso de Molina to Shaw and Max Frisch, are those of a figuration or compaction of verbal-musical elements made excessive, damned by its own vitality, by an ontological *libido* or hunger for embodiment of which the erotic is only one, perhaps contingent, expression. The pulse of life, of a spirit in felt motion, in Tolstoy's Natasha in *War and Peace* seems to reduce most of our own biographies to a ghostly grayness.

What is the price which the imaginary demands of us in exchange for its prodigality of giving? How much within us is simultaneously enriched and laid bare when a Falstaff, a Julien Sorel from Stendhal's *The Red and the Black,* become tenants in our own often nondescript lodging? Does the "un-real" (meaning what?) exercise a metaphysical and psychological vengeance on the claims to reality of the everyday? Epic singers and reciters profess themselves possessed, Dervish-like, by the voices, by the bodies of those whose tales they narrate. Actors readily bear witness to their own absorption into the vampire-visitations of the *dramatis persona.* Balzac, Dickens, Flaubert tell, non-metaphorically, of the invasion of their own physique, of their dreams and conscious thoughts, of the inmost tics and reflexes of their demeanour, by the men and women whom they are scratching onto paper. At one moment, Flaubert proclaims: *"Emma Bovary c'est moi!"* At another, he bellows that he would do anything to boot the "loathsome little bore" out of his work-room.

The facts are clear enough. But at best, our understanding of them is made up of intuitions and images. What is in question, is nothing less than the unyielding nub of epistemology. What is meant by attributions to the phenomenology of internal and external perceptions of either reality or unreality? Across our planet, and for millions, 221B Baker Street is the "most real" —itself an opaque, logically unsatisfactory superlative—address in London. Countless letters and visitors seek it out. In what ways, if any, is Sherlock Holmes's house-number either unreal or non-existent? Different metaphysics, different theories of nomination and cognition, different psychologies give different answers. They propose differing borders between the empirical and the imaginary, between verifiable objectivity and the free play of the subjective. From German Idealism to Husserl, in models themselves ultimately Platonic, philosophers have argued for the dismissal altogether of the naive, intuitive separation between subject and object, between the proceedings of the percipient-interpretative self and the "outside" world. To these abstract theses, psychology, ranging from the purely introspective to the clinical, has added an awareness of intermediate states. Dreams, hallucinations, compulsive fantasies, the teeming welter of apparently baseless phenomena arising out of mental unbalance or lesion, circumscribe a frontier zone, vast and shadowy, between ego and object, between what is taken to be fact and what is labelled fiction. The demarcations are at all points fluid: "Is this a dagger that I see before me. . . ?"

We most probably cannot revert to the epistemological innocence of Aristotelian or Cartesian constructs of certainty. These were underwritten, quite specifically, by assumptions of divine realiability, of a final rationality and comprehensibility of the relations between the human intellect and an empirical-analysable cosmos. Our sense of the often compelling internalization of vision and experience, the seminal rôle of unreason in vision and experience is, after Rousseau, after Nietzsche and Freud, too insistent. We know, with Schopenhauer, that our world is "representation" (*Vorstellung*); that even the theoretical and the applied sciences, although to a lesser degree, may be models grounded in the particular fabric and neurophysiology of the human cortex rather than in any guaranteed, immutable and independent truth "out there." Differently phrased, our uncertainties as to reality remain those voiced by the very earliest of attempts at systematic thought. Xenophanes' taunt that if cows had religion their gods would have hooves remains irrefutable.

Axiomatically, viscerally, it may be that we feel, that we share

with other "normal" sensibilities the "common sense" finding
that the *personae* out of literature and the arts do belong to a different branch of reality than those persons we crowd up against in
the underground. The provocation, however, remains: that alternate reality can exercise on our consciousness, on our daily lives,
a pressure of presence, an intrusive impact, a memorability altogether in excess of that which we define as the "actual," as the
tangible. These three rubrics are decisive. Klytemnestra and Lady
Macbeth, those sisters in blackness, are present to us, our eyes
being open or shut, are material to the antennae of our recognitions, far beyond the majority of women or of men whom we encounter in "real life" (at every turn, language traps us within the
labyrinth which we are calling on language to elucidate). Theatrical or cinematic presentations, illustrations by insightful artists
—Blake's Milton, Doré's or Dali's Cervantes—may provide our
personal experience of immediacy with more emphatic contours.
Indeed, we may resent to ways in which these great "imagin-
ers" anticipate or condition our own conceptualizing. But the text
alone can, and often does, prove more incisive. It engraves the fiction in the wax tablets or copper plate of the respondent psyche.
Something very nearly physical is occurring.

Intrusiveness heightens this conjecture. The child cannot
easily banish from his nightmares, from the patch of darkness
he must cross on his way to bed, the monsters out of fairy-tales.
Fictions will take a hold even where, most vividly where, they ter-
rify or unsettle. They are the faces at the unlit windows of consciousness and sub-consciousness. It may well be that all lasting
fiction known to literature, from Homer to Borges, is, in categorical essence, a ghost-story; that the characters narrated or acted
out are spectral, in the rational-pragmatic sense, but endowed

with a penetrative "thereness" which we cannot explain or justify causally. Our private lives may alter as we aim to imitate, to "become" this or that fictive being. In romantic Europe, numerous individuals sought identification with Goethe's Werther, with Hamlet. We are in some literal sense "taken over" (what analogies are there between this possession and that by music?). The imaginary will not vacate its tenancy. Dying, Balzac calls out for one of the physicians in the *Comédie humaine*. Insubstantial mass and intrusive impact relate directly to memorability. The fiction makes itself unforgettable. This may happen on the instant. Heard, read once, David before Saul cannot be unremembered. Rembrandt's version is only confirmation, a splendour of certitude. Heard once, the voice of Melville's Ishmael, the tapping of Long John Silver's wooden leg, the cold bark of the fox in D. H. Lawrence's story, takes root in the inner ear. These sounds can be as memorable as are the most consequential or intimate of personal experiences—often, far more so. The problem of how this process is initiated grows even more perplexing when we consider the negative side. Why are there acutely literate, imaginative human beings who remain wholly immune or hostile towards the fascination of this or that imagined presence, who are left cold by this or that motif, landscape, dramatic scenario? Wittgenstein, abundantly responsive to Goethe, to Tolstoy, can "make nothing of Shakespeare." It is Shakespeare's characters, the normal touchstone, which strike him as factitious.

Some proceedings can be made out. As Aristotle ruled, a need to mimic, a pleasure in *mimesis* and *imitatio,* is universal to apes and to men. The mirror is an endlessly fascinating window, even where it mocks. In the representative arts, in literature, most evidently in the inception of dramatic genres, imitation may have been the well-spring. There is an elemental impulse to draw pictures on the cavern wall, to tell and re-enact stories and situations, to reproduce landscapes and their human or animal fauna, in short to re-create life in the recognisable guise of the life-like. Thus realism remains the stubborn node, the legacy of an instinctual reproductive need, in even the most fantastic, non-objective devices (the centaur remains half-man and half-horse). In particular, mimetic observation breeds characters. The fiction mimics noticed, recorded, explored actuality. All art is, at some level, *à clé*. It is more or less transparent to its source-material, to the manifold raw material of the extant. *Personae* customarily are a composite of diverse bits and pieces, as in a mosaic. Except in caricature or *ad hominem* satire, they are not a one-to-one facsimile. *Collage* and *montage* are means of impersonation much older than Homer. Here again, the process is combinatorial. No one, including the author, can tell how many fragments out of life, internal and external, how many natural resources, have gone into the assemblage of an Achilles or the brewing of a Malvolio.

The nearer to the photographic, to the seamlessly "glued," the further will a character be from the secret of the autonomous, from the quantum leap into an orbit of its own. The masters insinuate into their creatures the asymmetries, the roughage, even the contradictions to be found in the organic. Lasting architecture incorporates the irregularity. Imitation, reproduction, recreation are also, as we have seen, functional in a wider sense: language, art, music vary on what may, in the final analysis, be a finite thematic set. Star Trek varies on the Argonauts. Therefore there is a case, positivist and disenchanted, for arguing that even the most vivid and memorable of aesthetic products are to be regarded under the heading of mimetic, perhaps in some manner immature, play (this was Freud's view). The concept of originality in its true essence, of origination *de novo,* would be little more than a self-flattering illusion, a day-dream. Reality, however philosophy and the sciences define it, the *given* world, in either a religious or materialist concept of donation and pre-existence, will always be the controlling source and inventory of the imaginary. The camera lens at work in the aesthetic is doubtless subtler, more penetrative, more resourceful in its apertures and filtres than any which optics could conceive of. But when we believe ourselves to be imagining, let alone creating, we take pictures.

Artists, writers, philosophers in an idealist or romantic vein (Schiller, Schelling, Coleridge, Emerson) feel otherwise. Coleridge's distinction between Fancy and Imagination bears directly on the gap which separates the mimetic assemblage, the combinatorial and merely inventive from the genuinely creative, from that "esemplastic" power which enables the great artist, poet, and playwright to shape living forms. These are organic and transcendental in that no anatomy of their constituent elements, no technical dismemberment of their gestation and possible sources can account for the vitality of the whole, a vitality whose sum radically exceeds that of all discernible parts. Exhaust every insight into historical-social context, into philology, into formal and stylistic components, ransack the author's biography, his own readings and encounters—the life-secret of the persona which he "bodies forth" will elude you. Just as does that of the men, women, and children who people the "other" (the lesser?) "reality principle" (in Freud's somewhat uneasy demarcation).

Endlessly fascinating are the glimpses which writers allow us into the work-shop of individuation, into the making of the Golem. Often, Victor Hugo draws, etches his personage before "wording" him or her. Balzac is a *pointilliste,* letting his *figmenta* emerge into view, into communicative intelligibility via minute depictions of their locale, of the street or house which pre-figures and defines their physical and psychic lineaments. We can follow, cadence by cadence, the tormented search for phonetic and syntaxic rhythms, accords, modulations which are the matrix, the coming to laboured birth of Emma Bovary or Fréderic Moreau. A grammatical orchestration sounds the identifying note, the unfolding fugue—the plot-narrative—of a Flaubert agent. In Proust, one can show how the effects of integral presence grow out of verb tenses, out of the *imparfaits* and *passés simples* which inflect Albertine or Swann into motion as does gravity when it bends light and curves space in relativity. In Simenon's notebooks, height, weight and exact address are given to the imagined *personae.* The intrigue arises out of these "police-blotter *signalements.*" The names seem to follow. Henry James, on the other hand, hovers over lists of proper names. These are the stellar dust out of which a Lambert Strether, an Adam Verver condense into luminous mass. *Middlemarch* is, in some respects, a reflection on the rôle, both lyric and mendacious, which the letter *l* plays in the names and destinies of the protagonists.

Whatever the triggering impulse, whatever the generative turn, writers insist on the resistant, even mutinous autonomy of their principal incarnations. Balzac is incensed at the unexpected, unwilled twists of mind and of behaviour taken by the women and men who enter and re-enter the thronged space of his *Comédie humaine* (that re-entry being itself undeniable proof of their continued existence in time). Tolstoy complains bitterly about his incapacity to control Anna Karenina's voice and actions towards the close of the novel. She has "escaped from him" and defies pre-vision. These are *not,* insist the begetters, complacent metaphors of anthropomorphism. We do not understand the "genetics," but the shock of rebellion from within the planned scenario is as un-nerving to the author as it is to his readers. How late, how much against his will, did Proust "discover" the treachery, the sleaze in his beloved Saint-Loup?

To this mystery, the hoped-for listener, spectator, or reader is accomplice. It is by virtue of the openness and empathy of his reception that the fiction is validated, that it inhabits individual memory and cultural transmission. The instruments of response are decisively collaborative. Where they are not forthcoming or ephemeral, the work dies. Unpublished, unperformed, Shake-speare's *Hamlet* would have died with Shakespeare. There may in some Borges-land be a limbo of brilliant characters and fic-tions which never stepped out of dreams, private fantasies, or lost texts. The psychology of reception, of the responding moves in our senses and mentality are at once perceptible and almost un-decipherable. We have seen that they comprise self-identification, the reader's identifying lunge towards the *persona* whose glory, whose anguish, whose social, moral, erotic, intellectual condi-tion we would imitate and "ingest" into ourselves (masturbation to the tune of the fictive is not only carnal). Fictions serve as looking-glass to our illusions, to our most covert dreams and am-bitions. They can also be the seed of nightmares. It is not only the child or adolescent who dwells on terror in books, in drama, in film. Haunted recollection draw from a well, whose deeps are probably related to sexuality, a particular *tremolo,* a shudder in the soul. Somewhere in this intricate concatenation and abyss lies the answer to the nagging question of the pleasure we derive from tragedy, to the compulsion we manifest when wanting to re-experience fictions of pain, of catastrophic loss.

Thus there are fundamental energies of identification and of recoil, of imitation and of avoidance, at work in the aesthetic collaboration between maker and audience. At more or less informed, discriminatory, contextually alert levels, every spectator, listener, reader provides the fiction with its incorporation. The dramatist, the novelist instigates. He or she initiates the paradox of fertile, innovative echo, resounding in every recipient and across time. This echo substantiates and reciprocates, enabling the work of art, of literature, of music not only to realise and multiply its intentions, but (ideally) enriching it with significations, which a continuum of relevance and renewal of which the author, artist, and composer may not have been aware. There is no better example of a dialectic yielding new truths. The burning of Virgil's Troy now comes after that of Dresden in fresh immediacy. Like the performer—the actor, the musician, the dancer—the awoken, participatory reader has an executive function. He too, as French has it, "signs the page." Or as Peter Shaffer put it to Arnold Wesker:

> furious, inchoate energy funnelled through shape (and only so) reconstitutes itself as furious energy in the brains and psyches of its *recipients*. Reconstitutes itself because of you. The fire which started in the playwright's head must get dimmer and dimmer as it grows in the communal imagination of an audience. Your job is to convey sacred flame in a vessel. You can say, looking at that vessel smoking on the stage: "How miserable. I have seen the *Volcano*,

and all I caught is one wretched tongue of fire." But that tongue properly placed and focused upon, *is* the Volcano. Your power to concentrate fire for an audience will make them feel it, and be burned by it, even though they don't know the volcano, and never can. . . . what one writes can detonate in a viewer's head with the same resonance that it had when one first put it down on paper . . .

It is the actual process of this import into ourselves of imagined beings, of landscapes, situations, objects more various, often more memorable, than those in the external world, it is the psychology (the neurophysiology?) of reception, which elude us. How do we "make flesh"—the eucharist-metaphor is obviously kindred—semantic suggestions? By what recognitions or concessions do we ascribe to them truth-values, a mode of existentiality so credible as to make ghostly so many of the women and men and empirical facts we come across "out there"? One recalls Shelley's exultant sorrow when he declares that those who have loved Sophocles' Antigone will no longer love any living woman comparably. To what extent is our conceptualization of the fictive made plausible by, added to by our everyday experiences? Does our immersion in the factual "flesh out" the imaginary? What liberties of collaboration are taken from us when a great illustrator—a Doré, a Rackham—is so resourceful that he has "imagined for us," making his rendition of figures and settings henceforth inescapable? (Children's editions of the classics should not be too well illustrated.)

It may be that these instrumentalities of realisation—of "making real"—are minutely cumulative. We add to our sense of present density, of "thereness," each time we re-read the novel or see the play staged (in even the finest of films, for reasons which are unclear, this presence fades after a certain number of repeated viewings). We may forget this or that character and episode, this or that name, only to have them leap back to life later, just as in mundane affairs. Where have they dwellt meanwhile? For many authors and readers, a *persona* is mainly image. For others, the lasting incision is the sound of a voice, a mannerism of speech. Working against metaphor, within the Judaic iconoclastic heritage (the *Bilderverbot*), Franz Kafka is matchless in his thinning to emptiness the image of his personages while making totally unforgettable their voices and the rustle of their shadows. In each and every act of aesthetic reception there are elements both cultural-collective and private. It is precisely the mark of enduring art and literature that it summons to re-enacting and generative echo the universal as well as the particular. But the aetiology of response and the psychic moves involved are as difficult to theorize as are those of the poetic act itself.

Hence the perennial resort, which I have already underlined, to theological allegories. These are licensed by the resonant obscurity of *Genesis*. There is no convincing reading, except in terms of the revealed, of the divinely axiomatic, of the proposition that God created man "after His own image." That He made man, as it were, in facsimile. What we know of the human animal renders any such postulate almost blasphemous. It has always been more plausible to suppose that it is man who has "made God" after his own mortal contours (Michelangelo's bearded patriarch on the Sistine ceiling). Such an inversion is altogether within the logic of the anthropomorphic.

Nevertheless, it is on the biblical affirmation or on the figure, ubiquitous in mythology, of the shaping of clay by the Master Potter, of the infusion and breathing of life into the clay, that poetics relies. In the begetting by writers and artists of fictive creatures, of *figmenta* imbued with vital attributes, aesthetic theory and practice have found a close analogue to the divine creation of organic forms. The poet, playwright, or novelist names his characters as Adam names the animals around him; in either case, nomination entails both truth and "real" existence. The successful dramatist or story-teller or painter is "God" in large miniature. He or she ushers into the world agents out of the imaginary, out of some dust of pre-existence, whose subsequent fate, whose freedom of action can, precisely as in the mystery of free will accorded by God to His creations, challenge the maker.

Where such *dramatis personae* are male and female, they may indeed be, and in some measure at least, have been drawn in the craftsman's own image. There must be *something* of Shakespeare in both Iago and Cordelia—a catholicity of self-projection which seemed to Lamb or to Hazlitt god-like, but whose neutrality appalled Tolstoy and Wittgenstein. Art and literature are possible because they mime, though on an evidently humbler level, this humility being that of all fiction as set against truth, the divine *fiat*. Even the kabbalistic trope of God's solitude, of His wish to create man so as to have company, has its counterpart in the longing of the artist to "people this little world" with presences at once familiar and resistant to him. Alexandre Dumas gazed with paternal pride at the rows of tin soldiers which gave visual markers to the legion of his characters (he wept at their "deaths"). Having fathered Natasha and Anna Karenina, Tolstoy came to doubt his own mortality.

These allegoric analogues are talismanic to artists and to theoreticians of the poetic. They point towards "creation" and away from "invention." They infer the organic, the life-given autonomy of the begotten, rather than the assemblage, the combinatorial, the "fancied" (Coleridge's dissociation) which would characterize the invented. *Poiesis,* as we have seen, lays claim to primary making. Infused by the breath of the Muses, the rhapsode, the epic poet, the composer of the Prologue in heaven to Goethe's *Faust* in turn breathes a dynamic, intrusive, and unforgettable *élan vital* into a constellation of words in action. The scenario of divine precedent empowers him or her to make fruitful a process whose innermost springs remain impenetrable. In turn, this precedent, validates the experience of the receiver who "suspends disbelief" and allows a Faust or a Mephistopheles to take up residence within himself. Thus, at the highest pitch, in some sense beyond metaphor, the artist is indeed god-like to himself and to his public. He creates.

Is this conceit, using the word also in its historical-rhetorical meaning, now under pressure? Are the "great stories" going to continue to be told, will the characters which enact them continue to be born?

IV

To Plato, the point would have been self-evident. It is inconceivable that one should question the life of the mind without addressing mathematics and the sciences which, in the main, derive from the sovereignty of mathematics. Since Galileo and Descartes, this injunction has become theoretically and pragmatically inescapable. It is in mathematics and the sciences that the concepts of creation and of invention, of intuition and of discovery, exhibit their most immediate, visible force.

The difficulty, however, is twofold. Mathematicians and scientists "get on with the job." Like the proverbial millipede wary of introspective paralysis, they avoid too close a scrutiny of the epistemological foundations of their disciplines. They do not inquire too probingly into the justifying or subversive presuppositions of their manifestly triumphant progress. Even so elemental a challenge as the debate on the axiomatic and logical foundations of pure mathematics, on the internal consistency of axiomatic systems, at the turn of the century, is left in abeyance. There is simply too much to do. In turn, the application of even abstruse mathematical theories to natural sciences and technology reinforces habits of empirical confidence. The "thing works," whatever the arcane philosophic vexations at its originating depths.

The second difficulty is one of access. The non-mathematician, the outsider to the sciences, can hardly begin to grasp, let alone gauge, the arguments and controversies such as we have them as to the nature of mathematical scientific creation or invention. Ignorant of the languages of mathematics and of their translation into the exact and applied sciences, the listener can scarcely make out even the rudiments of the debate as to whether or not the objects of mathematical operations are, in essence, intuitions, mental artifacts, or realities in an existential sense. One needs considerable familiarity with mathematical symbolism in order to follow the controversies on whether or not there are in pure mathematics "discoveries" or, instead, an autonomous unfolding of *a priori*, as it were tautological, systems generated from within the human intellect and its deep-seated instinct for speculative, other-worldly play. *Homo ludens.* If, as Galileo ruled, nature speaks mathematics, far too many of us remain deaf.

Though almost a century old, Henri Poincaré's paper on mathematical creation is still considered a classic. Poincaré was attentive to the dynamics of algebraic intuition and resolution within his own eminent research. He brought to bear on them both wit and self-observant finesse of an unusual acumen. His autobiographical record of the moments, of the circumstances of seeming hazard, which triggered his famous memoir on Fuchsian functions—Poincaré was putting his foot on the platform of a provincial omnibus when the seminal hunch and concomitant solution struck him—remains exemplary. The "lightning flash" resulted from a lengthy process of prior but unconscious or subliminal work. It was the outcome of a concentrated process of analytical technique below the threshold of Poincaré's daylit awareness. Enigmatically, argues Poincaré, the sub-conscious self, somehow impregnated with algebraic impulses, has a tact and operative delicacy "in no way inferior to the conscious self." It is at this subliminal level that decisive choices are arrived at as between a congeries of possible, though rule-bound, combinations. "The true work of the inventor consists in choosing among these combinations." But how does the sub-conscious choose? Poincaré's answer is not altogether satisfactory: "The privileged unconscious phenomena, those susceptible of becoming conscious, are those which, directly or indirectly, affect most profoundly our emotional sensibility."

What is arresting is the move towards the aesthetic. A "special sensibility," unknown to the layman, defines the creative mathematician. The "useful combinations," where "useful" signifies the generative strength which will lead to further propositions, to related theorems and general laws, "are precisely the most beautiful." A false idea, an intuition leading to an impasse, "had it been true, would have gratified our natural feeling for mathematical elegance." Thus there may be multiple solutions to the problem—that, most recently, of Fermat's "last theorem"—but the one to be pursued will also be the most beautiful.

In this context, "beauty" is no vague analogue borrowed from the arts. It is rigorously equivalent with truth, as in Keats's equation. It possesses economies of sequence, transparencies of demonstration, potentialities for ramification, which give to "beauty" a substantive, though untranslatable meaning (as in music). The proof is true because it is beautiful; it is beautiful because it is true.

I find nothing more frustrating, more humbling, than my incapacity as a mathematical innumerate, to grasp this lucent realm of "truth-beauty." I am only able to simulate indistinctly by trying to experience, by trying to analyse, the presence of beauty in the style of certain chess masters, in the configuration and solution of certain end-games and chess problems. But here the beauty of the truth is, in some complicated ways, also trivial. That of mathematics is not. Yet again, music enters the dialectic. How is one to define *its* non-triviality, its uttermost seriousness, with its affinities, in encoded, formal structures, and possibly in psychic origins, with those of both mathematics and chess? Or how is one to account, in this constellation, for the unsettling fact that certain combinations in chess display obvious beauty yet can be unsound? There is no beauty to mathematical error.

G. H. Hardy in *A Mathematician's Apology* strikes the same aesthetic chord as does Poincaré. "A mathematician, like a painter or a poet, is a maker of patterns." Hardy takes these patterns to be more permanent than any in literature or art because "they are made with ideas" whose verity, whose consistency can be established forever (Descartes worries lest this eternity may be held to abrogate divine omnipotence). Taking up the analogy with chess, Hardy finds that the beauty of mathematical patterns, e.g. Euclid's proof of the existence of an infinity of prime numbers by a transparent *reductio ad absurdum,* surpasses that of any chess game or problem. The difference is one of *seriousness,* of consequential interest and eventual application—although the latter is a contingent bonus somehow suspect to as pure a mathematician as was Hardy. None the less, it is the sheer beauty of the mental map or configuration, the aesthetic quality of the pattern, which are paramount. Those incapable of attending on this recognition and the delight it conveys are tone-deaf.

Against the claim of total, disinterested purity, which Hardy pressed to provocative extremes, John von Neumann put the empiricist case. Not even the most abstruse of mathematical developments is wholly independent from some empirical foundation, from needs and impulses originating in the real world. Elements of the "nonmathematical, somehow connected with the empirical sciences or with philosophy or both" do enter "essentially" into the mathematical experience. But von Neumann concurs with Hardy in arguing that in both physics and mathematics the criteria of success, the proof that the right road has been taken, "are almost entirely aesthetical." The simplicity and elegance of a chain of mathematical deductions aim to satisfy criteria common to all creative arts. Whatever the empirical, factual roots of his constructs, the atmosphere within which the mathematician operates ("atmosphere" being von Neumann's term) is most akin to that of "art pure and simple."

The trouble is that these authoritative testimonials do not distinguish between creation and invention. In everyday parlance, one does hear mathematicians place creativity above inventiveness. But, so far as I am aware, the distinction is impressionistic rather than definitional. What underlies this *ad hoc* usage is, precisely, the epistemological uncertainty and foundational controversy to which I have already referred. Are mathematical operations, particularly after the calculus and non-Euclidean geometries, concerned with the architecture of the imaginary, with what I would call "truth-fictions"? Do they generate arbitrary, although rigorously deductive, fantasms? Or are they, on the contrary, reflections, descriptions, however refined, however abstracted and theorized, of the world "out there"? In what manifold regards are real numbers "real," were transfinite cardinal numbers waiting to be found as are islands or galaxies in unmapped spaces?

Only some agreement on this immensely challenging issue could provide uses of the concepts of creation and invention with demonstrable substance. The wonder, even to philosophically untroubled mathematicians, lies in the modulations, often wholly unexpected, from autonomous mental play, from the joyously "useless," to subsequent material application. Via relativity theory, Levi-Civita's tensorial calculus, an algebraic by-way lying, as it was, in blameless obscurity, lead directly to the nightmares and to the benefits of nuclear energy. If pure mathematics does spring from sub-conscious intuitions—already deep-structured as are grammatical patterns in the transformational-generative theory of language?—if the algebraic operation arises from wholly internalized pattern-weaving, how then can it, at so many points, mesh with, correspond to, the material forms of the world? How do imaginary maps become the atlas of the everyday? Does the notion of "discovery" throw light on this, apparently paradoxical, coincidence (Leibniz would adduce a "pre-established harmony")?

And can we, albeit from outside, come any closer to the insistence of mathematicians themselves on the aesthetic ideals of their craft, on its primordial parallels with poetry?

2

The demarcations, always fluid, always interactive and negotiable, between pure and applied mathematics, are suggestive in respect to literature. By far the greater part of literature is "applied." It arises from, it addresses occasion. It narrates, surveys, inventories, ornaments, satirizes, calls to memory, strives to give intelligible shapes to the givenness, to the "thereness" (*Da-sein*) of our existential context, i.e. the world. Even where the fictive is most implicit, in romance, in the evocation of the supernatural, in the collages of surrealism, literature remains, in essence realistic. This pervasive realism, so profoundly entrenched, as Aristotle saw *contra* Plato, in the verb *is,* in all predication, is analogous to that of applied mathematics. Also the latter calibrates, catalogues, formalizes intelligibly and sets in efficaceous motion that matter of the world, be it in building a pyramid or dispatching an inter-stellar rocket.

We have seen that the means of literary production are com-binatorial. Inherited lexical, grammatical, and semantic coun-ters are combined and recombined into expressive-executive se-quences. The liberties of combinatorial arrangement are vast, but not unbounded. There are axiomatic constraints, though subject to innovative enlargement, on the limits of signification. The per-formative utterance seeks to be understood at some level. (Hence the inherent triviality of so much of surrealist or automatic writ-ing.) As in applied mathematics, there are postulates and conven-tional algorithms—metrical forms, for example, or identifiable genres such as the verse epic or prose fiction. Applied mathe-matics indexes and fuels human practice. So does literature. The maps it makes of consciousness and its *imitatio* of the human con-dition are active. They alter the landscape. There is a novel *eros* after Dante, a deepened politics of human relations after Shake-speare, the topography of war has changed after Tolstoy.

Pace Hardy, the fertile drive, the harvest of applied, which is to say "impure," mathematics empower our lives. The application of mathematics to the measuring of an acre or the engineering of a nuclear reactor, enacts reason itself. In their turn, applications, the algebraic geometry which organizes our uses of space, the functional analyses without which economics, sociology, tech-nology would be impossible, open out into further problems and solutions. So it is with the dialectical reciprocities between text and context, between word and world. Both applied mathemat-ics and most of literature inhabit, activate the worldly genius of the prosaic. The category of progress, as it informs science and technology, does not, as we shall see, pertain in any immediate sense to literature. That of development, of what might almost be termed "laws of motion," does. Literary periods, literary and artistic movements together with the radicalism and reception of individual works, prepare for, indeed compel in style and in substance that which comes after. No less, moreover, than in thermodynamics, the exchanges of energy between the writer and the language, between tradition and the individual talent, entail loss. There is entropy in the aesthetic. Conviction seeps out of what were major constellations, such as the heroic epic, the chivalric romance, or verse-drama. Rather enigmatically, and as if the relevant tongue had grown weary, national literatures decay, as do particles. They become inert, at least for considerable periods of time.

The crux is this: "invention," in our social history, in industry and technology, taken in their comprehensive sense, is, more often than not, applied mathematics. Invention is answerable, as Edison emphasized, to specific needs, to pragmatic possibilities as these are offered by the availability or manufacture of new materials (re-inforced concrete for the modern metropolis, titanium for the Museum at Bilbao). Invention fills a niche in evolving totality as do rare metals in the table of elements. It is, again in the best, most energized sense, "interested" and "useful." The inventor seeks patents.

It may be that "invention" in literature and the arts is, at some distance yet illuminatingly, kindred. Aesthetic inventions, that of a new form such as the sonnet, the fugue, oil-painting or the pointed arch, are the technologies of sensibility (though one dreads Stalin's definition of the true writer as "an enginner of the soul"). They provide signifying shapes and raw material for consciousness when it seeks both recognition and self-recognition. Inventiveness, which Coleridge called "fancy," maintains an unbroken dialogue with the extant, psychological as well as material. It furnishes being as *technē* furnishes a house. At the routine, ephemeral level, that of ninety percent, say, of current fiction, of *Unterhaltungsliteratur*, this furniture is *kitsch* or pastime or an ornament for conspicuous consumption. But at its finest, literary invention instructs us to enrich, to complicate heuristically, the bounds of common, unexamined habitation. It installs windows through which it invites us to look on new terrain, on new sources of light. It tells the tales by which we come to hear the voice of our private and communal identity. It sees to it that the "library at Babel," Borges's fantastication so solidly grounded in the geometry of comic sections, remains at once inexhaustible and open-ended.

But the poet says: "I never invent."

Nor, one suspects, does the pure mathematician. The existence, the history of pure mathematics ought to be the occasion for (exultant) wonder. Our species has, at best, a chequered record. We come at the close, if it is that, of an epoch of singular bestiality. But there are four domains, whose possible interrelations and affinities lie at the heart of this study, in which men and women seem to surpass their condition. They are those of music, of poetry and the arts, of speculative metaphysics when it is at the pitch of a Plato, a Spinoza, or a Kant, and of pure mathematics. Together with music, pure mathematics, in its disinterested irrelevance, is probably the crowning enigma of our so often dubious presence in this world.

Yet, strictly considered, it is not or need not be "of" this world. By virtue of a quantum leap into the strange dignity of the useless, a leap whose psychological-cultural motivations elude us, ancient Greece conceived of axiomatic constructs or "imaginaries" liberated from utility, from application, and from empirical experience. Nevertheless, of a reality so luminous, so evident to the privileged intellect, and of such beauty, as to give proof—as Plato intimates, a necessary and sufficient proof—of the human soul's latent access to the transcendent, to a logic and harmony surpassing all modes of bodily life. In the realm of pure mathematics, in number-theory above all, the mortal mind is at play. It imposes on itself rules, constraints of utmost rigour; yet it experiences a freedom, an abstention from compromise (from all that is approximate, profitable, vulgarized by exploitation) bestowed, otherwise, only on the gods. Hence the perception, which legend ascribes to Pythagoras, that the human soul is "at music" when it engages in pure mathematics, or Aristotle's identifications of mathematics and the divine.

The dilemma, we saw, remains unresolved. There is the belief that the pure mathematician comes upon realities of an especially guarded, abstract sort, but pre-existent to his inquiry. This would be Plato's view. And the contrasting belief that pure mathematics creates its material, proceeding by regulated intuition from problem to problem, from theorem to theorem in an internalized motion towards the generalization of the particular. Where every worthwhile generalization, in turn, directs analysis towards new particularities, as in the icon of a branching tree, with its central trunk, its criss-cross of reticulations, all growing autonomously from the far unknown of its roots. Hardy is jubilant at this autonomy; von Neumann finds it disquieting. Indeed, is there something "in-", because "non"-human in the indifference of pure mathematics to the commonplace of existence?

To Plato, to Descartes, the non-mathematician is, unavoidably, a non-philosopher, almost thoughtless in the basic sense. All he can attempt to do is to draw crude mental pictures for himself of what makes pure mathematics not only possible but dynamic, constantly unfolding towards ever more complex and, we are assured, ever more beautiful truths.

I arrive, in ignorance, at a paradox. The combinatorial possibilities in mathematics do seem to be unbounded, or bounded but also infinite as is Einstein's universe. The quality of the mathematician lies in the choices he makes, as does that of the chessmaster when selecting a move from among myriad allowed possibilities. The economy, the discipline of discard, implicit in such a choice is inseparable from the beauty of the solution (so far, the chess-computer tends to use what is called "brute force"). It is difficult to escape altogether from the intimation that there is indeed some sense in which the manifold components of the mathematical operation do pre-exist, in which they are external and prior to the human intellect. Are there not vast areas of the cosmos, both macroscopic and microscopic, as yet unseen and, most likely, never to be seen by us, yet undoubtedly extant?

But there is another sense, no less coherent, in which it is the act of mathematical imagining, the process of infinitely serious play itself, which calls into being, which gives existence to, the elements and laws of its generative patterns. As in that "invention of melody" which haunts Lévi-Strauss as the most irreducible of mysteries, it is discovery that creates. Only perception can grant being (Berkeley). Pure mathematics creates what it discovers, yet also discovers what it creates. Fichte's ontological idealism is the philosophic conjecture most at ease with this *aporia,* with this undecidable paradox. It is the self, conscious and sub-conscious, which constructs the world it will discover. But though their origin and causation are those of the human mind, they constitute a demonstrable and compelling reality, what Fichte called a "non-I." What epistemology has never resolved satisfactorily is the obvious question as to the correspondence between human consciousness and the active mirror "out there."

From this paradox and duality stem the wealth of theological, even mystical metaphor which shadows, or lights, the philosophy of mathematics. From it derive the suppositions, themselves often playful and helplessly ironic, as to the mathematical proclivities of the deity. Shared by Plato and Descartes, but also by Leibniz and by Einstein, is the suggestion that the existence of, say, prime numbers, whatever the true nature of such existence, or the solution to the Goldbach conjecture, relate to a "Prime Mover" (the pun on Aristotle's term does, in this instance, seem to me permissible). This relation is stronger than in any other human pursuit. Thus there is, in even the most resolutely atheist or agnostic of pure mathematics something of a covert remembrance or celebration of God.

Knowing of the mathematician's emphasis on the poetic, on aesthetic criteria, can the layman look any closer into the workshop?

3

In pure mathematics, the abstention from worldliness is inscribed in the algebraic codes. No contamination from empirical and sensory constraints, no polysemic imprecision need intrude. Even where their inception is considered to be, in some sense, intuitive, the findings of functional analysis or algebraic topology can be counter-intuitive in the extreme. "Common" sense is left to its innocently representational, mundane, and demotic illusions. Musical notation aspires towards an analogous purity. It too can abstract and abstract from, which is to say detach itself from, mundanity and the material. But to a lesser degree than pure mathematics. For even the most formally autonomous of musical patterns induces, in the listener's reception, an unwilled sequence of images, of more or less naive but irresistible associations with the external world and its prodigal sounds. Our listening is drawn, voluntarily or not, at the conscious or sub-conscious level, towards the cinematic. Pictures, meaningful shapes, representational echoes arise. At lower and programmatic levels, musical sounds and devices provoke a multitude of sensorial, historical, private associations and connotations. They sound our world. There is, in consequence, be it in the most formalized or other-worldly of musical compositions, such as a Bach exercise or one of Webern's a-tonal miniatures, the eventuality of a "programme"; of an imagined content translatable, precisely as pure mathematics is not, into mimesis. The impulse towards illustration and application is always latent.

In respect of impurity, of invasive realism, language is totally vulnerable. No immaculateness is possible. We have evidence that experiments in systematic neologism, in automatic writing, in surrealist dissolutions of syntax, end in triviality. We have seen that even the most inventive, innovative of writers cannot escape from the locale and temporality of the language which he inherits or acquires, from the native state and history of lexical-grammatical priority. Language is immeasurably saturated. Words, grammatical forms, phrases, rhetorical conventions are saturated, nearly to the level of the phoneme, by usage, by precedent, by cultural-social connotation. A speech-sound sets off concentric and formally unlimited chimes. It collides with every neighbouring semantic particle in an echo chamber, rather as do the church-bells of Venice, some off-beat, some out of tune, unsynchronized, as they set each other off, drenching the air with their concordant and conflicting voices. A master of language *can* energize the medium into a quantum leap. But the new orbit is, in turn, teeming with associations not of his choosing. That the "world is too much with the poet" is not so much a result of mundane temptation, of self-investment in the transitory and opportune. It is a completely unescapable corollary of language itself. Which transports with it, whether we would or not, the cargo that is the world. The pure mathematics in language could only be silence.

Nevertheless, a persistent thrust towards purity, towards liberation from the bonds of the already extant, does inhabit literature, and lyric poetry first and foremost. Like pure mathematics, like serious music and the poetics of abstract thought which constitute metaphysics, poetry seeks to be only itself. It would leave behind the world of dross and of dirt—*e fango è il mondo,* says Leopardi, a poet obsessed by the temptations of infinity. Poetry would circumscribe for itself a free-zone of self-reference. This aspiration defines Platonism and its theological-philosophic legacy in the West. It commits us to an always baffled engagement with transcendence.

But defeat is, to a greater or lesser degree, pre-ordained. Language allows no immaculateness. The most uncontaminated of lyric texts, the most abstract, meta-geometric of Spinoza's propositions, cannot altogether break its moorings from the denotative-connotative impurities of the vulgate. The anchor of lexicon and grammar, of diachronic and synchronic usage, drags language back from autonomous renewal. Yet what matters most in poetry —prose can, although rarely, also turn its back on *orbi et urbi*—is the sinew of this striving for liberation from imposed, borrowed, eroded reference. It is the effort to pierce the unsayable, to proceed at exceeding risk through its circle of fire as does the Pilgrim, eloquently speechless, at the close of the *Paradiso*. Beyond the necessary demands of the prosaic, via gradations of transgressive intensity, lies the realm of the *absolute*. Sartre writes of Calder: "[H]e suggests nothing. . . . His mobiles signify nothing, refer to nothing but themselves: they are, that's all; they are absolutes." Thus what I call "absolute" poetry enacts a radical paradox: it would escape from the historical-social burden and ready-made in its own language. In a major lyric poem there is a loving enmity to language. More exactly, the poet aims to cross the frontiers of his (of all) language so as to be indeed "the first that ever burst into that silent sea."

Is this condemned paradox the hallmark of creativity in literature? Is even the most accomplished of poems the lamed shadow, the transcription into saturated discourse, of that which it set out to be? In which case, the persuasion of the poem, its claim on our repeated readings, would entail the latent presence, the proximate pressure, of the poem that is not (yet). This pressure of formed absence, of a promise of unfulfilled but always incipient revelation, is the crux of religious and mystical experience, as it is that of idealist philosophies. It defines the absolute in poetry. Can we, keeping the pure mathematician very much in mind, say anything of its genesis?

There is, *stricto sensu,* no finished poem. The poem made available to us contains preliminary versions of itself. Drafts, cancelled versions, work-sheets internalize what Leibniz termed the "great mystery of that which could have been." In both positive and negative senses. Shown, at Oxford, the draft for Milton's "Lycidas," Charles Lamb felt terror at the thought that that poem could have been otherwise. At the other end, so to speak, the poem as we have it will induce an apprehension, more or less substantial, of what it could be if it were to achieve the full measure of its intentionality, which is the surpassing of its medium. We recall Leibniz when he alludes to the enigma of that which "will never be" though it lies so near. The richer, the more enduring the text, the more vivid, the more palpably circumstantial, will be this sense of a potential self-surpassing into a sphere of absolute freedom. "Read me, look at me, listen to me," says the significant work of literature, art, and music, "and you will share in the joyous sadness, in the constantly re-newed wonder, of my incompletion. You will derive from this incompletion in action what evidence is given to the human spirit of that which lies beyond, *just beyond,* my highest reach" (once more, it is the *Paradiso* which most incisively articulates this proximity).

Such near absence and some of the ways in which it informs yet beggars the prodigality on offer are the underlying trope in Shakespeare's Sonnet 122:

> Thy gift, thy tables are within my brain
> Full charactered with lasting memory,
> Which shall above that idle rank remain
> Beyond all date, even to eternity;
> Or, at the least, so long as brain and heart
> Have faculty by nature to subsist;
> Till each to razed oblivion yields his part

Of thee, thy record never can be missed.
That poor retention could not so much hold,
Nor need I tallies this dear love to score;
Therefore to give them from me I was bold,
To trust those tables that receive thee more:
   To keep an adjunct to remember thee
   Were to import forgetfulness in me.

Note the theme of donation in "gift," in "date" (the "given"), in "yield," in "give," in "adjunct," in "import," with its twofold connotations. The sonnet incorporates the superfluous but indispensable exercises of remembrance which are also its own prior versions and impulses towards coming into public being. In "razed oblivion" there is "erasure," very nearly as it is invoked in current deconstructive theory. It is, by necessary paradox, the acceptance of "oblivion" which legitimatizes the gamble on "Beyond all date, even to eternity." Remembrance is, as Helen Vendler observes, ubiquitous in our text. The particle *re* is sounded over and again. But, in a turn characteristic of Shakespeare, what we *re*member, perhaps most vitally, is also the futu*re*. It is the poem immediately beyond the one we have on the page in the voyage to perfection, unattainable but undeniably *there*, which will "subsist," past any "faculty of nature." Which will divest itself of the cliché of time "even to eternity." Love knows of absences more vehement, more expressive of the promise of hope, than is any presence.

The internalization within the finished work, where "finished" is perhaps the antithesis to "completed," of preceding, alternative, discarded performative solutions, can be made out, as we saw, in drafts, in sketches, in the sequence of preliminary maquettes. The ultimate source, together with the ice-berg mass of hidden labours, of trial and error, is, at the outset, sub-liminal. Any record, therefore, of the compositional process, however fragmentary, however cryptic its shorthand, is already a fairly late stage. It is a provisionally disciplined vestige and tracer of pre-conscious proceedings. This is as true of Beethoven's famous sketch-books as it is of the preliminary designs, often corrected radically, which x-ray and infra-red examination reveals under the surface of a Titian. Relatively few, moreover, of the "foul papers" of artists, composers, or writers have been preserved. But where such drafts do survive, where cancellations, revisions and hesitant simultaneities of expression can be made out, the insights provided are absorbing.

Consider the "roughage" in progress towards Yeats's "Lullaby."[1] The germ cell consists of five words set down vertically:

> sleep
> alarms
> deep
> bed
> arms.

This "haiku of possibilities" already encapsulates the stages of composition and the poem to be. Over successive drafts, these cellular words will attract, as if by aural and thematic force of gravity, ambient associations and figures (both of speech and of personified myth). The node-crystal generates facets as from within. "Thus a mother sang asleep / The child her breasts had fed," a sleep "beloved and as deep / As daring Paris did." For a stage in the exploring process, Paris energizes the formative motion:

1. The drafts are reproduced in Curtis B. Bradford, *Yeats at Work* (1965).

> The sleep that Paris found
> Towards the break of day
> Under the slow breaking day
> That first night in Helen's arms

There is not, and will not be for some time yet, any punctuation. Eventualities of rhyme and cadence are postponed. The trigger-words must be allowed untrammelled circuits and collisions across the shadow-lines which divide the sub- or pre-liminal from the willed tests of composition. "Arms" will draw "alarms" into fruitful proximity. "Sleep beloved sleep / Sleep where you have fed / Forget the world's alarms." The "feeding," "bed" modulating into "fed," the "arms," Helen's but also those of heroic combat, the depth of sung-to sleep, are now in mutually activating reticulation, like the swiftly spinning vane which generates power out of the wind.

A third mythical persona enters the phonetic and rhythmic plot. "Sleep beloved with such sleep / As on the hunter Tristram fell." A "utilitarian" move interposes, as if to assist the reader. Yeats identifies:

> Sleep beloved the sleep that fell
> On Tristram the famed forester
> When all the potion's work was done.

As so often and programmatically in Yeats, the classical, Homeric legacy counterpoints the Celtic. Out of the humble *Ur-wörter*, the seminal units in the prologue-list, out of a nameless mother's lullaby, majestic shades have risen: Paris and Helen, Tristram and Yseult. In a beautifully lucid progress, whose begetting roots nevertheless remain hidden, what has been until this point a phonetic sonority, a dictate of vowels and incipient measure, extends towards argument. Tristram's magical sleep brings it about that "birds could sing, the deer could leap / The oak bough and the beech bough stir / And the world begin again." As in Whitman, a cradle-song, a lullaby, becomes an *aubade* in the fullest sense. It attends on, it celebrates, the never-fathomed marvel of new life, though that *vita nuova* co-exists unsettlingly with the fatalities manifest in the destiny of the illustrious lovers.

That "beginning again of the world" will be discarded from subsequent drafts. It tells of a poem which could have been, and which I imagine myself preferring to the self-indulgent signature-tune privileged by Yeats. The sleep in "Lullaby" is made such as "From the limbs of Leda sank." As it appears in *Words for Music* (1932), the poem is tighter but, to my mind, more conventional. Now Paris, Helen, Tristram, Leda are emblematic, one might say heraldic, of the ambiguous grace of sleep, infantile and erotic. The motif of auroral renewal and rebirth is still present —"Stag could leap and roe could run"—but in a less declared and consequential key. What will find its place in the Macmillan edition canon, is something of an eclectic text (cf. Bradford's analysis).

This, we saw, is the condition of all poetry in regard to its genesis, whether or not we can document and thus try to reconstruct its embryology and growth. What makes the building-site of Yeats's lyric so enlightening is the visibility of deployments from the five initial words to the published song. Equally instructive is the suggestion of a constricting code of personal allusion. For Yeats, the evocation of Helen and of Paris, which is to say that of the mythical causes of the catastrophe at Troy, forced, as it were, the introduction of Leda. At this exact juncture, it seems to me that the achieved economy and musicality are those of invention, of a resort to a previous investment in assured craft. There was the light of creation—taking the word in its generic and in its biblical-mythological connotations—in that "beginning again of the world," and its unfolding harvest. These are dropped, leaving us uncertainly aware of the poem which might have been (the conceit of rebirth will, to be sure, be enacted in other and more telling of Yeats's poems).

Some texts seem to emerge ready-made. They are, truly, *objets trouvés*, subject to scarcely any amendment. In the main, these are shorter lyric poems. But Byron testifies to the composition of lengthy stanzaic sequences, hardly to be altered, in a single, definitive rush. In neither case, of course, do we know of the process of internal drafting and shaping memorization preceding the actual voicing or script. Such immediacies (this can be shown in Byron's *Don Juan*) do appear to share certain attributes. They incorporate visual "snap-shots"; they are memoranda on the instant; they exhibit wit (does God, the creator, make jokes?). They compare to the solution, lightning-like, of a lesser mathematical equation or a chess problem, in providing the pleasures of enclosure, of end-stopped demonstration. The poem can be terse because it takes as given the matter of the world, of known sentiment, of social occasion or historical background to which it refers, even where it does so obliquely or tangentially. It is just these characteristics of wit, of embeddedness in the data of experience and recognition, of circumscription, which pertain to invention.

Philip Larkin's "Wires" came "in one shot":[2]

2. A. T. Tolley, *Larkin at Work* (1997), p. 144.

The widest prairies have electric fences,
For though old cattle know they must not stray
Young steers are always scenting purer water
Not here but anywhere. Beyond the wires

Leads them to blunder up against the wires
Whose muscle-shredding violence gives no quarter.
Young steers become old cattle from that day,
Electric limits to their widest senses.

A minimalist allegory of impotence which is also, principally
perhaps, a poetic exercise on the harshness, on the rasping
sub-text of the *r*-sound. In the workbook, "the cattle" is made
"old cattle," specifying the arch-Larkin theme of senescence.
"Scenting" purer water replaces "glimpsing." The first half of the
fourth line hesitates. "Anywhere" replaces "world," a distinctively
"Larkin" tuning-down and *diminuendo*. In l.6, "agony" gives place
to "violence." A grammarian is in charge: "agony" is experienced,
whereas "violence" is inflicted. Initially, the closing verse reads
awkwardly: "Electric wire staked round their widest senses." Naively, one wonders whether wildest, no doubt something of a romantic and enhancing banality, is the ironic contraction in "widest." The latter is a more thought-provoking solution and one
representative of Larkin's fastidious detachment.

Other Larkin vignettes are re-worked. In progress, the close
of "How" had people "separated," "widely separated," or "parted"
by estates "of children / With violent shallow eyes." The changes
made in the final version appear slight, but they are persuasive:

How few people are,
Held apart by acres

> Of housing, and children
> With their shallow violent eyes.

Probably only a fellow-poet could weight for us the suggestive strength of "acres" or of that insertion of "their." But in their very integrity and transparency—those "high windows" in Larkin's best-known poem—these amendments, and the text as we know it, tell of invention. They are resolutely, if ironically, grounded in the substance of the everyday. Theirs is a spirit of place emphatically English. The "electric limits" which they set for themselves are mordant and self-teasingly parochial. It is only "young steer" (a Roy Campbell, a Dylan Thomas?) who blunder up against those shredding wires. Even the violence is shallow, which may make it grimmer.

Almost programmatically, an annotator of common ground such as Larkin, excludes from his register the gamble on futurity, on the transgression of current speech and ready intelligibility which is risked, often to the breaking-point, in poetry and art of the first order. It is the poem as yet unrealised within the poem, the poem which "will not be" yet exercises its imminent pressure —Plato's speculative inclusion of non-being in being—which solicits the demarcation between invention and creation. To Larkin, to the reasoned and disenchanted findings of common sense, with its esteem for the prose of the world, such Platonic paradoxes are suspect obscurantism or outright pretentiousness. They must be substantiated, if at all, by actual examples. Such as those provided by Paul Celan, denier of invention.

A Celan poem is an absolute, though he himself came both to postulate and to rule as impossible its realisation. It is an absolute at odds with its language; at odds with the enterprise of literature; at odds with prevailing criteria and practices of communication.

A polyglot—Celan is a masterful translator out of six or seven tongues—this most innovative and far-reaching of German lyric poets after Hölderlin, experienced as nearly unendurable his own resort to the German language. Could he not, should he not, have written in Rumanian, in French or, ideally, in Hebrew? German is the language of the butchers who exterminated his parents and the prodigally humane world in which Celan grew up. German is the language which formulated Jew-hating obscenities and a will to annihilation without precedent. It unleashed from within itself the bellowing of the inhuman while, at the same time, laying claim to its eminent philosophic-literary heritage and while continuing, at many levels and in the domesticities of the everyday, to function normally. For Celan, no artifice of purgation, no packaged forgetting, can remove from German the virus of the infernal. The notion of dismantling German altogether suggests itself, but is wholly impractical. Much closer to hand lies the alternative of silence. Here Celan's dilemma has its premonitory antecedent in Kafka's torment over a "false mother-tongue."

In consequence, a Celan text is the locale of an unspeakably painful embarrassment, of an internal contradiction literally "not to be said." How can a poetry, a prose whose parataxic subtlety, whose radical precision touch on magic, but whose abiding source and sub-text are Auschwitz and the spectral condition of the Jew thereafter, adorn, enrich, perpetuate the life of the German language? How is it possible for a Paul Celan to afford this parlance out of hell access to his formative sub-conscious, to the shaping needs in the inmost of his being? Can anyone carry German poetry after Hölderlin, whose kindred presence is talismanic throughout but always to be re-negotiated, to new heights of lyric power? To qualify such a situation as "ironic" is to trivialize it. The abyss is too determinant. It enforces a finally suicidal tension between the act of expression and its immediate medium; between an imperative of articulation—what *must* be uttered—and the lexical-grammatical-semantic means of that articulation. To no other writer, except Kafka, was the production of a text, however inspired, however memorable, so costly a humiliation (just because of the inspiration and memorability). Because it is the public instrument of the text, German prevails (once more). Thus the seminal motion in a Celan composition is one of thwarted repudiation. The poem would free itself of its linguistic phenomenality, leaving only an unvoiced shadow in the burnt grass. Wherever a Celan poem falls at all short of its absolute, German has prevailed. Wherever it does attain its absolute, German profits. Again, "irony" is far too glossy a concept.

Correlatively, a Celan lyric is at bitter odds with "literature" and all aspects of literary life. It flinches at the glorification of "great writing" and its begetters. Celan's hair-thin vulnerability to the indiscretions and vanities of literary-academic chit-chat, his contempt for the *littérateur* and the modish virtuoso, became legend. He defined true poetry as an "absurdity," given its incapacity to better human conduct, given its proclivity to embellish, to mask such conduct. A hand-shake matches, probably out-weights, any poem. Yet poetry is also an absurdity as indispensable as the air we breathe, as the redemption which will, most likely, never come. What, now, is its task? "To think through, to take to its logical conclusion, Mallarmé."

By which, I conjecture, Celan to signify a programme for absolute poetry, for a textuality which will break its leasehold on language in so far as language—*les mots de la tribu*—is at one with the demands of mundane discourse. It is, says Celan, the task of the absolute poem (that "absurdity") "not only to be itself," but to speak "on behalf of the other" (*in eines Anderen Sache*). This "other" can be a living presence; in effect, it will usually be that of the unremembered, nameless victims, their ash wind-scythed to oblivion. An authentic, an absolute poem reveals, declares itself solely "at the edge of itself," at that border-line which I have tried to define as the marker of necessary transgression, of metamorphosis out of the hitherto known and intelligible.

At this point, Celan is, deliberately as it were, untranslatable: "*es ruft und hohlt sich, um bestehen zu können, unausgesetzt aus seinem Schon-nicht-mehr in sein Immer-noch zurück*" (Martin Heidegger's idiolect often underwrites that of Paul Celan). To metaphrase grossly: "in order to persist, the poem calls on itself, it conveys itself from its already-no-more, from its in-built ephemerality and forgettability, back into its every-yet." It recuperates its being towards an eventual lastingness. Such self-summons or "auto-vocation," leaves the poem "in solitude"—as, of course, it does the poet. The poem is "solitary and under way" towards an undefined rendezvous which it will, more often than not, miss. But whose calling, in every sense of the word, is its imperative secret and *raison d'être*.

All this puts with incisive finality what I have sketched as the relation of an absolute poem to its "fore-words" and to its potential alternatives, the "ever-yet" of its fulfilment. The absolute poem, the literary text, the work of art, the musical construct are under way towards a yet-to-be. The poet, says Celan, is the "accompanist" (*mitgegeben*) on the journey.

The last antinomy is the most difficult to elucidate or to justify. Particularly in its later phases, Celan's poetry can be at odds with intelligibility (though he himself strenuously denied such hermeticism). What is being said? To cite the precedent of Mallarmé is deceptive. Mallarmé's elusiveness, his teasing obscurity is often tactical. It pertains to an esoteric tradition, to willed preciosity. There is in Mallarmé a rhetoric or anti-rhetoric of secrecy which invites decipherment. A fair measure of Celan's opacity does relate to this aesthetic. Indecipherabilities will yield to knowledge of the biographical and referential context, to exact chronological and geographical placement. Indeed, details out of Paul Celan's personal, private life, out of fraught encounters, out of elected landscapes and historical anniversaries—that, for instance, of Hölderlin's death—act as a sub-text, comparable to that of classical mythology in Hölderlin's or Keats's odes. But there are poems to which no external information, no contingent circumstance, seems to give entry. They remain, till now, essentially closed even to arguable interpretation. Their un-understandability is, as I have tried to show elsewhere,[3] ontological. This is to say that it is their enacted substance and, it may be, motivation.

What is at stake is Celan's deepening distrust of communication in any current category. Communication or, more precisely, the will to communicate, the intentionalities of the expressive, be they public or private, are fatally flawed. To communicate readily, let alone eloquently, is to falsify. Language is leprosied with cliché, with individual and social hypocrisy, with glib imprecision. It has served (brilliantly) the demands of genocide and of political enslavement. Its reserves of apologia and of mendacity, of factitious embellishment, and of amnesia, look to be inexhaustible. Language can say: "there was no Auschwitz" or "Celan is a plagiarist" (the hysterical accusation which sickened his later years). On the most intimate levels of love and of friendship, lan-

3. Cf. *On Difficulty* (1978).

guage betrays and betrays itself. How, then, can it be entrusted with that supreme "under way" towards the truth, towards the "transfinite," to borrow a wondrously suggestive mathematical notion, which is the absolute poem? How, then, can verbal discourse, the speech-act, be a legitimate pointer to that which lies beyond it?

Celan allegorizes this dilemma in his prose-parable of August 1959: *Gespräch im Gebirge* ("Conversation, Talk in the Mountains"). Here is the agonizingly exact transcription of an exchange (with Adorno) which had been envisaged but never took place. Which could not have taken place by virtue of its utter necessity — in a remark often trivialized, Adorno had expressed doubts as to the validity of a lyric poem after Auschwitz. Again, one thinks of Leibniz's concept of that which *is* because it will never be. The crux, out of Heidegger, is the light-years of separation between *reden*, "to talk," to engage in *Gerede*, chit-chat, and *sprechen*, "to speak," in an attempt at authentic significance or *Sprache*. The latter goes unheard as it addresses itself to "no-one and No-one," that *Niemand* which is Celan's despairing short-hand for "God" in reference to the Shoah. Our works and days are lunatic with *reden* and *Gerede*, with loquacity and its "palpable designs upon us." This articulate cacophony deafens. Hence Celan's more and more defeated cry: "*Hörst du . . . hörst du?*" How can one hear any longer what vestiges endure of *Sprache*, of tongues which were once of fire, but have been obliterated to mute ash? There will be no *Gespräch* in the mountains, only an *Entgegenschweigen*. This "remaining silent," in both an adversative and an "encountering" sense, is Heidegger's coinage in the last letter he wrote to Celan.

What to do? The banal objection: "why write poetry and, if written, why publish?" does have its force. Celan was morbidly susceptible to it. Time and again, he ironized or deplored his vocation, validating it solely in regard to the ineluctable burden of remembrance, of the naming of the nameless dead. At other points, however, he exalted the mysteries of his craft above all other endeavours. The contradictions must have grown insuperable, the asymmetries beyond resolution. Whence, I suggest, the advance into a darkening degree of incomprehensibility; the *Lichtverzicht* or "renunciation of, abstention from light." Celan's neologisms are unmistakable: *Nachtglast, Sperrzauber,* expressions charged with the night-time of meaning and the violent, magical act of closure. Now the poem must ache its way through the swinging stone gate so as to reach the dark, itself "ripe with necessity":

> ein von Steinwut schwingendes Tor noch,
> gesteh's der
> notreifen Nacht zu.

Observe that "rage of stones," that "lithography" and writing on stones. "Stonespeech," a crucial "Celanism," now has a silent truth denied to human chatter. It is one of the premonitory indices of a possible epiphany. I have already quoted Celan's invocation of a "language north of the future." Until that language can be spoken and, what matters far more, heard, the absolute poem entails a deferral of any assured sense, of an order of intelligibility which can, even haltingly, be metaphrased or paraphrased. All that authentic poetry and what is most absolute in art and in music can accomplish is to say: *"komm mit mir zu Atem/ und drüber hinaus."* "Draw breath with me, and go past, go beyond that breath." This going beyond, this literal transcendence being that which I am seeking to define: the motion in progress towards realisation and the incompletion which this motion must make sensible. Incompletion as the denial of "finish," with its connotations of "polish," of "veneer," of high gloss.

Thus invention comes very near to achieved intelligibility, to the domain of the understandable (the "applied") and its manifold triumphs and uses. Creation, infinitely rarer, can, indeed it must, open on to "the *terra incognita* of the soul" (Coleridge). Its avenues are those of the trackless. It can, as Walter Benjamin argues, wait for us to follow, to catch up with it, although it is implausible to suppose that we will do so. "*Eingedunkelt die Schlüsselgewalt*": "darkling, be-nighted is the power of the key." A door locked yet open as in Kafka's parable of the Law. Where the act of hearing language itself rather than what we have made of it would give proof of the messianic.

René Char was among the poets whom Celan translated. Char and Celan look to Heidegger. No poet was more inebriate with the promise implicit in the fragment than was Char. His best poems, many cast outwardly in prose, are contracts with the unknown. As in tales of secret service and decoding, their edges are torn. They will yield their meaning, they will disclose their message, only when the matching half is found and fitted seamlessly to their edges. Till that "joining," obscurity, the oscillating instability of options, are inevitable and legitimate:

> Demain commenceront les travaux poétiques
> Précédés du cycle de la mort volontaire
> Le règne de l'obscurité a coulé la raison le diamant
> dans la mine

René Char's poetics are emphatically those of the open-endedness of creation. They comport a scrupulous provisionality of statement and also of understanding in respect of the immediate. "*Il convient que la poésie soit inséparable du prévisible, mais non encore formulé.*" Poetry lives "in perpetual insomnia" lest it succumb to the inventive facility of mere dreams (such as those cultivated by the Surrealists whom Char left behind, though Surrealist painters continued to inspire him). Poetry must stay awake so as to be ready for its meeting with the parties to the contract. Who are they?

Like Heidegger, Char, at moments, invokes "the gods":

> Nous ne jalousons pas le dieux, nous ne les servons pas, ne les craignons pas, mais au péril de notre vie nous attestons leur existence multiple, et nous nous émouvons d'être de leur élevage aventureux lorsque cesse leur souvenir.

At other moments, the matching portion of the text yet to be revealed is held by death, with whose prodigal resources Char had become intimate during the Resistance. Or the one to be met, at the cross-roads towards Delphi, on the way to Emmaus, is, in René Char's "trans-realist" idiom, stellar Orion.

It is the poet's pre-eminent task to struggle against the temptations and constraints of the finite (*la finitude*). Therefore, the appeal to

> Orion,
> Pigmenté d'infini et de soif terrestre . . .

The destined rendezvous may, as with Heidegger, be at the frontier of emptiness (*le vide, das Nichts*). It is the dangerous privilege of the true poet, who is a secret agent of perception, to make of his border-crossings, simultaneously clandestine and luminous, an instigation to plenitude, to fulfilment. Put this way, such phrasings are abstractly portentous. But in Char's texts, they take on a compelling clarity. The movement of transit, of a darkness "in passing," sounds an unmistakable note:

> Dans un sentier étroit
> J'écris ma confidence.
> N'est pas minuit qui veut.
>
> L'écho est mon voisin
> La brume est ma suivante.

The lapidary pride in that third line has been hard-earned. Not everyone has a right to midnight, to an unsafe-house in the no man's land of the unknown. An absolute poem is born of the "summons to becoming" (*l'appel du devenir*). It must venture "into that rebellious and solitary world of contradictions" which Char associates with the riddling depths of Heraclitus. Where creation is on trial, there is no choice, for "how is one to live without the unknown before one?"

4

Only mathematicians can assess the respective claims to creation, to invention and to discovery in the mathematical process. Only a mathematician can gauge whether or not these concepts apply, whether or not they can be discriminated between, in the drafts, in the work-books leading to a mathematical paper or treatise (where such material is, in fact, preserved). I have no qualification to do so. If I adduce, tentatively, a "mathematical moment," in the gist of a *moment musical,* it is because of the insistence of mathematicians themselves, as I have cited them, on the poetic and aesthetic impulses in their craft. It is because mathematicians and philosophers of mathematics invite us to seek analogies between their constructs and those of the poet, artist, and composer. Can the layman evaluate, even innocently, the proud postulate of Paul Erdös (regarded by his peers as the twentieth-century's greatest pure mathematician and numbers theorist):

> mathematics is the only infinite human activity. It is conceivable that humanity could eventually learn everything in physics or biology. But humanity certainly won't ever be able to find out everything in mathematics because the subject is infinite.

Observe the overlap of a technical and of a general or metaphysical invocation of the "infinite." Erdös ironized, uneasily, the presence of a totality of solutions in what he called "the Book," kept in the hands of a godhead at once bountiful—he created an infinity of prime numbers—and malign—he denied us the understanding of many of their attributes. Ramanujan, a magician among theorists, came at the same image, but from an opposite vector: "An equation for me has no meaning unless it expresses a thought of God." What are the bridges to the poet, to the metaphysician, to Bach's definitions of the source and purpose of music? Again, mathematicians testify.

With reference to what are known as Abelian integrals, Mittag-Leffler writes: "The best works of Abel are truly lyric poems of sublime beauty . . . raised farther above life's commonplaces and emanating more directly from the very soul than any poet, in the ordinary sense of the word, could produce." In a similar vein, Edgar Quinet remembers:

If I was smitten by algebra, I was dazzled by the application of algebra to geometry. . . . The idea, the possibility of expressing a line, a curve, in algebraic terms, by an equation, seemed to me as beautiful as the *Iliad*. When I saw this equation function and solve itself, so to speak, in my hands, and burst into an infinity of truths, all equally indisputable, equally eternal, equally resplendent, I believed I had in my possession the talisman which would open the door of every mystery.

These are exaltations in the romantic vein. No less than in literature or the arts, there are in the history of mathematics styles and conventions of sensibility. Algebra, analysis have their romantic as well as their baroque and their classical moments. To a somewhat lesser degree, individual mathematicians deploy a personal manner, a signature comparable to that of the writer or graphic artist. Those competent to judge will say that they can distinguish, virtually at a glance, between the page of an algebraic paper by, say, Cauchy, and one by Riemann. A particular hand is visible. Thus what Aldous Huxley called "the mad dance of algebra" has its diverse and, in some measure, personalized beat.

Markedly so in the work of Evariste Galois. He stood, in both a general and a technical-formal sense, at the heart of revolutionary romanticism. Many had sought to prove the impossibility of solving algebraic equations of the fifth degree. Galois found the criteria for the resolution of equations of whatever degree, confirming from within this immensely powerful generalization that fifth-degree equations are indeed insoluble. Out of this finding arises almost the entirety of the modern theory of groups and algebraic topology. Numerous problems, previously unrelated, were shown by Galois to be "grouped." A process of synthesizing substitutions demonstrated their fundamental kinship and the shared conditions of either solubility or non-solubility. Galois's insight was to have a prodigious heritage. Points he made, hints he left, are still state of the art.

This "burst into an infinity of truths" was achieved by a twenty-year-old whose memoire to the Academy of Sciences in Paris had been rejected as unintelligible (such was its advance on established concepts). Trapped into a moronic duel, most probably staged by the police in order to eliminate a notorious political radical, Galois, who clearly foresaw the fatal outcome, had one night left in which to order his papers and announce his discoveries. He did so on the night of May 29th 1832, in a letter to his friend Auguste Chevalier. Set down at frenzied speed, this document is one of the most inspired and poignant in the records of the human mind. Even *visually*, Galois's letter towards imminent death suggests analogies with the last drafts of Keats or with what letters and sketches we have of the condemned Schubert.

The complete mathematical writings of Galois have been published, monumentally, by Robert Bourgne and J.-P. Azra in 1962. They include facsimiles of certain pages composed on that last night, together with their marginalia, doodles, and graffiti. Between the torrents of algebraic notations appear words such as *mentir* and *pistol* (presumably, for *pistolet*), all too pertinent to Galois's situation. The results which he can, which he must now communicate, have been "in my head" for at least a year. There is no time left in which to expand on his proofs: but "*On trouvera la démonstration.*"

It is the cry, twice set down, "*Je n'ai pas le temps,*" which makes a study of these arduous algebraic abstractions all but unbearable.

Pushkin had already fulfilled so much of his genius prior to the duel. Not so Evariste Galois: "*Mais je n'ai pas le temps et mes idées ne sont pas encore bien développées sur ce terrain qui est immense.*" Galois declares to Chevalier the simultaneous "beauty and difficulty" of his insights. He doodles what may be a self-portrait, a vestige imminently posthumous. But the outside world, the source of his suicidal circumstance, intrudes. The word *République* surges at us, in a lapidary script, from between the tumult of algebraic symbols. At one point, the inward dialectic, the interplay between the purely mathematical and the political becomes revelatory as in no other document I know of.

Between two lines of functional analysis dealing with $(fx)^2 + (\alpha - a)(Fx)^2 = 0$, comes the word *indivisible*. It is followed by *unité; indivisibilité de la république*. A further line follows: *Liberté, égalité, fraternité ou la mort*. At which point the algebraic notation resumes.

The crucial illumination is this: *indivisible, unité, indivisibilité, égalité* belong obviously to republican-revolutionary rhetoric and politics. They belong no less indispensably to the conceptual idiom of mathematics and to that revolution, no less "radical" —itself an algebraic-political term—that is Group Theory. The two currents of language and conceptualization are confluent, are close to fusion in Galois's stressed, generative consciousness. Transcribing, as it were, under inner dictation, Galois is cerebrating verbally *and* algebraically simultaneously. The two semiotic codes, that of natural language and that of algebraic markers, are meshed. At some threshold to consciousness, the political bears on the mathematical and the mathematical on the political. Fusion occurs at "white heat" in a common crucible.

This fusion extends to the graffiti, to the caricatural sketches in the margins. Later on the page, we find: "*Pas l'ombre.*" I take this to refer to the idiomatic "no shadow of a doubt." The phrase would apply both to Galois's axiomatic demonstrations and to his undoubted entrapment in a political ambush. We can make out two further words, written slantwise amid algebra: "*Une femme,*" pointing to the trumped-up, sordidly trivial motive for the murderous cartel.

These pages, desperate with incompletion, brought to "science one of the most capital moments we know of" (Jacques Hadamard, in his pioneering monograph on the psychology of mathematical discovery). Galois's theorem on the periodicity of a certain class of integrals anticipated by a quarter century or more on available concepts. At some only partially conscious level, these concepts were present and figurative to Galois. Is it at that same level that "equality," as a technical designation, entered into the utopian politics of *égalité*?

If this is so, Galois's results are, emphatically, those of self-discovery. The algebra and the ideology are at one in the forward motions of the psyche. And Leibniz is proved clairvoyant in his assertion that "Art is the highest expression of an interior and unconscious arithmetic."

5

The analogies in respect of creativity in absolute poetry and pure mathematics are intuitively plausible. The mathematical imagination may derive from the same areas in the maze of the pre-conscious as do music and the arts. Einstein was paraphrasing Schopenhauer (and could have been citing Leopardi) when he professed "that one of the strongest motives that lead men to arts and sciences is to escape from everyday life with its painful crudity and hopeless dreariness." Plato and Erdös put it more exaltedly: the true poet, the numbers theorist, the composer of the Goldberg variations no less than the deviser of the Goldbach conjecture, are spirits possessed by infinity. Theirs is, at significant points, a common pursuit.

None the less, the differences run deep and need to be clarified.

The enterprise of the theoretical and applied sciences is eminently collaborative. This is so on the pragmatic, sociological plane. There is, from the outset, a community of inquiry, of research, and of proposal. Even where they compete, even where they are intensely rival in their pursuit of intellectual priority and material benefits (the Nobel, the patent), scientists communicate with each other in a "cyberspace" of reciprocal awareness which precedes, millennially, today's actual networks of informational immediacy. The development of science and technology has been inversely proportional to that of solitude. The laboratory, the institute for research, the international colloquium are the requisites of collectivity. Even in pure mathematics, although it continues to be a category apart, publication is, today, very largely shared. An entire mythology has blossomed around those privileged to sign with Paul Erdös. In astrophysics, in molecular biology, in theoretical and applied thermodynamics, papers are appearing with up to thirty or more authors. There may be behind this multiplicity somewhat grimy motives of professional promotion and mutual aid. The underlying condition, however, is genuine: the investigation of scientific problems, the formalization of hypotheses, the discovery of relevant solutions and of technical realisations proceed along a tidal front. Numerous specialists and practitioners, similarly equipped, are at work simultaneously and across the developed world. As the tools of questioning, be it in the most abstruse domains, become materially more massive, become economically more voracious—the accelerators needed for the study of sub-atomic particles, the radio and x-ray telescopes which probe the edges of our universe, the genome-project in bio-genetics—team-work is the only possible arrangement. In turn, attempts at secrecy, for military, ideological or commercial reasons, have proved counter-productive.

This *communitas* of the sciences has, at certain historical moments, probably come as near to a politics of maturity, of disinterested progress as any in Western social history. The best of the Enlightenment was energized by the ideals and *praxis* of scientific exchange, of encyclopaedic ordering in regard to nature and manufacture. The communication of ideas and inventions took place across political and administrative frontiers, across religious divisions and differing traditions of literacy and sensibility. From the Royal Society in London to the anatomists in Pavia and in Naples, from the Paris Observatory to the gathering of "natural philosophers" in St. Petersburg, ran threads of information, of controversy, of collaborative suggestion. Scientific gazettes and, above all, a prodigality of correspondence, meant for circulation, created a cosmopolis for the intellect. From Mersenne and Leibniz to Condorcet and Compte, the ideal of a commonwealth of positive, beneficial truths, transcending the bloody, infantile conflicts of religious, dynastic, and ethnic hatreds, seemed within reach. Perhaps the sheer cost of scientific research, as we enter the new millennium, perhaps the deepening contempt of scientists for all forms of compulsory secrecy, of censorship, of entrapment within ideological or commercial constraints, will, once again, bring universality. The "ownership" of a scientific truth, of a technological solution, is a puerile notion. As Kepler reportedly said, in midst the massacres of religious wars, the laws of elliptical motion belong to no man or principality.

Does this mean that individual genius plays no part? There is much debate on this point among historians and psychologists of science. Can one discount the seminal rôle played by an Archimedes, a Galileo, a Newton, a Faraday, a Darwin, or an Einstein? It is perfectly possible to do so. Historians point out famous synchronicities, cases in which monumental advances are achieved more or less simultaneously by a Newton and a Leibniz (calculus), or a Wallace and a Darwin (natural selection and the descent of species). The break-through, the radical re-orientation of analytic imagining, "lay in the air." The great discovery would have been made sooner or later, possibly by minds, by observers and experimenters less gifted. Insights long dormant are exhumed. The Copernican model had been available to ancient Greece, there are eighteenth-century intimations of the descent of man from primate ancestors. What may prove decisive is a shift in the political-social power-relations, an increase of secular license, a loosening of the mind-set made sclerotic by eroded metaphors (what has been called a "change of paradigm"). Had Descartes worked a few decades later, he could have published some of his "heretical" findings. The ambient climate of cultural-social dislocation, of "relativity" in both the technical, Einsteinian sense and that of moral and aesthetic values, generated much of the atomic theory, of the uncertainty principle, of complementarity, as these burst into life, at incredible speed, during the 1920s and 30s. It is, specifically, difficult to imagine an uncertainty principle being argued prior to the collapse of confidence, of rational determinism in human affairs, brought on by the catastrophe of 1914–18. Einstein's conservative faith in order could never resign itself to the indeterminacies of quantum physics. As in Western civilization itself, a certain chaos had come again.

Thus the sum of scientific advances surpasses exponentially that of its individual parts, however inspired by personal genius. That advance—I will come back to this point—is indeed inertial and oceanic. It proceeds via an inner logic and propulsive necessity in many ways independent of individual initiatives. This forward-motion can be arrested or accelerated by cultural-political contingencies such as religious censorship or by lack of resources. Combinations of such negative factors may indeed explain the comparative lack of scientific-technological advances in the African, Islamic, and oriental worlds (cf. Joseph Needham's voluminous investigations of the anomaly of Chinese "backwardness" after an early brilliance). Across time, however, and precisely owing to the collaborative, pluralistic nature of the process, there is a strong sense in which scientific theories and discoveries can be thought of as anonymous. The vast tide comes in.

Paul Valéry writes, not without a touch of mysticism, of those

> existences singulières dont on sait que leur pensée abstraite, quoique très exercée et capable de toutes subtilités et profondeurs, ne perdait jamais le souci de créations figurées, d'applications et de preuves sensibles de sa puissance attentive. Ils semblent avoir possédé je ne sais quelle science intime des échanges continuels entre l'arbitraire et le nécessaire.

Leonardo da Vinci, proclaims Valéry, is "the supreme type of these superior individuals." This may be so. But the flying-

machine, the submarine, the hydraulic screw, or the understanding of vortices would have been arrived at had Leonardo not
sketched and encoded his pragmatic clairvoyance in his (essentially unavailable) notebooks. Science discovers itself.

Art history teaches us that several hands have been at work on
numerous paintings. Some of the pieces deemed most characteristic of this or that master are, in fact, composite. Assistants,
disciples, fellow-craftsmen in the *atelier* or civic commission have
provided the background, have painted in attendant figures or
motifs, and may have completed the canvass as a whole. In major
renaissance and baroque frescoes, the master's sketches and overall design are realised by his acolytes. The foundry is crucial to
the later Henry Moore, casting on a monumental scale what were
small, almost tentative maquettes. In architecture, various forms
of plurality are the rule. The architect, the builder, the furnisher
of relevant materials—today, the computer's holographic suggestions and solutions—are engaged in a combinatorial enterprise.
In music, the collaborative exercise of creation and invention is,
no doubt, much rarer. On the anecdotal level, we know of hybrid
scores assembled by more than one composer; we know of works
such as Mozart's *Requiem*, Puccini's *Turandot*, Busoni's *Doktor
Faust*, Berg's *Lulu* or Mahler's Tenth Symphony completed by the
composer's students or admirers. More generally, much of early
and baroque music consisted of summary melodic and thematic
outlines to be instrumented, to be given their ground-bass by
other composers and executants. But it is in the nature of the case
that most music does originate in individual sensibility rather
than in the collectivity of a workshop.

Even the most "autistic" of aesthetic acts, even the most
graphic of singularities, is phenomenologically social. It comes

into being under the shaping pressures and constraints of the available media. Language is simply the most obvious example of the collective matrix. Historicity determines the options of the imagination. One need hardly be a Marxist (though it sometimes helps) to grasp how formatively social, economic, and ideological data circumscribe, mould, art, music, or literature. The ancient epic is as circumstantial a product of highly specific ethnic, economic, and political requisites and opportunities as is, in its different manner, the prose novel. The milieu of the clan is as seminal in Homer as is that of mundanity in Proust. We have seen already that there is contamination by the psychological and social environment in even the most absolute and otherworldly of lyric poems. Communication, the pulse of feeling and of thought to be communicated, are social. As is soliloquy when it uses language—a socio-historical means, exceeding all privacy—to make of itself another. Spoken aloud, a Hamlet soliloquy manifests and makes honest the sociology of the self.

It is these everyday truths which underlie the claims of modern "reception theory." Unquestionably, the audience, the viewer, the reader are dialectically implicated in the genesis and on-going presence of literature, music, and the arts. Audience response, the record of successive and transmitted interpretations, the social history of performance, exhibition, and publication—what is made accessible or canonic where, when, to whom—are integral to the aesthetic and discursive once these have been externalized, once consciousness breaks silence. Those playwrights who invite audience intervention, as, on partisan occasions, did Brecht, or who solicit from the electronic web alternative chapter-endings to a work in progress, as John Updike has done, are pointing up, in a didactic-humorous strategy, the constancy of social participation in the creative mode. For so much of its history, more-over, *poiesis* has been nameless. The cave-painters of Altamira, the architects of the Pyramids, the composers of folk-music, of popular airs sung, orchestrated across centuries, remain anonymous. As do the begetters, no doubt numerous, of the oral epics, of the defining fables which decay into fixity and (imaginary) author-ship in the "Homer" of our *Iliad* and *Odyssey*. Our obsession with individual authorship, with the artist's signature, with the persona and thumb-print of the composer, our hunt for plagiarism, are a very late and, I will want to argue, temporary reflex. They declare that dramatization of the ego of which renaissance and romanticism were the foremost, inwardly kindred, expressions. Conceivably in Shakespeare, assuredly in J. S. Bach, the concep-tion of workmanship, of formal production, was professional and non-egotistical to a degree we find difficult to experience. Even the major work—in Shakespeare's case, we must except the *Son-nets*—was a generalization, a matt of shared technical practice, far beyond self-consciousness. Much of the Elizabethan theatre was nourished by multiple hands. These were at work, often *ad hoc*, often cannibalizing previous material, on the same script. Shake-speare begins as a collaborator in the *Henry VI* trilogy, most prob-ably in *Titus Andronicus* and *Edward III*. He will end as an inspired understudy to Beaumont and Fletcher in *Henry VIII*. Here, there are indeed analogies to be drawn with the participatory enter-prise of the sciences. More than any other aesthetic genre, the theatre always has something of the character of a laboratory, its doors wide open to society.

But although such analogies are instructive, they are far less significant than the parting of the ways. In the arts, in music, in the philosophic moment, and in almost the whole of serious literature, solitude and singularity are of the essence. The creative motion is as individual, as entrenched in the citadel of the self, as is one's own never collaborative, never interchangeable death. We shall see that this intimate kinship of *poiesis* and of death, of the individuation of the aesthetic-metaphysical act, and of the aloneness of personal extinction is central. It defines both processes by reciprocity. We create or come close to creation and we die in ontological isolation, in *soledad*. This term, associated with the poetry of Góngora, perfectly concentrates the pertinent values. It implies Latin *solitudo,* from which it derives. It comports isolation, exile into the waste places of the self, an apartness from other human presences as is that of the anchorite. It connotes the "soul's midnight," another baroque precision familiar to the mystic, the metaphysician, and the poet. Out of which the birth of the work brings either light or an even denser darkness. The *soledad* of the creator is, as Góngora has it, *confusa.* It is simultaneously an emptiness, a desert of the spirit, and a potential plenitude, pregnant with shaping impulses. The poet, the thinker are unutterably alone, yet under pressure of crowding possibilities. At the threshold of the silence within him lies the turbulence of incipient form, of the will to articulation. Coleridge's Mariner, who can serve as an elucidating model of the voyage towards imperative expression, is alone, alone to the point of madness, on a crowded sea.

The night-side of generative solitude has, since classical antiquity, been made emblematic by Saturn, by the characterization of the poet and artist as "saturnine."[4] Born under a lightless

4. The classic study remains Raymond Klibansky, Erwin Panofsky, and Fritz Saxl, *Saturn and Melancholy* (1964).

star, he dwells in melancholy. Milton's "Penseroso" assembles the traditional, iconic motifs with memorable economy. The philosopher's, the poet's lamp will "at midnight hour, / Be seen in some high lonely tower." By virtue of necessity, but also of wearied desire, he will become a hermit. Communing with the spirit, adverse or tutelary, of Plato, of "thrice great Hermes," patron of fictions, the cloistered maker will "oft out-watch the Bear" in the starry heavens. Robert Burton locates in the contemplation of lofty truths, of beauty and of myths, in the imagination wedded to the speculative, a prime source of *tristitia*. An excess of solitude, *nimia solitudo,* can lead human beings to a state of nothingness: *et nihil sumus.* But also a voluntary aloneness is conducive to the eclipse of reason: it "gently brings on like a siren, a shoeing horn, or some sphinx to this irrevocable gulf" (note the surrealist alchemy of Burton's images). Yet there are those, no less eloquent, who bear witness to the ecstatic yield of solitude. Who testify that only in severe aloneness is it possible to feel the pulsebeat of life at its most intense pitch. Who equate *soledad* with the very possibility of speculative and constructive labours of the first rank. This, we will see, is Montaigne's reiterated conviction in his tower; as it is that of Nietzsche's Zarathustra in the blinding aloneness of high noon.

The categories, the typologies of solitude, as they differentiate the informing dynamics of the aesthetic from those of the scientific, overlap. But five modes may be worth distinguishing.

Solitude can be by choice, though that choice may well be inflected by psychological and social constraints. Montaigne is exemplary. He made of his round keep a sanctuary of fertile isolation. Tibullus' verse could have been his motto: *"in solis sis tibi turba locis"* ("alone, be a world unto yourself"). Like Prospero—

there are similarities—Montaigne peopled his silences with the voices of books. Thus there are in Montaigne's legion of quotations choral and individual familiars; even the roof-beams in his study carry citations from Scripture, some of them subtly awry. When at work on the *Essais*, when steeped in his preliminary readings and argumentative reveries, Montaigne kept at bay even those closest to him. The canonic injunction occurs in Book I, xxxix:

> We should set aside a back-room [*une arrièreboutique*] reserved exclusively to ourselves, keeping it entirely free, and establishing therein our true liberty, our principal retreat and solitude. There our normal discourse should be with, addressed to ourselves [*de nous à nous mesmes*], so privy that no contact or communication with the outside can find a place there. We should converse and laugh as though we had no wife or children, no posessions, no followers, no servants. Thus, when the occasion arises that we must lose them, that loss should not be a novel experience. We have a soul which can turn inward on itself [*contournable en soy mesme*]; able to keep itself company; capable of attack and defense, of reception and donation. Let us have no fear of decaying in that solitude through idle boredom.

To "laugh in solitude": a complex, troubling stance—Prospero again, or Hamlet, who quotes Montaigne. But out of that (silent?) laughter must have bubbled the unquenchable wit, the mercurial ironies of Montaigne's leviathan monologue.

There *is* laughter in Emily Dickinson's elected aloneness, but of a muted register. She underwent, she celebrated the wealth of loneliness:

> There is another Loneliness
> That many die without—
> Not want of friend occasions it
> Or circumstance of Lot
>
> But nature, sometimes, sometimes thought
> And who so it befall
> Is richer than could be revealed
> By mortal numeral—

Throughout too lengthy stretches of social history, the destiny of the exceptional woman has been one of enforced isolation, either psychological or public. Dickinson is grimly exact: "This is my letter to the World / That never wrote to Me—." Lines dated c. 1863 make for painful reading:

> The Loneliness One dare not sound—
> And would as soon surmise
> As in its Grave go plumbing
> To ascertain the size—
>
> The Loneliness whose worst alarm
> Is lest itself should see—
> And perish from before itself
> For just a scrutiny—

Nevertheless, like Montaigne, Emily Dickinson knew that her solitude was crowded with presences: "Alone, I cannot be— / For Hosts do visit me— / Recordless Company—Who baffle Key—". These visitants rouse the poet's consciousness to rare insights and vivacities. They reach into a "Being under Lock." Like few other writers—Thoreau's hermitage at Walden does strike one,

by comparison, as shrewdly public—Dickinson makes of her isolation the fuel, the validation of an illumined strangeness, of angles of incidence which only such *soledad* and cloistered apartness
could provoke. Is there, I wonder, any lyric more saturated by the
perceptions of aloneness, though obliquely and quite impossible
to paraphrase and account for, than the early (c. 1859)

> Water is taught by thirst.
> Land—by the Oceans passed.
> Transport—by throe—
> Peace—by its battles told—
> Love, by Memorial Mold—
> Birds, by the Snow.

The genius of the first and last lines crystallizes for me the utter
sharpness of tranquil, mute light in the often autistic warren of
poetic and philosophic productivity.

"Warren" is precisely apposite to Ludwig Hohl, one of the
secret masters of twentieth-century German prose. Hohl, who
believed that creation in any fundamental sense, lies outside
human reach, developed acute powers of observation. He was
a *voyeur* into the nuances and tremors of sensibility. Hohl experienced physical and psychological phenomena as intermina-
bly fragmented. With disenchanted scruple, he fitted these fragments into a language-mosaic of exceptional lucidity. Hohl did
so from a literal underground, from a cellarage or below street-
level cavern in Geneva. There, the teeming notes and aphorisms
which constitute his opus (*Die Notizen*) in an always provisional,
mobile array, were hung on clothes-lines for inspection and revision. Hohl, whose very name is an omen, was a collector of
silences and solitudes.

He came to distinguish between aloneness as suffocation, as sterility, which he identified with the flatness and dour Calvinism of his years in Holland, and the festive, fruitful solitude of the Alps. There is a solitude of the peaks and one of imprisonment, one of horizons and one of intractable confines. Out of authentic isolation, release can occur via a chance meeting, notably with a talismanic text (e.g. Goethe's *Maxims and Reflections* or Spinoza's *Ethics,* to Hohl the text of texts). Paradoxically, "the greatest, who are the solitary ones, have trust in the world," a trust as in a brother. Theirs is the fraternity of the essential. This is Ludwig Hohl's methodological point. Only solitude, difficult, humiliating, even corrosive as it is, can safeguard art and thought from corruption. The media, the lust to communicate by socially sanctioned and rewarded means, the manipulation of discourse towards approval and success, are an irreparable waste of spirit. Communication with others is a secondary, almost unavoidably suspect function. Language is true to itself only when it strives (always imperfectly) to address the "truth-functions" within itself. Echoing Kafka, whose penultimate parable of the "Warren" or "Maze" so uncannily prefigures Ludwig Hohl's actual existence, Hohl believed that there is genuine communication only when the listener is "appalled" (*entzetzt*).

Montaigne's tower, Dickinson's nunnery of one, Hohl's lair—each a solitary confinement, but freely chosen in pursuit of veracity.

Solitary confinement can be involuntary. The second category of creative solitude is political. Throughout history, major literature and philosophic analysis has been produced by those incarcerated by despotism, censorship, and repression. From Boethius to Cervantes, from *Don Quixote* to Sade, the catalogue of lasting works composed in prisons has been prodigal. The summit of Chénier's lyric art is achieved within hours of the guillotine; and though the shadow may be retrospective, execution hangs over the finest of Lorca. The prison-letters of Gramsci or of Havel, the poems smuggled out of labour or death-camps, are all too representative of the twentieth century. Where there is tyranny—political, ecclesiastical, tribal—literature (music to a more fitful degree) is the agent of declared or Aesopian opposition, of subversive irony and clandestine hopes. It is, as Russian parlance has it, "the alternative state." Poets, thinkers, have been slain, their writings burned and pulped, their possibilities of publication gagged, since antiquity. In *Julius Caesar*, Shakespeare's irony is mordant: "I am Cinna the poet, I am Cinna the poet. . . . I am not Cinna the conspirator." No matter, the wretch will be "torn" for his bad verses. Whenever totalitarianism grows megalomaniac, which is a tautology, its antennae for the dangers posed by the voices of anarchy, of libertarian rage or laughter in literature, become excited. Stalin was not altogether mistaken when he regarded Mandelstam's epigram on the "Caucasian mountaineer" as an intolerable challenge. The ironists of the Enlightenment, of romantic liberalism, the guardians of protest such as Voltaire, Shelley, Heine, Zola, or Solzhenitsyn, either experienced the Bastille of barely escaped from it. Today, leading African novelists and dramatists are being ground to slow death in the jails of ludicrous dictatorships.

Exile has long been an instrument of inflicted solitude. The artist is banished into airtight seclusion; he is cut off from his own work and from anyone who might respond to it (consider the case of Ernst Barlach, playwright, graphic artist, sculptor, under Nazism). Normal intercourse and communication with the outside world were prohibited for a Bulgakov, for an Akhmatova. Systematic ostracism drove Tsevetayeva to suicide. The phrase is a cliché, but nauseating: "live burial." Of these punitive isolations, that from his native tongue is, for a writer, the cruellest. There are virtuoso exceptions. Lamenting, incessantly, his banishment from the treasure-house of his native Russian, Nabokov proceeds to brew an American English sumptuously his own. Borges could have flourished in several languages. Beckett did. But these are, very possibly, the privileged forerunners of a shift in linguistic consciousness, of a new freedom of discontinuity between the mother tongue and the poetic (to which I shall return). Very nearly up to the present, the writer unhoused from his language has been like a painter blinded.

No record of this deprivation, of this living sepulchre, exceeds in desolate awareness that of Ovid's *Tristia* (it is by right of suffering that Mandelstam will borrow that title):

> "Missus in hanc venio timide liber exulis Urbem:
>   da placidam fesso, lector amice, manum;
> neve reformida, ne sim tibi forte pudori:
>   nulla in hac charta versus amare docet.
> haec domini fortuna mei est, ut debeat illam
>   infelix nullis dissimulare iocis.
> id quoque, quod viridi quondam male lusit in aevo,
>   heu nimium sero damnat et odit opus!"

"I am the book of an exile and enter the City (Rome) full of fear. Blessed reader, extend your hand gently to the weary one. Do not flinch with fear of being ashamed of me. No verse in these pages teaches the arts of love. The destiny of my author is such that the unhappy man can conceal it under no witticism. Also, that work which in his youth, and as cause of his disgrace, he composed with playful ease—he now hates and curses, but oh, too late!" Now comes the bitter crux. Should the reader spot deficiencies in Ovid's once inspired Latin, let him remember that these lines are being penned in midst of a barbarian tongue and culture:

> "siqua videbuntur casu non dicta Latine,
>   in qua scribebat, barbara terra fuit."

Ovid can no longer hear nor use fluent Latin. His ears, his lips are being coarsened and atrophied by the harsh babble of the Black Sea tribes at this bleak end of the world. It is this which makes of Ovid's relegation, of the never-ending quarantine, a homicidal solitude.

Yet the paradox is undeniable. It is under extreme pressure, under political interdict and ideological censorship, it is underground, in *samizdat,* that so much of the best in our legacy has been produced. This is delicate ground, almost taboo to liberal presumptions. But freedom of intellectual and aesthetic expression, political-social tolerance for the independent thinker or artist have been, in historical fact, benign interludes. The Athens of Socrates (Aschylus, Euripides die far from home), Augustan and imperial Rome, the medieval theocracies, Tudor-Elizabethan England, the *ancien régime* of absolutism in Bourbon France, the petty principalities in Goethe's Germany, pressed on the life of the mind and of the arts with varying degrees and techniques of prohibition. The chronicle of Russian literature from Pushkin to Brodsky is one of survival under brutal repression. Much of the incandescence of current Latin American writing has originated in a climate of despotism. In each of these cases, however, censorship and worse have been, as Borges puts it, "the mother of metaphor." Art, music, philosophic allegory and speculation, literature first and foremost, can flourish at their peril. Where there is clear and present danger to freedom of imagining and expression, literature has no need to justify its vital functions, to dignify its motivations. There is, for the writer, an economy of the essential. He is made indispensable to himself as to others. A Molière, a Shostakovitch know themselves at risk. This affords their works, their choices of themes and of idiom, a logic of immediacy, however oblique or masked its encoding. Inversely, and no doubt at too severe a cost in human suffering, despotism, the tyrant-state, profoundly honours, by its fear and enmity, the poetry, the metaphysical questionings which it would eradicate (undying honour is done to a Socrates, a Giordano Bruno, a Spinoza).

It may well be that it is more difficult to generate aesthetic and intellectual work of eminence from within the unresisting vacuum of more or less complete, indifferent license. Populist democracies are not necessarily inclined to excellence. The patronage of the mass-media and the free market, the distributive opportunism of mass-consumption, could be more damaging to art and to thought than have been the censorious *régimes* of the past. What epigram could have reached, let alone affrighted, the White House during the Vietnam atrocities? Unawareness and condescension can cripple as effectively as prohibition.

Again, the distinctions to be drawn between the humanities and the sciences are seminal. Science too has experienced censorship, ideological hostility, and attempts at outright suppression. It has its exiles and its martyrs. After Galileo, after Descartes, however, the mechanics of interdiction have, almost invariably, proved futile, indeed risible. Witness the endeavours against Darwinism of fundamentalist unreason. Or they have turned out to be self-defeating, as in the case of Stalinist interventions in plant-genetics or Nazi efforts to cancel out Einsteinian physics. No totalitarianism can, over the long run, afford scientific-technological primitivism.

There is, furthermore, an absolutely decisive difference between the work of art or of philosophy and that of science. Had Copernicus, had Galileo been eliminated prior to the dissemination of their insights, these would unquestionably have been arrived at by others. Neither heliocentrism, nor Mendelian genetics could have been other than delayed (and probably not for very long). Science, as we will note, has its sequential inevitability. It cannot be localized and thus arrested by *ukase*. Philosophical reflection, aesthetic realisation, on the other hand, are totally vulnerable to contingent accident, to planned annihilation, to the silencing of the maker. The metaphysical treatise (Servetus on the Trinity), the painting, the symphony, the poem can be silenced once and for all. They can be incinerated or shredded beyond any possible restitution. Being singularities whose instauration and achievement are always occasional, are always unpredictable and, in substance, non-repeatable, the systematic pages of a philosophy, a musical score, a fiction attach to individual existence. Destroy, stifle, or corrupt the "onlie begetter," and the work will be obliterated. Indeed, we pay far too little heed to the utter fragility, to the lottery which determine the key artifacts, the canon, the seeming monumentalities of our culture. What has survived of antiquity is the merest tip of the iceberg. We shall never read the lost plays of the Attic tragedians, the ample list of whose titles are to us like a ghostly teasing. The bigotry or manic sadness which commits to the flames Byron's journals, Büchner's *Aretino,* part two of Gogol's *Dead Souls,* has prevailed. Bakhtin's theoretical work has, in large measure, perished under the Stalinist steamroller. Had Brahms's Fourth Symphony gone lost in the post. . . .

What I have alluded to as the "anonymity" of the sciences is also their re-insurance. Work can be entirely re-done; the missed opportunity recurs. Nor do the sciences require or benefit from the paradoxical stimulus of political oppression or censorship. Contrary to the humanities and the arts, an Inquisition, a Neronian or Stalinist despotism do not foster good science. Whatever its internal élitism and rarefaction of spirit, science is at home in an open society. Everyman is offered access. Whereas the poet, the philosopher in solitary, enforced bounds, must people his own world and that of his fellow-conspirators (his readers):

> And here is not a creature, but my self . . .
> My brain, I'll prove the female to my soul,
> My soul, the father: and these two beget
> A generation of still breeding thoughts.

Observe the perfect fit of silence and of continuity in that "still." Only murder, that of Shakespeare's Richard II, can put a stop to this fruitfulness. But murder *can* do so, and has done so throughout the waste and barbarism of our political-ideological history. In the sciences, no such irreparability, no such end-stopping, is feasible.

Aware of the productivity of adverse solitude, there are those who manage for themselves its actualities and its mythology. This is our third type of *soledad.*

Repeatedly, Rousseau affirmed that a dungeon would have been the best safeguard for his exacerbated sensibility; that only total isolation, as of a desert father, could protect him from the libellous malignity and persecutions of a traitorous society. In the 1760s, Rousseau proclaimed that solitude, the hiddenness of a quarry hunted by its foes, despised by the mob of general mankind, would henceforth be his condition. The initial sentences of the *Rêveries du promeneur solitaire* are a manifesto:

> Me voici donc seul sur la terre, n'ayant plus de frère, de prochain, d'ami, de société que moi-même. Le plus sociable et le plus aimant des humains en a été proscrit par un accord unanime. Ils ont cherché dans les raffinements de leur haine quel tourment pouvait être le plus cruel à mon âme sensible, et ils ont brisé violemment les liens qui m'attachaient à eux.

Rousseau finds himself to be on this earth "as on an alien planet," on which he has been thrust from the one in which he dwelt. Even Montaigne's solitude was, implies Rousseau, by comparison tempered, even factitious. Did he not intend his *Essais* to be savoured by others, whereas the *Rêveries* are destined solely for their author. Who must henceforth abstain from human company.

It was Rousseau's genius to make of this flight into the desert, with its pathological motivations, with its origins in a more or less cultivated persecution mania, a general scenario with very nearly incalculable impact and consequence. The hunted dreamer finds solace

> soit couché dans mon bateau que je laissais dériver au gré de l'eau, soit assis sur les rives du lac agité, soit ailleurs, au bord d'une belle rivière ou d'un ruisseau murmurant sur le gravier.

Bewitchingly, the cadence of the sentence mimes the dream-motion of the boat. From Rousseau's melancholy pastorale derives *"le sentiment de l'existence dépouillé de toute autre affection."* There is no overstatement in saying that this finding and its phrasing are one of the hinges on which the history of Western consciousness has turned. That "feeling of being," which will translate via German idealism and the romantic movements into Heidegger's *Stimmung*, that ingathered plenitude of reflecting self-consciousness, arises out of solitude and out of those landscapes of aloneness which Rousseau identified for us. We walk the hills, we hymn the forests, we drowse on moonlit waters, in Rousseau's wake. Our tourist solitudes are his.

Also to Nietzsche, the high lone places are paramount. But whereas Rousseau's itinerary of isolation is that of the foot-hills and lakes, the setting of *Zarathustra,* coming after Byron's proto-Nietzschean *Manfred,* is that of the glaciers and perilous summits. Several factors went into Nietzsche's ever more alarmed self-exile from the flatlands and the world of common men. States of rapturous vitality, of energy more than human, alternated with physical break-downs and the coming of near-blindness. An incensed fastidiousness, an aristocracy and courtliness of soul susceptible to unforgiving irritation made all but quite exceptional human contacts difficult to endure (vulgarity made Nietzsche ill). Very soon, moreover, Nietzsche was forced to realise that those works of his to which he attached supreme significance, which he described to himself and rare intimates as regenerative acts comparable to Scripture, were smouldering in silence and perfect indifference. Despairingly, he combed the horizon for echo, even hostile. Titles, now among the towering feats of psychological intuition and linguistic expression, were quickly remaindered or returned to the author (who had financed their printing and publication in the first place). This ostracism from response reached a particular pitch during the composition of *Zarathustra* in the early 1880s. The tension of spirit demanded by this labour drove Nietzsche from refuge to refuge, from the lake of Garda to the Pennine Alps, from Airolo and the Gotthard to what was to become his elect, talismanic sanctuary—that of Sils-Maria and the upper Engadine. Nietzsche proclaimed *Zarathustra*, and Book IV especially, to be the "highest gift" any mortal had bestowed on his fellow-men. The silence which received the book was almost total:

> After the kind of *call* that my Zarathustra was, a call from my inmost soul, not to hear a single peep by way of reply: nothing, nothing, only the soundless solitude multiplied a thousandfold—there is something terrible about that, beyond all comprehension; even the most robust person could perish because of it—and, oh my! I am not among the "most robust"! Since that time it is as though I've been staggering about mortally wounded; I'm amazed that I still live.

In undisguised need, Nietzsche wrote to Burckhardt, pleading for some reply concerning *Zarathustra* and other writings, for some sign of hearing. Burckhardt countered with urbane evasion. More and more, the "hermit" of Sils-Maria sensed a depth of isolation which would induce madness.

Yet he knew that this very isolation was both the source and the proof of his stature. The pendulum swung dialectically within Nietzsche's self. Like Zarathustra, he thirsted for a descent into the companionship of society, even, perhaps, that of disciples. But he divined that such descent would jeopardize the absolute rigour of his dithyrambic vision, of what he pictured as a blinding exchange between the eagle and the sun: "I draw circles and sacred boundaries about me; fewer and fewer climb with me up higher and higher mountains—I am building a mountain chain out of ever-holier peaks." Here again, as with Rousseau, a radically specialized, even pathological complex had its extraordinary effect on sensibility at large. Nietzsche's solitudes and alpinism of the spirit were mimed by generations—exactly as Zarathustra had hoped and dreaded. Such was Nietzsche's will to power that even his collapse into the long night of speechless derangement proved iconic. Like that of Hölderlin, it exercised a troubling spell over those who sought to test the proximities of high creativity to unreason. There is a tragic propriety in the fact that no insight should be truer of Nietzsche, though recorded in a wholly different context, than Virginia Woolf's unforgettable: "The loneliness which is the truth about things."

Blinding migraines may have accounted for something of Nietzsche's fragmented, aphoristic presentation. The fourth order of *soledad* being that imposed by mental or physical infirmity on the artist or intellectual (where any distinction between the mental and the physical is often virtually meaningless). This domain is too extensive to be concisely summarized. It is, moreover, plagued by anecdote and folk-wisdom. Long before Plato's *Ion*, no doubt, the rhapsode was regarded as prone to manic possession. In numerous cultures and societies, poetic inspiration has always been associated with more or less pardonable lunacy ("the lunatic, the lover and the poet" in Shakespeare's good-humoured triplet). Heir to German romanticism, with its galaxy of literary and philosophic derangement and suicide, legatee of Hölderlin, Kleist, and Nietzsche, Thomas Mann came near to equating creative genius in the arts with sickness. There are "Olympian" exceptions, most notably that of Goethe; more often than not, aesthetic accomplishments of the highest kind are bred by a cancer of the psyche, by excesses of perception (Blake's maxim) and technical risk whose dynamics are pathological. Who but an epileptic could have experienced the states of illumination, of second sight into the abyss of human psychology and of social history manifest in *The Possessed* and *The Brothers Karamazov*?

The isolation, the exile inward caused by physical lesions is obvious. What is extraordinarily difficult is the demonstration of the actual correspondence, if it exists, between a handicap and the work produced. The witness borne by a Beethoven, by a Smetana, to incipient and worsening deafness, rends the heart. But just what was its effect—structural, thematic, tonal—on the late music of the two masters, on their most accomplished quartets? How does Goya's deafness translate into the howling violence and autism of the so-called "black paintings"? What relates the hallucinatory idiosyncracies of Van Gogh's Arles and St. Rémy paintings to the recurrent bouts of insanity, of schizophrenia (?) recorded in his letters? What is cause, what is effect?

The motif of blindness, of an exchange of sight for insight— as in Sophocles' Oedipus, as in the myth of Tiresias or Shakespeare's Gloucester in *King Lear*—attaches stubbornly to the history of epic: to Homer, to Milton, to Joyce. But what, if any, are the links between Borges's blindness and his often miniaturist mnemonic devices? I am ignorant as to the existence of any mute poets, though such a condition could be made intuitively plausible. Gray's "mute inglorious Milton" does, at any rate, seem hauntingly inappropriate.

Of strategies of solitude founded on illness, that of Proust is among the most consequent. The crux is not the psychosomatic aetiology and tenor of his asthma, of pulmonary crises which rendered any normal existence impossible after the years of mundanity. It is the immensely productive use to which Proust put his self-incarceration (the ambiguity of captivity, the eros of reclusion are, of course, the express scenario of the later part of *La Recherche*). Out of his sound-proofed, fumigated hive, Proust secreted a multitudinous society, a city for thought and for feeling rivalling Dante's. By force of sub-liminal book-keeping—precisely the same budget was adhered to by Kierkegaard—Proust bent his physical life and the life of the *magnum opus* into coincidence. Both terminated, at the same programmatic moment. In every sense, death allowed Proust to return to worldliness.

The sciences have no comparable and determinant intimacy with mental and bodily affliction (there are dramatic exceptions such as that of Hawking). The caricature of the "mad scientist" is exactly that: a folk-fiction originating in an intimidated apprehension of the scientist's seemingly occult powers and concentrated distraction. Staring at the heavens, Thales tumbles into the well. Legend and a handful of actual instances hint at the autistic solitariness, at the neighbourhood to dementia, which may affect the pure mathematician, the mathematical logician *in extremis*. But, almost throughout, sanity and the collaborative are instrumental to the sciences, theoretical and applied. The drama of pariahdom enacted by Rousseau or Nietzsche, the sufferance or cultivation of isolating sickness so manifold and, it may be, fruitful in the arts, in literature or music, would, in the sciences, be counterproductive. A certain democracy of well-being looks to be essential to scientific progress.

The final rubric of creativity out of solitude is that of the theological or transcendental, both experienced and metaphoric, which I touched on at the outset of this study.

The human artisan, the builder of thought, finds himself alone but not alone during the creative process. He is alone, often to the point of unbearable stress, and isolated *in propria persona*. This utter aloneness in the burrow of the self, as Kafka's allegory has it, can be physical, psychological, social. It can derive from the untimeliness, which it to say originality, of the work or the doctrine. There is simply no one "out there" equipped to decipher the performative means, the philosophic message, the *novum* of style or logic. There is no echo to an immensity of expressive need and vocation (the "voicing" outward from the innovative depths). Only a counter-silence or derision. And yet, there is, ineluctably, a "secret sharer," another presence. Which can solace, or strike terror or both. Indeed, the solace and the terror are strictly inseparable, as in Pascal's midnights or in Rilke's *Duino Elegies* (the master-text of modern ontological solitude).

A religious sensibility which has been, as we have seen, at the centre of aesthetic and philosophic acts in our civilization, registers, more or less consciously, the enormity of its "pro-creation." To attempt creation, to augment or alter the sum of being already on incommensurable offer, is blasphemy however loving. However ardently it celebrates a world already "charged with the glory and grandeur of God." The anathema, in genuine monotheism, on the making of images, be they mimetic, combinatorial, or systematically discursive (e.g. in the *Timaeus*), simply legislates that intuition. Who, we have already asked, is man to rival His creator? Simultaneously, however, this celebratory blasphemy, this never-ceasing wrestling with the Angel, comports an intimacy like no other, a polemic eros, in Hölderlin's analysis, more brimful of psychic risk and exultation than any.

During the late sixteenth and the seventeenth centuries, God would appear to have been a somewhat more frequent visitor to the workshops of the poets, the hermitage of the metaphysicians, than He has been of late. Poets such as Donne and Herbert, the virtuosi of the visionary and analytic in baroque Europe, document, with acute psychological notations, the shock and recompense of divine visitation at the creative hour. Thus the poems of St. John of the Cross are a close record of solitude at once total and overwhelmed by encounter with the transcendent. The creative, one would almost say "creating" face-to-face, transpires in the *noche oscura,* "with no one in sight." It takes place *en secreto* and hidden from all view (*que nadia me veía*). The "deepest caverns of the soul" are made bright by the collision. The poet's observation is sharp: his spirit is *tan embedido,* "drunken-reeling" in Roy Campbell's masterly translation. In this mysteriously violated solitude, violated by the imminence of God, the feared but beloved competitor, and out of the soul's inebriation, rises the poem (the painting, the cantata, the metaphysical conjecture). Volcanologists report that surging lava hums a primal tune.

Such invaded solitude has its secular analogues. There is the Muse at one's back, the daemonic inhibitor making of the "writer's block" a palpable intruder. When the compositional process is in spate, when formal obstacles seem to yield so that the pen can scarcely keep up with the informing rush, poets, novelists, composers tell of working "under dictation." There is a voice within their voice. In turn, playwrights, writers of fiction, tell of their meetings, often fraught or even hostile, with the *personae* of the play or novel in progress. The solitude of the executive moment and locale becomes crowded with the insistent presence of the imagined. In what is psychologically far more than an anthropomorphic conceit, the character takes on a "thereness" exceeding that of empirical reality. The incarnate shadow both attenuates the author's or artist's aloneness and increases it in respect of his fellow-man. What sociable weight can the men and women met in the street or in his home have had for the begetter of Cordelia, of Iago, of Ariel on the day Shakespeare wrote this or that scene?

The "drunken-reeling" of the creative hour, the autistic vertigo incurred by sustained thought of the first order, have their hang-over. Solitude redoubles with generation. Something essential and organic has been torn away. It is no longer wholly the poet's, the artist's, the thinker's own. "Go, little book," says the poet in ambivalent valediction. Writers, painters, tell of a desolation, a *tristitia* as of *post coitum*. Works have been destroyed, theories kept silent, in order to remain with their author.

To be sure, pure mathematics and the pursuit of formal or mathematical logic can entail comparable solitudes, spells of hypnotic solipsism (to the point of mental collapse) and their ennervated aftermaths. But these similarities to the poetic are external. There is no jealous God, no rival maker to whom the solution of a diophantine equation could be conceived of as a provocation. A demonstration of the continuum hypothesis or an unravelling of Russell's paradox of the class of all classes, does not take on the possessive and possessed contours of a literary persona. There is no Pygmalion. The theological drama has no bearing and "transcendence" is a technical designation. It is, I believe, this metaphysical neutrality or even inertness which differentiates, at great depths, the creativity of mathematics from *poiesis*. In the scientific project in general, moreover, and in its applications via technology, secularization and sociability are at once inherent and progressive. Science and technology are in constant and ubiquitous commerce with the existential, with the worldliness of communal circumstance. Science is ontologically indifferent—hence Heidegger's often misunderstood saying that "science does not think." And it is, by very definition, collective.

Thus absolute poetry, art and music, the enduring in philosophy, do look to be cognate with solitude, with those categories of *soledad* which I have cited. Such solitude is rendered paradoxically more exigent by its inclusion of the rival maker, of the inspiring or forbidding *daimonion*. "What is most to be treasured is as difficult as it is rare," declared Spinoza in the closing *scholium* of his *Ethics*. During the late 1650s and the 1660s, Spinoza immersed himself in near-total reclusion. Out of which aloneness he engendered a blueprint for human reason, for human justice, for the making vulnerable of the soul to rigorous truth, as yet unsurpassed. Spinoza's library included a Góngora.

6

Concepts of time are as diverse as is human experience. Phenomenologically, they *are* human experience. The periodicity of oscillations in a cesium atom, by which today's sciences determine exact time-measurements, is no less an historical convention than was the marking of time by the incense clocks of the ancient Orient. The atomic time-piece is merely more precise within its given framework. Both metaphysics and common sense have always perceived the seminal distinction between "time" and "duration" as these were polarized by Bergson and fused by Heidegger. "Times" are codes of mensuration standard-ized at given historical-technological stages, in given societies, towards public and pragmatic ends. "Durations" are the current of individual experience, as fluid, as anarchic as is consciousness. There is no fully shared, absolute chronometry to the duration of pain, of nightmare, or of pleasure. To put it more accurately: clock-time relates to existential duration in a kind of irrelevant parallelism. On the clock-face, the hand traverses identical divisions during the torture-session and the making of love. This identity may be invoked ironically or allegorically. This identity remains irrelevant; it proceeds across an abyss of indifference, where "indifference" re-appropriates its neutral meaning.

The ideal of mathematical time attaches directly to a necessary presumption or fiction of unchanging eternity. There is motion, governed, measured by immutable laws (until very recent particle-physics and cosmological models of alternative universes). The paradox of motion within or under the governance of the immobile, of the unmoved mover, authorized much of science, but also of theology and metaphysics from Plato and Aristotle to Newton. Postulates of eternity, of universality—itself a notion inseparable from immutability—continue to operate successfully in the determination of scientific principles and technological prescriptions, though there are, as I have just mentioned, uncertainties and unresolved strangeness at the far edges.

These temporalities, however, have scarcely anything to do with the flux and eddies, with the torrential and the stagnant, with motions in reverse or circularity, which characterize subjective duration. The clocks, the calendars within the psyche are as variably, as unpredictably "on time" as are the infinities of pulsations, of thrusts forward and backward, of broken rhythms which cadence our inward lives. Hence Plato's fierce gamble on eternity and distaste for the anarchic horology of emotions. Hence the incapacity, so definitively formulated by St. Augustine, to define duration to ourselves and to others. In semantics and grammatology, the debates over the status of verb tenses persist. Past, present and future in any nonscientific context look to be essentially linguistic. They are not homologous, or not altogether so, in their pacing of psychic and social experience across different cultures (politically, symbolically, Chinese time is not ours). I have tried to show in *After Babel* that the concept of hope is indivisible from the development of the future tense which, in turn, has its lexical-grammatical atlas and history. How do these relate, if at all, to Platonic intemporality?

What I aim to consider summarily is how time and duration help us grasp the fundamental differences between the dynamics of the creative in the arts, in music, in literature and those in the sciences.

It is no hyperbole to say that each work of art, music, and literature generates its own "time-world," its own temporal space. Nominally, the "space-time" in relativity catches up with insights as ancient as aesthetic and poetic theory itself. In the arts, the time-constructions are as manifold and nuanced as are the forms and objects produced. Naively, Italian Futurist paintings and sculptures seek to represent dizzying sensations of speed, of *accelerando*. At the opposite pole, much of abstract art and of monumental statuary professes the belief that "time must have a stop." It communicates, as in Henry Moore's lineaments of titanic repose, themselves dreaming of Michelangelo, immobilities and sleeps of time. Within an artist's oeuvre, the "time-zones" energized by, signified by different paintings or sculptures can be utterly diverse. Using what would appear to be closely similar geometric divisions and chromatic codes, Mondrian can suggest either total rest and timelessness or the frenetic beat of jazz and modern dance. Some of Giacometti's stick-men are trapped or at home (or both) inside bleak, unbreathing stasis. Others, nearly identical, are blown into haste by those cruel winds "from under the earth." Paul Klee's conjectural landscapes, which stem from the alertly dreaming eye, hint at time-reversals, at arrows in backward flight, out of some chronometric arrangement on the hidden side of the moon. I have referred already to the enigmas of silence in Giorgione, to Giorgione's ability to "paint silence." I suspect that this particular gift relates closely to his renditions of duration, of suspended narrative. Where, in Giorgione, song and musical instruments are involved, the play of duration against time lies obviously to hand. But how can one account for the wonderfully translucid presence, *vibrato* of distinct, though related, gradations or planes of time in the painting known as that of *Three Philosophers*? By what spiritual-technical means does Giorgione intimate the muted menace of wordly time, of time charged with incipient violence in the foreground, as against the pastoral-mythological inadvertence of time and sovereignty of duration in the far background of *The Storm*?

Pace its suspect punning, T. S. Eliot's "music moves / Only in time" is a truism. Intensity, pitch, harmonic function and timbre are the components of rhythm, which is time organized. Accentuation cannot be separated from the length of the note or of the interval (the silence) where length is temporal. But in music length and brevity, speed and slowness, are both time-bound and time-free. The metronome marking relates to the conventions of objective, idealized time. But the length, the cadence of the musical unit and structure as performed and heard are impossible to systematize or standardize exactly. There are intricate acoustic factors depending on the actual space in which a piece is performed; no two instruments produce perfect uniformity. These factors interact with psychological expectations and receptivities, with executive conventions which are simultaneously cultural or public and intensely private. Such terms as *allegro* or *adagio* are inextricably historical, technical, and subjective. A close sequence of musical configurations conveys a sensation of *vivace;* where such configurations are fewer or extended, we derive an impression of slowness. But at every bar, as it were, composer and executant can subvert the expected effect. There are Webern miniatures, some taking less than a minute of "standard time," which affect the ear as slow and spacious. There are *largos* in Beethoven whose formal repose seems to generate an intense compression of time. I have heard Richter play a lightning-quick trill in Liszt in a way suggesting the unending. In no other mode of human expression are the possibilities of synchronicity and of discord between time and duration as manifold, as productive as in music.

There is, moreover, a twofold "timeliness" to any piece of music. The piece enacts a duration specific to itself. It organizes the relations between the metronome, the acoustic phenomena, the psychology of audition and of recall (a richly complicating component) in its own singular manner. This combination differs with each performance. Thus the time of a Bach fugue cannot be multiplied into that of a Chopin *étude*. A Bruckner *andante* cannot divide into a Haydn *scherzo*. The same artist playing the same piece in the same studio and at a brief interval will not achieve the same exact length of clock-time nor of formal-psychological duration. The pressure on the string, the touch on the key, the flutter of breath on the mouth-piece are unrecapturably unique in each and every instance. It is their mechanical isochrony, their sameness to themselves which make recordings go dead for many composers and performing artists.

The difference from the sciences is drastic. We have seen that the timepieces of science are Platonic. They require an infinitely divisible but invariant eternity. The nano-seconds postulated in quantum physics are no less objective, are no less precisely calculable than are the billion light-years in cosmological models. A vital part of the history of science and of technology has been that of a constantly improving exactitude in measurements of time. Where time enters the equation, an operation, an experiment must coincide, to the maximal degree with that of the same experiment carried out at any other place or date. This exact repeatability is crucial to the entire scientific and technological enterprise. Otherwise the constructs of reason would collapse into chaos.

There is no need to dwell on the components of time in the languages of literature (as in all language). Such categories as cadence, rhythm, stress, repetition, or thematic variation are as functional in poetry and in literary prose as they are in music. Devices, effects of swiftness and of retardation, of harmonic resolution—as in the formal closure of a sonnet or in rhymed couplets—are common to musical and to linguistic structures. As are those of tonal, structural, and conceptual discord. Is there in any art form a subtler practitioner of bar-divisions, of rests, of key-shifts and, above all, of silences than is Beckett?

Nor is there any need to labour the limitless varieties of the relations of literary narratives, oral or written, to time(s). From Homer to Proust, Mann or Joyce, Western literature has built its worlds around the realms of the past tense, around grammatologies of remembrance. Correspondingly, utopian and science-fiction writings remember the future. More especially, the history of the novel in the West, as it deconstructs and re-invents that of the verse epic, is one of narratives which not only proceed within a given time-frame but whose unifying theme is time itself. From Cervantes and Defoe to the moderns, our novels enact the effects of time on the individual and on society, on consciousness and locale. *O tempora, o mores.* Again, just as in music, the abstractions of chronometric time, of the calendars, chimes and clocks "out there," play against the authenticities of psychological, fictive duration in the work. This is as patent in the pseudo-Aristotelian "unity of time" which compacts neo-classical drama into twenty-four hours as it is in the time-capsule which gives to Virginia Woolf's *To The Lighthouse* its charged immobilities. The prodigal reflections on, the metaphoric animations of, time in Shakespeare, most incisively in the *Sonnets,* constitute an anthology of perceptions comparable only to those in Dante and in Proust. There is, one hazards, a poetics and a metaphysics of temporality to be harvested from the mere listing of the word "time" in the Shakespeare concordance.

The intentionality of literature in reference to the *topos* of survival, of "immortality," is one which I want to consider in the closing section of this book. Here, I want to look more closely at the distinctions between the relations of creativity to historical time in the arts and in the sciences. There is, demonstrably, a history of the sciences, of the creative and inventive proceedings in the sciences and in technology. Is there "art history" or a history of poetry in any analogous sense? Or is an altogether different historicity at issue?

We have seen that no work of art, however abstruse, however hermetic and inward, is autonomous. The most private lyric, the most counter-figurative painting are embedded in their historical-social context. Whatever signifies, in however radical a privacy of focus, belongs to history and public circumstance. This applies, most obviously to material possibilities, to the dialectic between concept and expressive form. We noted that words and musical notations, oil-paints and titanium, initiate, condition, and, in so far as all executive forms are techniques, determine the potentialities, the actual realisation of the text, of the sonata, of the Cézanne still-life or the Guggenheim Museum at Bilbao. Materiality is social history, as is *technē*. Likewise, receptivity and interpretation are historical and social phenomena. They anchor the arts and literature in common time. Thus the survival of the book or the partita, of the statue or the painted landscape, seems to hinge on a beautifully paradoxical movement. The original, circumstantial body of reference, the local code, go lost or become imprecisely conjectural. The sitter for the portrait, the occasion and performative means (vocal, instrumental) of the musical composition, the referentialities, implicit and explicit, in the poem or play or novel, ebb from remembrance. We cannot, to any thorough, reliable degree reconstitute the conditions—material, social, psychological—under which an Aeschylean tragedy, a Bach oratorio, a Velásquez portrait, were first composed, made public, and received. We do not see a film of the 1930s as did its contemporary audience. What did Fra Angelico and his ecclesiastical patrons means by "fine art"? Yet here is the key paradox: in some elusive but compelling sense, contextual knowledge seeps out of the work so as to induce, to make room for a most difficult-to-define but decisive timelessness. Mallarmé says it all in his celebrated: *Tel qu'en lui-même l'éternité le change.* Each time the Greek or Shakespearian drama is re-enacted, each time the baroque or classical piece of music is performed and heard anew, each time the *quattrocento* Annunciation is viewed in a chapel, gallery, or museum, the errors inevitable in our response, the misunderstandings unavoidable in our interpretative archaeology of feeling, invest in the work its novelty, its intemporality (the young Lukács dwells on this paradox in his fragmentary Heidelberg *Aesthetik*).

Loss makes new. The original message has been silenced. Or it becomes a retrospective convention, a mythology of meaning. This allows, indeed necessitates the fertile misprisions of renovating response. It is precisely those works, those aesthetic systems which programme "eternity," which plan timelessness, that will fade altogether or retain only an archival presence in vapid sublimity. Encased, as it were, in its now irretrievable local habitation and historical date, wholly concordant with the technical means available to it, a Dante *canto*, a chapter out of Rabelais, a political allegory in Dostoevski, will necessitate, will remain open to, the impassioned ignorance and restorations—always to be renewed—of later reception. The "strange, secret savour," as Lukács puts it, of what has, very largely, become unrecapturable, remains none the less so as to solicit new appropriations.

There may be casual analogies in the histories of science and of technology. Curators and archival scholars re-construct medieval astrolabes or edit, with every philological-documentary refinement, the writings of Galen or Copernicus. But their intent is, very precisely, to inhibit erroneous interpretations, to falsify opportunistic re-appropriations. No sane teacher of planetary orbits will substitute a Ptolemaic *almagest* for a modern textbook. Anatomies, physiologies prior to Vesalius or to Harvey are, in the exact sense, of historical, perhaps aesthetic interest (Vesalius' plates retain their iconic force). They have no persistence of transformative rebirth as does an ode by Pindar or a Rembrandt etching. There has been irrefutable progress and a concomitant erasure of what lies behind. Science and technology are in incessant progress. Their condition of being is that of an advance across measurable time. Which truism brings us to one of the most challenging of epistemological-aesthetic questions: Does this primary concept of progress, of advance, apply to *poiesis*, to the history of realisations, of executive forms in the arts, music or literature?

Even preliminaries are difficult to sort out. We know that aesthetic judgements are a maze past unravelling. They are woven of subjective intuitions most probably founded in the sub-conscious, possibly in certain aspects of neurophysiology. They are consequent on social-historical consensus and pressures for conformity. They reflect the unstable, often irrational caprice of fashion. The canonization of the aesthetic, the ascription to a work of classic and lasting values, engage power-relations at once pedagogic and ideological, political, and mercantile. No aesthetic values are value-free or, despite Kant, wholly disinterested in an ideological sense. Taste, moreover, is at all times subject to correction, to revision, and even complete reversal. We have seen that its most confident, historically and collectively empowered dicta are strictly unprovable. No dissent, however eccentric, scandalous, or solitary—Dr. Johnson on Milton's "Lycidas," Tolstoy on Shakespeare—can ever be refuted.

At the same time, a readiness to make discriminations, to experience and to state that A is superior to B, is essential. It makes possible a vital economy and, as it were, hygiene of attention and response. To direct a brief lifetime on mendacious or ephemeral trivia is, indeed, an "expense of spirit." There is so little time in our ordinary lives for that which justly overwhelms and transmutes consciousness. To equivocate on the relative significance, on the life-giving stature of, say, the *Missa solemnis* on the one hand and the latest top-of-the-pops on the other, is to impoverish both individual existence and the body politic. But I repeat: however self-evident this persuasion, however fervently one may act upon it, the valuations which it proclaims are not subject to proof. The contrary view can be urged with equal commitment. The mass-market does so daily. It is this intuitive status that so intimately relates an aesthetic credo to theological beliefs. Both are inherently fallible assertions from the unplumbed depths of the spirit. They are jubilations against despair, neither refutable nor irrefutable.

When we have arrived, via individual response and the almost determinant force of inherited tradition, at a taxonomy, at a classification of aesthetic works and forms according to "greatness," "universality," "impact," "lastingness," "metamorphic potential" or what we will, the question arises: Is there progress? Do C and D constitute an advance on A and B by virtue of time? We have seen how obvious the answer is in science and technology. Nuclear physics surmounts alechemy; molecular biology supersedes the physiology of humours. The same pertains to applications: e-mail improves on the semaphore, a supersonic jet outstrips a galleon; chloroform dramatized the ascent of man out of unimaginable pain. No winds of fashion will blow science or technology backward. Phlogiston theory will not return to replace Maxwell equations. Flat-earth adepts may be intractably obstinate, but they are mumbling sheer nonsense. A man or woman who states sincerely that Mozart could not compose a good tune is *not*. The distinction is fundamental and dismaying. Scientific theories are indeed open to overhaul, correction, and dismissal. But the next paradigm is demonstrably better in its explanation of the relevant data and in its capacities for experimentally testable prediction. Scientific and technological knowledge is cumulative. It "adds up." In fact, it is this augment by addition and refinement which defines and validates the very category of knowledge. To repeat: today's sixth-former or high-school student can manipulate tools and concepts closed to Galileo, to Isaac Newton, and, very soon, to Einstein.

What, *per contra,* is an advance on Homer or Sophocles, on Plato or Dante? What stage-play has progressed beyond *Hamlet,* what novel surpasses *Madame Bovary* or *Moby Dick*? Does any lyric by, say, Rilke or Montale improve on one by Sappho or Catullus? Is Stravinsky superior to Monteverdi? Do Picasso or Bacon excel Giotto? Even to pose the question in this way is to invite a sense of absurdity, of misdirected asking. The temptation is great to say "No"; to situate the aesthetic and philosophic in intemporal constancy, and have done with the argument (underlining, once more, the abyss of differences with the sciences). The issue, however, is more resistant than that. It does compel a closer look.

There is no need to revert to the historicity, which is to say evolution, of the materials and means of aesthetic production (philosophy abides by the perennial poverty of words). Such evolution is evident in architecture and in music, the arts most kindred to the sciences and to technology. The development of Plexiglas, of light-weight metals, of holographic simulation and computation does enable a modern architect to conceptualize and achieve projects unimaginable to Vitruvius or Palladio. The development of the modern piano, of the electronic synthesizer does enable a Debussy or a Stockhausen to explore, to externalize tonal possibilities and sound-worlds inaccessible to Haydn or even to Liszt. In this, undoubtedly important sense, there *is* progress and there can be enrichment. But does this mean that a Frank Lloyd Wright house or Jean Nouvel's art-centre in Lucerne is an advance on, a supersession of, the Parthenon or the civic square in Sienna? Have Debussy's *Images* improved upon Bach's *Welltempered Clavichord* or Chopin's bagatelles? Again, the impulse to impatient denial needs to be qualified. Sculpture has benefited from an evolving technology in regard to raw materials and their shaping (the "flights" open to Calder were not available to Bernini). There are those who would contend that the development, in the West, of a geometrically underwritten understanding of perspective, together with the introduction of oil-based pigments, made art better, richer, more persuasive. Furthermore, and this may be vital, new materials, new techniques—the pre-stressing of concrete, the welding of metals—initiate imaginings. In the dialectic of electronic music, the synthesizer puts on offer, as it were, acoustic eventualities, tone-clustres and tints which a Boulez can probe, incorporate or discard in the creative process. But will this expansion in any conceivable way make Berlioz, say, or Sibelius dispensable? Virtual Reality, as the computer-screen generates and reticulates it, sits at the architect's elbow. Has Wren become obsolete? It is arguable that the typewriter has modified certain elements of poetry; will the word-processor and pc alter the future of the novel? Each of these questions poses fruitful difficulties.

But because its sole medium is language, literature, more than any other aesthetic form, invites the concept of perennity. Languages have their history. Given periods—French during the sixteenth century, Elizabethan-Jacobean English, American English today—and, for reasons not wholly understood, different languages manifest different levels of energy and acquisitive confidence. But overall, their instruments are the same in perpetuity. The watchman waiting on the roof at the start of the *Oresteia* uses words, grammatical rules, and rhetorical devices fundamentally the same as those used by the menials waiting for Godot some two and a half millennia later. In what ways, if any, can Beckett's play be deemed to be an advance on Aeschylus'? Indeed, does such a question make any sense?

All aesthetic forms, all works of art, music, literature, are produced in diverse orders of relation to their precedents. This relation may be one of diffuse generality or of highly specific notice. It may entail imitation, rejection, variation, travesty, pardody, citation direct and indirect. The modes of allusion, of declared and covert reference are truly incommensurable. No work, however iconoclastic, however "original" (what, exactly, does that term signify?), comes to itself or to us unforeshadowed. There are audacious leaps, but no quantum jumps. Certain features in the decorative arts, in geometric symbolism, notably in Islam, prepared, perhaps made logically inevitable, across a thousand years, the non-figurative, the cubist experiments in the modern West. The Schoenberg-revolution embodies much out of Brahms and Debussy. The *Iliad* is heir to a very long history of oral predecessors. In this, highly important, sense, there is in the aesthetic, in *poiesis*, an on-going history, a phenomenology of the additive and of accumulation. Had we but Picasso, we could reassemble a transformative inventory of graphic and plastic arts from Alta-mira and its cave-painters to Manet and Cézanne.

Contrary, however, to the imperative of progress in the sci-ences and in technology, the relation of the new work to the sub-stantive and formal past, to the tradition of previous paintings, statues, symphonies, buildings, poems, or novels, is thoroughly ambiguous. The wealth of the canon, of the exemplary, is simul-taneously generative and inhibiting, seminal and constricting. It provides alphabets, short-hands of recognition, of immediacy, of recall and comparison so pervasive as to both underwrite the shaping act and so as exercise on it enormous pressures. In Joyce's *Ulysses*, in Derek Walcott's *Omeros*, in Thomas Mann's *Doktor Faustus*, it is these re-insurances and pressures which are made the explicit theme. Thematic variation, as we saw, is fundamen-tal to aesthetic organization and reception. A major proportion of literature, of the arts and of music is built of more or less vivi-fying, metamorphic quotation and re-iteration (how much there is of Dickens in as radically new a work as Kafka's *Trial*). The etymology strikes deep: to "re-peat" is "to ask again," to pray a second, a third, a hundredth time as does Dante to Virgil, as did Virgil to Homer, and Homer to. . . . Where the ballast of the past grows too heavy, where it sifts into pre-digested conventions—as in much of the antique mythology and re-modellings in, say eighteenth-century poetry and heroic painting—the particular lineage stales. When retrieval and reproduction of the teeming catalogue out of the past come near to overwhelming a present culture and sensibility, creativity may experience crisis. I will re-turn to this eventuality.

But note the utter flexibility of the uses of duration open to the aesthetic. A Mann, a Joyce, a Pound, or a Stravinsky may "invent backward." Like innumerable forebears, they can deliberately archaicize, both in medium and setting. Indeed, the cultivation of patina, of the stylistcally and substantively by-gone, is itself as old a device as that body-shield in the *Iliad* with its bronze-age intimations. Artist, writers, composers set modernity of technical means and expectations against the reborn presence of the distant archetype, be it a Mayan figure in Moore, a renaissance motet in Stravinsky, or the voice of Dryden in T. S. Eliot. Correlatively, the arts, and literature in particular, have at their disposal all manners of futures. Science-fiction is as old as the myth of Icarus. Narrative utopias—the Arcadian, the Golden Age in the garden of man—may well have been a cliché by the time of the redaction of *Genesis*. The deep-seated mechanism is always there: the future as a remembrance of a lost past, as a satire on the present, as a figuration, at once fantastic and rational, of evolving technology.

To these time-games and flexibilities, there is no plausible counterpart in the history of the sciences. A working astrophysicist cannot couch his paper in the idiom of Laplace. No biogeneticist calculates "pre-Darwin." The pressures of history at his back annul and consume themselves as they thrust him forward (the principle of the jet-engine). A modern physicist can hardly make out even a translation of Newton's *Principia;* but he does not need to.

Given this essential difference, we ask again: In aesthetic creation, does the fact, highly significant and informing as it is, that B comes after A make it better? Is A superseded?

The answer is, I believe, a categorical No. All texts, all works of art and of music empowered by survival and transmission, open to renascence and renewal by virtue of reception, possess values neither superseded nor cancelled out by later works. Neither historical chronology nor technical sophistication renders a classic obsolete (this being the definition of a "classic"). They will modify, often profoundly, the ways in which an earlier work is perceived and interpreted. *King Lear* currently comes to us in the light or shadow of Beckett's *Endgame* and Pinter's *Homecoming*. The placement of a work within the life of inheritance will alter. There can be periods of eclipse, of forgetting. Major acts of imagining—the novels of Stendhal—will recede into limbo, into what the French call their *purgatoire*. But if they have in them sufficient life-force and insolubility, if the questions they ask of themselves and of us remain unanswerably insistent, such works re-emerge, often with re-doubled impact. The Metaphysical poets are re-discovered, as is baroque music, or the so-called "primitive" arts of Africa and the American Northwest. The hieroglyphs slumber, then wake to eloquence.

At the decisive level, the notion of progress, of supersession in historical time, reveals itself as factitious. Serious works are neither outstripped nor eclipsed; major art is not relegated to antiquarian status; Chartres does not date. The difference with science and technology is of the essence. In the arts, in literature, in music, duration is not time. Formal and meta-mathematical logic does move forward and amend prior findings. Philosophy does not. The questions argued by Plato or Descartes or Kant are as pertinent today as they were at their inception. Only certitude ages.

The timely timelessness within the web of history which situates *poiesis* and metaphysical questioning, which can be "dated" but does not "date," is at once evident and difficult to analyse. From within the matrix of common, historical (chronological) temporality, the maker and the thinker can, if sufficiently endowed, achieve contemporaneity with their predecessors, with actual contemporaries and, most enigmatically, with works and insights yet to come. Steeped, *in concreto,* in the minutiae of his own historical moment, so many of them irretrievable to us, Juvenal is already contemporary to Swift. Both are made "more themselves" by Karl Kraus. The clocks of transformative reception, of restoration to relevance and felt immediacy, keep their own time (where "keeps" has the full meaning of preservation). Avantgarde can be, often turns out to be, epilogue. The formally retrospective and technically conservative, on the other hand—those alexandrines of Baudelaire—can generate utmost radicalism. The artist, the philosopher are at liberty to be behind the times or ahead of them. The motion is never one of mere linearity. It can, I intuit, be seen as that of a spiral, of a helix in which ascent and descent are equivalent.

It is this paradox of timelesness within the context of historical time which legitimizes the perennial claim of the maker to immortality, which validates that *exegi monumentum* which has been the password of the humanities in the West. It is this conceptual eternity and reversibility in the grammars and calendars of creation—as insoluble and sovereign as is the "When Abraham was, I am" of the Fourth Gospel—which have underwritten Western education and taste. They define our network of reference and recognition since Babylon and the dawn of ancient Sumer. Hence the power of *Gilgamesh* or of the statue of the kneeling scribe over the inward of present-day consciousness. Every valid act of humane literacy, argument, and realised form is a past made present and a present charged with recollections of the future. Such propositions and the valuations they entail cannot be proved in any formally logical, let alone experimental sense. This may well be the mark of their life-giving truth.

We can now put forward a central postulate. Only two experiences enable human beings to participate in the truth-fiction, in the pragmatic metaphor of eternity, of liberation from the eradicating dictate of biological-historical time, which is to say: death. One way is that of authentic religious beliefs for those open to them. The other is that of the aesthetic. It is the production and reception of works of art, in the widest sense, which enables us to share in the experiencing of duration, of time unbounded. Without the arts, the human psyche would stand naked in the face of personal extinction. Wherein would lie the logic of madness and despair. It is (again together with transcendent religious faith and, often, in a certain relation to it) *poiesis* which authorizes the unreason of hope.

In that immensely significant sense, the arts are more indispensable to men and women than even the best of science and technology (innumerable societies have long endured without these). Creativity in the arts and in philosophic proposal is, in respect of the survival of consciousness, of another order than is invention in the sciences. We are an animal whose life-breath is that of spoken, painted, sculptured, sung dreams. There is, there can be, no community on earth, however rudimentary its material means, without music, without some mode of graphic art, without those narratives of imagined remembrance which we call myth and poetry. Truth is, indeed, with the equation and the axiom; but it is a lesser truth.

But is that greater truth of the arts secure in the ways in which we have known and lived it up to now? Has *poiesis* its classic future? It is to these questions I want to turn.

V

We have seen that the concepts of "creation" and of "invention" are always in context. Their semantic field is that of history in its social, psychological, and material components. That which purports to deal with eternity is itself time-bound. We saw that even the most solipsistic of formal constructs, that even the most private and neological of articulate acts, has a social and collective matrix, most emphatically when it sets out to subvert, to transgress that matrix. A nonsense rhyme, a Dada *vocalise*, an aleatory composition in music, will use inherited, more or less public and conventional markers in order to unsettle expectation and "make new." Its shared legacy, its eventual intelligibility are facts out of an historical, communal, technical surrounding.

Such temporality and rootedness in the available—no Calder mobile prior to certain technologies of welding—seems to pose no barriers to the concept and enterprise of invention. Invention is the child and motor of historical time in its perceived and statutory linearity. The relations of the experience of temporality, of the sequential calendar of history, to the idea of creation are, in contrast, acutely perplexing. The theological "background noise" in the areas of meaning of "creation," the rhetoric of timelessness and irreplacable everlastingness which attaches to poetry, to the arts, to music, to metaphysical discourse would seem to postulate a "time outside time" only tangential to that of history and of science. This postulate organizes the Western tradition of the classic and the canonic. The Homeric epic, the Platonic dialogue, the Vermeer townscape, the Mozart sonata do not age and grow obsolescent as do the products of invention. A nineteenth-century steam-engine is now an historical curio. A novel by Dostoevski is not. The distinction is at once obvious and intractable. It suggests highly problematic but trenchant differences in the existentialities of time in individual consciousness and in culture. If the past, present, and future of Dante's *Commedia* are not those of the Riemann hypothesis, what are they?

No element in our experience of formal and substantive phenomena stands still. Vitality, which includes decay and closure, is a function of perception and interpretation in motion. Thus the history of the psyche is that of incessant change. Within this flux, there are episodes of mutation, of revolution or, as current mathematical models have it, of "catastrophe." The underlying shifts are tectonic, as in continental drift. But they can also manifest energies of acceleration, of metamorphosis so vehement, so far-reaching as to make our analyses, our explanatory theories homeless or, at best, conjectural. The defining perspectives, the maps, have been transformed and re-drawn. What seemed stable has been made uncertain recollection.

I believe that the current changes in the experience of communication, of information, of knowledge, of the generation of meaning and of form, are probably the most comprehensive and consequential since *homo sapiens'* development of language itself. There is, to put it in shorthand, a new locale for man after von Neumann or Turing. Without reference, however tentative, to these overwhelming alterations in the environment and means of articulate consciousness, of conceptualization and representation, any study of creation and invention would, now, be antiquarian. The "great stories" are today being dreamt and told, if at all, in an entirely new way.

Language, in an overall sense, is a rule-governed system of arbitrarily conventional markers, vocal and graphic, whose function it is to communicate and record significance (which is, in this case, a more neutral and inclusive term than "meaning"). The permutations of these markers, their "character," where the play on words is illuminating, are formally unbounded. They can be lexical-grammatical phonemes, pictograms of the most diverse sort, musical notations, ideograms, mathematical-logical symbols. Thus the rubric "language" applies fully to music, to mathematics, to formal logic or the notation of a choreographic figure. It applies also to works of art, although there is here a certain transfer of usage. We read a text, a musical score, an algebraic theorem. We also read a painting or sculpture or piece of architecture. It is this legibility which makes possible the conveyance, the suggestion of sense and the elicitation of every order of response from the most abstract to the most emotive. We inhabit language-worlds (Heidegger) or language-games (Wittgenstein) in so manifold and intimate a way that our sensation of being is primarily semiotic. It is made "sensible," in the strongest connotations of that word, by encoding. Hence, we have seen, the analogies between genetic, biomolecular sequences and the decipherment of an alphabet and syntax.

The conventions of the acts of signification conveyed by gestures, "body-language," have been remarkably stable across time and cultures. Certain gestures in the cave-art of Altamira are eerily familiar. For its part, the triad of emission, communicative medium, and reception has informed human existence since the instauration of remembered history. Fundamentally, the generation of messages and their receptive interpretation—which is always translation, even within the same language—have been a constant. This empowers us—do we pause long enough to be startled?—to make out, to respond intellectually and emotionally (however imperfectly) to inscriptions, images, architectural remains, texts emitted thousands of years ago by individual men and women, by communities of which we have only the most shadowy intimations. The begetters of *Gilgamesh,* of the *Exodus* narrative are emphatically legible, audible to us, even where complete philological confidence or decodings of sensibility may prove elusive. We read Euclid and Phidias in some respects very differently from, in others very much like, how they were read by their contemporaries. Archaic tongues, millennially unspoken, can be acquired by the interested scholar. Like energy itself, and the parallel may be of the first importance, significance and potentialities of transmissible meaning are conserved.

The conjecture that this dynamic stability and conservation may today be in question looks to be implausible. It entails the suggestion that certain fundamentals of human consciousness, of mental proceedings and habits of feeling are susceptible to alteration in depth. Moreover, given the very gradual, normally imperceptible modifications in human evolution, in the history of "being human," the hypothesis of any "catastrophic" break does seem irresponsible and melodramatic. The time-scale looks wrong.

I am aware of the force of these objections. Nevertheless, I put forward the intuition, provisional and qualified, that the "language-animal" we have been since ancient Greece so designated us, is undergoing mutation. It seems to me that recent technological developments, technology inevitably implicating metaphysics, come near to enforcing some such supposition. Caught, as it were, in the slip-stream and turbulence of changes which are occurring at a fantastic rate, our misunderstandings and imperceptions are unavoidable. But if that "death of man" proclaimed by Nietzsche and Foucault is anything more than an histrionic shibboleth, what we have known of both "creation" and "invention" will have to be re-thought. And it seems common sense to initiate this re-thinking at the nerve-centre which is language.

2

Geologists report enigmatic signals premonitory to earthquakes and volcanic eruptions. Some animal species seem to register as yet imperceptible tremours; the light changes. What I would call, tentatively, the seismic shocks and fractures in language, the breaking of the primordial contract between word and world, did have their fitful, occasional precedents. Ancient logic gnawed at the seemingly insoluble paradox of the Cretan liar, of the self-defined liar affirming a true falsehood or false truth. There are challenges to the capacity of language to describe verifiably, to arrive at any empirical decidability, in the ruminations of the Sceptics. Montaigne has his playfully incisive doubts as to the demonstrable verity of any linguistic proposition. But in both classical and renaissance scepticism, the means of inquiry and debate in which doubts and subversions are expressed remain, themselves, intact. Indeed, in *Paradiso* XXXIII, the failure of the mortal word to articulate, to conceptualize divine radiance—

> Oh quanto è corto il dire e come fioco
> al mio concetto!

—places the word at the very threshold of the transcendent and the absolute. Whereby the *dignitas*, and bounty of God's bestowal of language on Adam and his fallen progeny, are jubilantly reaffirmed.

The closest we come to a total negation of the semantic, to

a *logos*-nihilism and annullment of man's pact with saying, occurs towards the final moments of *Timon of Athens*. In an abyss of life-denying despair, of ontological nausea—it is being *per se* in nature and in man which offends Timon unendurably—Timon bids "language end." His epitaph, necessarily verbal, is to be washed away by the cleansing seas. Taken generally as calling for the termination of all speech, Timon's laconic imperative would, in the Western tradition of thought and *poiesis*, be virtually unique. And it has its paradoxical source in the art and sensibility of the most resourceful "speech-agent" of whom we have record, in Shakespeare.

But the tidal wave of *Sprachkritik*, of the critique of language root and branch, in Central Europe between the turn of the century and the 1940s, is of another order. It enlists philosophy and literature, sociology and political science, psychology and the arts. It leaves no aspect of our language-humanity untouched. The consequences of this destabilization, of this slippage of elemental trust in the word, may prove to be more far-reaching than those of the political revolutions and economic crises which have marked our age. It is only now, often dimly, that we can begin to make out the new landscape.

Dated 1901, Hofmannsthal's *Ein Brief*, better known as the "Lord Chandos Letter," has lost nothing of its finality. The eponymous hero, a brilliantly endowed young Elizabethan aristocrat, writes to Francis Bacon. He has already, at nineteen, composed mythological poetry. Much is expected of him, for both world and word have been prodigal. But now "the capacity to think or to say anything coherent has deserted me." At first, this loss bore on those abstractions which normal human beings mouth so readily. Lord Chandos found himself unable to utter such words as "spirit," "soul," or "body." Articulate pronouncements and judgements became literally unutterable. On Chandos's lips they turned to rotten fungi. Even to hear fluent propositions babbled by others became intolerable. "Words swam around me; they turned to eyes staring at me, and into which I had, in turn to stare. Words whirl and it makes me dizzy to look into their incessant spinning, beyond which one enters on emptiness."

Chandos can no longer relate to simple objects and artifacts. A watering can, a dog lazing in the sun, a modest rural cottage on his estate can become "a vessel of revelation" (*Gefäß einer Offenbarung*) so charged, so brimful with existentiality, as to make impossible any adequate response. Even an assemblage of trivia confronts Chandos with the terrifying presence and unfathomable proximity of the abyss. All that is itself mute overwhelms his bewildered psyche bringing at once terror and benediction. When the moment of epiphany has passed, Lord Chandos is thrust back into the void. During anguished nights, there arises the phantom of a supreme *desideratum:* of a mode of human thought and perception "in a medium more immediate, more fluid, more glowing than is the word. This medium too is made up of whirlwinds and turning spirals; but unlike language these do not lead into the bottomless, but somehow into myself and into the deepest lap of peace." Chandos dreams of a tongue in which the mute presence of the world can address him truthfully and in which he may, after death, make himself answerable to an unknown judge. This will, in any event, be his last letter to his eminent friend.

The ironies are many. A confession of speechlessness is dispatched to Francis Bacon at the very moment of the high noon of the English language. At every point, the fact of Shakespeare lies between the lines. Hofmannsthal's *Sprachkritik* hints at the possibility (it is explored in Wittgenstein) that there is something almost blasphemous in Shakespeare's total, never to be surpassed, linguistic virtuosity, in Shakespeare's sovereign trust in the power of the word to say the world and all that it contains. It may be that there is in that seeming power an illusion, a vaunt, ultimately hollow, that human discourse and parlance can penetrate and transmit the essence of being. To which the everyday world of Chandos's experience, unsettled by Shakespeare's omnivorous eloquence and loquacity, retorts by affirming its mute intractability, its "unspeakable" openness to the abyss. Pascal, as it were, *contra* Shakespeare.

For Karl Kraus (who prized *Timon of Athens*) that abyss yawned. His reading of omens was unnerving. He foretold, in midst of the confident froth of the *belle époque*, that a time was nearing in Europe when gloves would be made of human skin. He understood the First World War to be far more than a demographic, political, and social hecatomb. It marked *die letzten Tage der Menschheit*, the irreparable termination of what was humane in Western civilization. The garish twilight in which Kraus made out the collapse of *civilitas* had been prefigured and, at signal points, generated by a crisis of language. Philosophy, law—law above all—the arts, the striving after truth and personal responsibility in private and public communication, had been fatally sapped. Speech-acts and instruments trivialized by mass consumption and publicity, falsified by the jargons of the bourse, of the educators, of the bureaucrats, of the men of law, had become incapable of telling the truth.

Of this incapacity, the propaganda, the deluge of lies, the "Newspeak" of 1914–1918 (Orwell is Kraus's heir), had compounded a nauseating rhetoric of hatred and of death. Kraus's venom-

ous but heartsick *pastiches* of Austro-Hungarian and German imperial communiqués, of the greasy idiom of the profiteers, of
exalted ladies and whores excited to hysterical chauvinism, remain matchless. As do his investigations into the sadistic hypoc-
risies of the language of the law-courts, into the empty logorrhoea
of parliamentary debates, into the inflated gossip which passes
for most of philosophic arguments or literary and art-criticism.

Kraus's is a world gone mad with vacant but virulently con-
tagious chatter. No trillion-*Mark* note during the Weimar inflation represents as macabre a devaluation of human needs and
hopes as does the devaluation of the word. Mass circulation has
effaced whatever authentic meaning the coinage of words and
syntax might once have possessed. The monstrous inflation, the
embezzlement of diction, have made the truth speechless.

This apocalypse was soon to produce the dialects of the inhuman in Nazism and Stalinism. It breeds the manipulative
infantilism in the mass-media of an unbridled capitalism. Its
power-house and matrix of emission is the press (we print money
as we print lies). Kierkegaard had observed, as early as 1848,
that the new scriptures, the holy writ of modern man in the
West, would be that of the newspaper. We add to these, today,
the planetary web of the graphic and electronic media. Kraus expended his incensed talents on analysing, excoriating, parodying
the languages of the press. Here, disseminating shock-waves so
constant, so childishly seductive, as to saturate awareness, was
the "anti-matter" to the word in its answerable, truth-functional
sense. Here was a detergent so smoothly erosive as to package
and routinize all falsehoods, all bestialities—the latest torture of
a child, yesterday's ethnic cleansing—and to merchandise all art
and thought. "In the beginning was the Word," proclaims the

Fourth Gospel. "In the beginning was the press," amends Karl Kraus.

The logical empiricists and logical positivists of the Vienna Circle were Kraus's exact contemporaries. Primary demarcations are to be drawn within language. Authentic meaning pertains solely to propositions which can be empirically verified or falsified, as in the sciences (Popper); in the strictest sense, truth is a function of the productive tautologies of formal logic and mathematics (Carnap), although even there absolute internal consistency remains impossible (Gödel). The key triad, "language, truth, and logic" coincides functionally only within these conventions of verification, of trial through experiment or formal resolution. Where such verification and resolution are impossible, linguistic utterances and propositions may have great emotional, ideological, or aesthetic reach. But they are *stricto sensu* devoid of decidable meaning. Thus propositions of a theological or metaphysical order belong with fictive narratives and poetry. They are "non-sense" however exalted, metaphoric, or suggestive. They belong to the domain, no doubt vast and more or less consoling, of the imaginary, of the subjective, of the irrational. In a virtually technical sense, this domain remains infantile. It points to the slow adolescence, biogenetic and cultural, of the mind (a view strongly at work in Freud).

It is the task of analytic *Sprachkritik* and logical empiricism to discriminate stringently between these two worlds of language-use in order to secure an impregnable foundation for and classification of the exact and natural sciences, to anchor mathematics in the axiomatic and to ascertain what can demonstrably be said to be or not to be the truth. True meaning must generate proof. Talk about "God" or "transcendence" or the "soul and spirit of things," as it has filled our ears from Plato to Schopenhauer, is more or less self-deluding gossip. No philosophic assertion, no poetic image, is susceptible of proof. The Pythagorean theorem is.

The bearing of this partition on the early Wittgenstein is evident. The all-too-celebrated, subtly histrionic finale to the *Tractatus* marks the essence of demarcation. That "of which we must be silent," which is external to systematic logical and scientific predication, in fact comprises all that matters most. The *gravamen* of the *Tractatus* itself is its unwritten (unspoken) half. Wittgenstein insists on this paradox. The philosophic issues which vex human consciousness, the anguish of being—the first Wittgenstein and Heidegger on *Sorge* are not far apart—the moral dilemmas "to which the sciences give no answer," are of the essence. As is the sphere of the imaginative, of Tolstoy's tales or Brahms's chamber-music. But they cannot be spoken of if language is taken to be a code, ultimately transparent and subject to empirical or logically formal proof. The close of the *Tractatus*, therefore, and the meta-algebraic idiom Wittgenstein strives for (whatever its literary antecedents in Lichtenberg), divest human discourse of much of its responsible status. The iceberg translucency and purity of the logical and the scientific rises, as it were, above the mass, fundamental but indeterminate and undecidable, of the "not to be spoken of." Ideally, the subjective questionings, the introspections, the stream of the imagined which make up the measureless lives of natural language should belong to the mute. This is the exact point where *Sprachkritik* entails a mystique of silence.

Though there is a touch of absurdity and internal contradiction in any discourse, let alone eloquence, about silence, this mystique bred arresting works. In Hofmannsthal's *Der Schwierige,* the protagonist, who has survived live burial during trench-warfare, is no longer capable of enduring mundane, unexamined speech. The fluent resort to such unfathomable words as "love," "existence," "consciousness," "the self," in daily parlance, in the lingo of the drawing-room, strikes him as ethical and intellectual "indecency." The long-standing, pre-1914 claims to spiritual sense and communicability have been lost. Thus mundane chit-chat merely prolongs barbarism. Above all, the lexicon and syntax of love in the West, old as the Fourth Gospel and Dante, have been made mendacious.

The stratifications of significance, the challenges to interpretation in Kafka's brief parable of "The Sirens," are as demanding as any in modern literature. The ontological *Sprachkritik*, the putting on trial of language is, as throughout Kafka, terminal. It is conceivable, Odysseus being the dubious exemplar, that the song of the Sirens can be borne or rendered inaudible by some contrivance, such as wax in the mariners' ears. "But the Sirens possess a weapon more terrible than their song, which is their silence. It is perhaps conceivable that one has been able to escape their song, but assuredly not their silence."

The ambiguous loftiness and terror of the unsayable, of that which divides the doomed triviality of fluency and rhetoric—the "journalistic" signifying the daily—from the non-communicable spheres of the essential, as defined in the *Tractatus* are the crux of Schoenberg's *Moses und Aron*. The God of Moses is defined by his absolute inaccessibility to verbalized thought, to conceptual articulation or any imaging. His is the rigorously "inconceivable, unimaginable, unsayable" presence out of the Burning Bush. His truth is tautological, as in pure logic and mathematics: "He is that which He is." Any attempt to represent, to analogize, to metaphorize, in short "to speak Him," is not only vain folly: it is blasphemy. Thus Aaron's golden tongue, his oratorical acrobatics, whatever their political, pragmatic utility, are a damnable betrayal of the Sinaitic revelation. The Mosaic deity dwells on the other side of silence, precisely as does all transcendence in the *Tractatus*. Moses comes to realise that he is unable to articulate convincingly this decisive partition. Schoenberg's opera, whose incompletion testifies at once to its theme and to its honesty, ends on Moses's despairing cry: "Word, thou Word, that I lack" or "which fails me."

Freud's iconic self-identification with Moses is familiar ground. Vital, but difficult to delineate, are the relations between the critique of language and psychoanalysis. The praxis of psychoanalysis is saturated in and by language. There can be neither a mute patient nor a deaf analyst. It is the decoding of linguistic associations, references, and lapses; it is the "archaeological" excavation of hidden, suppressed or falsified meanings and intentionalities which constitute the psychoanalytic project and its hermeneutic findings. In the Freudian model and therapy, the legible yield of both the lives of the psyche and of their interpretation is lexical and grammatical (Lacan will press this assumption to extremes). The unresolved paradox is that of Freud's "trusting distrust." Utterances, texts, are to be approached with utmost suspicion; they are to be unravelled in depth just because their surface is so mendacious. At the same time, Freud was convinced that such unravelling, save in the case of the psychotic, was feasible. Analysis could tease out of discourse authentic significance, however covert and deep-buried at its inception. Freud's ultimate confidence in language is, at many points, almost innocent. He was a positivist epigrapher and grammarian of what he took to be the many-layered but decipherable palimpsest of the human soul. Thus there is an important sense in which Freudian psychoanalysis is a celebration of the omnipresence and communicative powers of the linguistic.

But in another sense, and one that follows on Nietzsche, Freud's doctrines and techniques constitute a *Sprachkritik* of radical consequence. Polysemic, many-layered, sub-surface, and leading into the turbulent, inaccessible energies of the unconscious, language, as Freud presents and uses it, has lost its classical luminosity, its ready correspondence with intent and with truthsaying. Again, to echo Quine's question, we must, certainly in the immediate and quotidian act of communication, neither mean what we say nor say what we mean. Hence the salutary privilege, in Freud as in the Vienna Circle, of scientific, empirically verifiable propositions. Hence Freud's scarcely concealed unease with the poetic and his almost frantic struggle for acceptance among the clinical, biological sciences. This master of narrative and of myth ached for neuro-physiological validation (which has never come). Non-scientific language and speech acts were the very means of his genius; but the utopia Freud strove for, the "adulthood" of civilization, was one founded on the verifiability criteria of the scientific.

Psychoanalysis has fractured the crust of speech; the magma of repressed material now boils up, as it were, from below. The classical, rationalist postulate of the ability of the human mind to determine and confine the range of meaning is impugned (in the analytic perspective there is always more being said and less than is purposed). Nietzsche's speculative play with language as lie had prepared the ground. Freud went much further. Language has been made richly fragile.

It is too early to attempt even the most summary assessment of the impact of psychoanalysis on the Western sense of verbal and written communication. Certain particular linguistic tools such as the pun, the joke, the Aesopian reversal of manifest intent, the resort to ambiguity are, in our current semantics, post-Freudian. Whatever the uncertain future of Freudian conjectures and of psychoanalytic therapy, it seems unlikely that the Freudian postulate of the verticality of language, as pulsing between depth and surface, will be altogether discarded. The principle of verticality is, to be sure, an ancient one. It was re-inforced by kabbalistic and scholastic techniques of stratigraphic readings (those forty-nine levels known to the Kabbala). But Freud has given it a secular force. He has insinuated into our encounter with dreams, with the spoken and the written word and sentence, a dynamic of indeterminacy. That also is *Sprachkritik,* and solicits a re-negotiation of the broken contracts between word and world.

There would be so many documents—philosophic, sociological, psychological and literary—to enlist. Among them the wonderfully patient, morally and politically informed, probing of the limits of language, of the incapacity of language at its most inspired to heal human suffering, in Broch's *Death of Virgil.* In an almost Wittgensteinian sense, Broch's Virgil comes to realise, to apprehend existentially, the fact that the essential, the revelation of death, lies precisely on the other side of the word. Only action, moreover, not words, may give to death a humane significance.

Fritz Mauthner's *Beiträge zu einer Kritik der Sprache* first appeared in 1901–02. Prolix (it runs to three volumes) and lacking in intellectual rigour, its influence was, none the less, far-reaching. Having drawn more amply on Mauthner than he cared to reveal, Wittgenstein turned dismissive. Borges studied the compendium. In it, Mauthner urges *Sprachkritik* to extremities. Language is simply powerless to express any fundamental, deeplying truths. Natural language can never refer unambigiously or describe exhaustively (Lord Chandos's bitter finding). It is, asserts Mauthner, an illusion to believe that logical propositions are either value-free or innocent of distortion. Abstract logic is itself founded on the grammars, conventions, and algorithms of common speech. It cannot escape the implicit presuppositions and ideological bias. Nor can we have any experience of innate ideas and modes of consciousness other than as facts of language. Substantives mislead systematically; no adjective is defining. Only when it is intentionally manipulative of the outside world, only when it addresses and serves our mundane needs, which is to say when it is, in the true sense, rhetoric, is language being (dis)-honest with itself and its users. Whenever it touches on either the non-tautological or the non-pragmatic, it becomes falsehood and obscurity.

Mauthner's critique culminates in an agnosticism of silence. Such silence would restore man to nature, which is itself silent. Would that "language were ready to die freely" as on the bleak shore in *Timon of Athens*. Only thus would there be liberation from the dead weight of self-deception and untruth. At which point, Mauthner is at one not only with the texts I have cited from Hofmannsthal, but with the coda to the *Tractatus* and with Schoenberg's Moses.

Thus the classical definition of man as "the language-animal," the conviction that the singularity and excellence of his condition are linguistic, a conviction and belief central to Western rationality and culture, were revoked by the Central Europran language-critics and advocates of silence. I am suggesting that this profoundly tragic, apocalyptically "totalizing" motion of arguments constitutes a seismic dislocation. I believe this dislocation, this tidal wave against the word, to be more severe and consequential than any other in modernity. Indeed, it may define the essence of modernity as that which "comes after." If, as our Hebraic-Hellenic creed had it, the Word was in the beginning, there will be a "death of language" and silence at the end. *O Wort, du Wort das mir fehlt.*

What brought on this cataclysm?

We are as yet too near the genesis and unfolding of the *Sprachkrise,* too caught up in its turbulent, open-ended wake, to give any comprehensive answer. Certain deep-lying fractures and tectonic collisions in social consciousness, in the foundations of sensibility, may elude us. We can only conjecture.

Already it is difficult for us to gage fully what were the monumental pressures of classical loquacity, of normative rhetoric and of textuality on Western civilization. We can hardly measure the millennial weight of a logo-centric system on both the collective and the individual psyche. It is manifest that that weight of "verbality" (the term had its positive aura in the 1840s), of textual precedent in law, in education, in literature, in political discourse, in the Judaeo-Christian canon and liturgy, was mountainous. As was the avalanche of print, of the bookish, of the encyclopaedic, as these codified the proceedings of the intellect and of the body politic from the medieval and renaissance period onward. Life in the West was organized around spoken and written power-relations. These were authorized—again we note the seminal, generative concept of an "author"—by a virtually unchallenged confidence in the perennity and truth-potential of the word. An empowering syntax had legitimized history, knowledge, prayer, and the articulate stream of introspection. Futurity had its explicit grammar.

Obstinate spectres, predators at the outer edges, together with such technical innovations as photography and limitless reproducibility, had begun, during the nineteenth century, to gnaw at the citadel of speech. Photography in particular raised little understood but intuitively unsettling questions as to the descriptive capabilities of language, as to the partitions of veracity as between word and image (would the word become caption?). Schopenhauer had proclaimed the especial transcendence of music, its likely endurance beyond man—a notion which seemed embodied in Wagner. Well before Freud, psychopathology and the nascent clinical investigations of the cortex had signalled the "local" lineaments of speech-functions and the utter fragility of verbal rationality. Hitherto unexplored immensities of psychic "undergrowths," of lesions potentially destructive of reasoned discourse and the insurance of logic, which is always a grammar, were coming to light. The intimation that foundational myths in some manner are prior to language as we know it, that the indispensable progress towards verbal and written codes had left behind much that was of seminal importance, antedates Jung.

But these often fragmentary, even esoteric subversions—witness the sparks of insight in Novalis, in Blake—do not gather force until a twofold, closely interrelated revaluation. We have seen that both the exaltation of language, of the "logocratic," and the crises of radical doubt are inseparable from a theological grounding and programme. Monotheism and textuality, be they Sinaitic, Pauline, or Islamic, are instrumentalities of word and script. The postulate of the existence of God is, in the deepest and absolute sense, a speech-act, however inadequate the reach, the predicative authority of that act may be. As were speech-acts the Adamic nomination of the living world, the dialectic of Plato or the inventory of the ego in St. Augustine. With the decay of a theological, canonic world-order throughout ever-widening areas of Western existence, the informing source, the normative claims of the primacy of language, of its sovereign at-homeness in creation, weakened. The "face of God" towards which the semantic marker had turned for legitimacy, dimmed, withered to decorative fable, or was erased altogether in decisive spheres of Western thought and sentiment. Newman's *Grammar of Assent* is a rear-guard action, acutely alert to every implicit linguistic-phenomenological issue, but ultimately frustrated.

Intimately related to this decline was, as I have tried to show, the exponential advance of science and technology after the industrial revolution. Wherever the sciences, pure and applied, wherever mathematics came to map, to energize, to expand human experience and possibilities, the retreat from the word proved correlative and ineluctable. It was simply no longer feasible to "speak," to circumscribe in natural language ever-growing domains of the existential, of knowledge and application, without resorting to the codes of the mathematical and the meta-mathematical. It was not only nature which "spoke mathematics" as in Galileo's famous maxim; it was all science, technology, economic analysis and, by derivation, logic. Hence, as we noted the interactions between *Sprachkritik* and the exact sciences and mathematics in the Vienna Circle, notably in Popper, Wittgenstein, and Carnap. Almost fatally, more and more of philosophical-metaphysical discourse seemed to withdraw into the zone of the metaphoric, of the literary. It returned, often ill at ease, to its origins in the doctrinal poetry, in the versified thought-narratives of the pre-Socratics. Thus there are distinct ways in which the *Tractatus*, Heidegger's *Sein und Zeit* or Sartre's *L'Etre et le néant* are nearer to Empedocles and Parmenides and Heraclitus (strikingly in the case of Wittgenstein's aphoristic powers) than they are to Descartes or Leibniz. It is only a sense, be it intuitive and diffuse, of this ebbing of language from the centres of proof which will help us understand Darwin's observation that he found Shakespeare boring and childish.

From Hofmannsthal and Karl Kraus to Noam Chomsky, from Mauthner, Wittgenstein, and Roman Jakobson to Derrida, the master-players in the critique of language, in philosophic and formal linguistics have been Jews or of Jewish origins (the exception is that of Saussure). This is no accident.

No moral and intellectual tradition, no ethnic history, has been more fiercely attached to the authority of the word—as revealed text, as law, as incessant commentary—than Judaism. Often rootless and harried in space, the Jew has made of the oral and written text his homeland. Philological minutiae, the conservation of lexical-grammatical inheritance and purity, have been at the core of Jewish existence far beyond the bounds of liturgy and rabbinic teaching. That "logo-centrism," that identification of the spirit with the letter, come close to defining both Jewish consciousness and the fraught miracle of its survival. Where a single letter or accent has been erroneously transcribed, the scroll is to be destroyed. As no others, therefore, Jews have perceived themselves and have been seen by others as being "the people of the Book."

A compelling logic generates the language-crisis from within Judaism. There could be no more radical, no more absolutely subversive a challenge to the language-saturated, prescriptive, obsessively verbalized construct of Jewish life and values (those commentaries on commentaries). To rebel against the holiness of the revealed and originating word (Derrida's "there are no beginnings"), to put in question the Adamic equations between name and substance, to reject the unambiguous finalities of bequeathed meaning in the law, in prophetic mandates, to query the coherence and intentionality of narrative—was to seek emancipation at the most uncompromising level. Whatever its scientific validity, the Freudian concept of an "oedipal revolt," of an uprising against paternal governance and confinement, brilliantly illuminates the *Sprachkrise*. Death to the textual fathers. From the doubts of Lord Chandos, the desolate mockeries of Kraus or Kafka's parables on silence all the way to derridean deconstruction, modern Judaism has mutinied against its patriarchal-paternalistic legacy of textual prepotence. It is in the non-verbal idioms of mathematics, of physics, of pure logic that twentieth-century Judaism has made its peace with meaning and with truth.

The *fin-de-siècle* intimation that language would no longer be adequate to and concordant with human experience, that its corruption by political falsehood and mass-consumption vulgarity would make of it an instrument of bestiality, was fulfilled. A clairvoyant dread, a feel for incipient horror, lies at the heart of the critique of language, of the anguished rebellion against the word. This decisive turn can be richly documented. I have cited Kraus's appalling foresight into the uses of human skin. Kafka's *In the Penal Colony* is unbearable in its anticipations. But the psychological, diagnostic well-spring of these premonitory precisions remains enigmatic. At crucial, synaptic points, the polemic with human discourse and the rejection of the millennial dominance of the *Logos* seem to have sprung from the intimacy of emancipated Central European Judaism with the German language. At once at home and not at home in German, too fluent an exploiter of its lyric and philosophic prodigality, Jewish sensibility came, as it were, to unleash the repressed energies of the inhuman in that language (we find them, nakedly, already in Luther). Freudian philology, the psychoanalytic descent into the abyss, may have played a significant, as yet little understood, rôle in this unleashing. All too soon, the Jewish anatomists and ironists of the word were to be consumed by the jargon of Nazism.

Thus I would conjecture that the classical and Judaic ideal of man as "language animal," as uniquely defined by the dignity of speech—itself a facsimile of the original and begetting mystery of creation—came to an end in the anti-language of the death-camps. Perhaps one can come near to identifying the moment of no return. Dying of thirst, an inmate watched his torturer slowly spill on the floor a glass of fresh water. "Why are you doing this?" The butcher replied: "There is no 'why' here." Signifying, with a concision and lucidity out of hell, the divorce between humanity and language, between reason and syntax, between dialogue and hope. Speaking and writing had become, at the nadir of history, an expression of absurdity and of disaster. There was, *stricto sensu,* nothing left to say.

The transmutations set in motion, the issues posed—metaphysically, aesthetically, socially, psychologically—by the unprecedented questioning and de-humanization of language in the West are too recent and multiple to allow of any confident survey. The "after-word," with its own dynamic possibilities, has barely begun. Epilogue is also prologue.

However, what is already perceptible is the fact that the concepts of creation and of invention which are the objects of my argument are being fundamentally affected. The changes are dramatic in the sphere, pivotal to the past, of textuality, of the reading, remembrance, and representations of our lives, both inward and social, both imaginative and empirical. The "Book of Life" and of "Revelation," *le Livre* that was to index the universe in Mallarmé or Joyce or Borges, are today vulnerably allegoric. As are those images and connotations of creativity, of authorship which, since the outset of literacy and magisterial narrative, attach to them. Standing at the cross-roads of Judaism and the Germanic, Heine foresaw that the burning of books would lead to the burning of men and women. We may now be witnessing a larger (also creative) conflagration.

3

Literature is only one mode of expressive form and of making present. Music and the figurative arts are to a greater degree universal. Within literature itself, moreover, oral composition and transmission based on orality immensely outweigh, both in time and in volume, the uses of the written word. The narratives which have shaped collective identities, which reach back to the seminal shadow-lines of the sub-conscious, were spoken. From the clay tablets of *Gilgamesh* to books on-line and on the Internet, the time-span has, in terms of the sum of human articulacy, been brief. Some five millennia at best, following on an unrecapturable but still dynamic prelude of orality. Indeed, the reflexes whereby we tend to confound concepts of creativity and invention with textualty, with the legible, are, in the main, those of Western cultures. We saw that such iconic notions as "the Book of Life" or "of Revelation" are Hebraic-Hellenic in origin and inheritance. They have never been customary, let alone immediate, to the major part of humanity. Borges's "Library at Babel" is precisely that.

None the less, any fundamental changes in the status of the textual, of the book conceived of as the mind's idiom or the "life-blood of the spirit," touch, and touch radically, on the nerve of our inquiry. "The people of the book" is a designation reaching far beyond Judaism. It draws into its orbit the substance of Western philosophy, law, political doctrines, history, and literature. It includes the sciences from Euclid to Newton's *Principia* and Darwin's prose. Our experience of the past, our practice of remembrance are *bookish* in the most thorough sense. So are our prognostications. I have already pointed to challenges and counterclaims. To the explicit orality of Socrates and of Jesus. To Plato's (partially ironic) rebuke to writing. To the indictment of book-culture by certain romantics—an indictment itself, however, eminently literate and scripted. There are impulses towards book-burning in some strains of Russian nihilism. Hatreds of ungoverned, secular literacy inhabit fundamentalist creeds, be they fascist, Koranic, or Maoist. Where a single sacred tôme has harvested and ordained the meaning of the human condition, libraries can be dispensed with.

But these have been dissents and vandalisms on the margin. Almost unthinkingly, we intend, we image books when we adduce creation and invention, the relations of thought and of imagination to time, the storage of knowledge and of error. Thus to question this primacy, to ask whether it is drawing to a close, is to ask where we are going. It is to test the hypothesis of a *Sprach-krise,* of a retreat from the word, where the pressures are most graphic ("graphic" having become a term of extreme instability and complication). It is, perhaps, to try and break the seven seals of a paginated apocalypse. Here, if ever, new techniques and technologies comport a new metaphysics. Furthermore, if the questions are rightly put, they will embrace parallel mutations in the arts, in music, in all the formative symbolic processes which concern the grammars of creation and of invention.

From the outset, the issues in question are inseparable from the pragmatic existence and uage of the book, i.e. the scroll. It is in the sixth century that Heraclitus is said to have deposited his writings in the temple of Artemis, giving symbolic expression both to the aura of the esoteric—"these works are intended for the few, for those qualified to gain access"—and to the trope of survivance, of a legacy beyond the mortality of the writer. Protagoras, according to Plato, entitles one of his treatises *aletheia,* signifying "truth," "the truth disclosed," a claim whose pride is vivid and emblematic still to Heidegger. As it originates in sixth-century Ionia, the scroll already declares its (immense) promise: its content, its message will survive death and reach those unseen by, unknown to its author, be they as yet unborn.

We know that this promise is contested. The dialectic of conflict and co-existence as between the spoken *logos* and the written *gramma* is richly intense. In the *Parmenides,* Socrates, master of the unwritten, listens to a citation from a philosophic text and asks to have it repeated, a formidably consequential move. The choices made between orality and textuality might, perhaps, have gone either way (as they did in so many other civilizations which have relegated writing to enclosed, ceremonious spheres). The play of alternatives is instrumental throughout Plato. The very notion of dialogue entails speech. In its generic immediacy, dialogue excludes writing. Hence the witty, elaborate scenarios of indirect report, of memorization at the start of Platonic dialogues. The genre, exceedingly ancient, is mobile, dramatic, self-correcting, occasional as is a modern "happening." But Plato's final opus, the voluminous *Laws,* has become a book in the full sense. In its textuality, the dialogue-convention is as much a formal artifice as it is in the narrated dialogues and orations of Herodotus and Thucydides. Note how the third party to a dialogue, the listener, has become the reader. The quality and function of his silence have altered profoundly.

A tidal motion, with its eddies and counter-currents, takes us from frank orality to the scriptural. The philosophic poems of Empedocles or of Parmenides, the narrated mythologies of Hesiod, still bear the stamp of oral modes, of rhapsodic presentation and mnemonic devices. But the dynamics are those of an advance, if it was that, towards a written state. The same evolution marks metaphysical arguments. It will, I believe, sustain the deepening emphasis on the transcendental, on what lies beyond the empirical, in Plato and Neo-Platonism. The bias of idealized vision, the wager on eternity, does attach, functionally as it were, to the vital abstractions and intemporality of a written, reproducible text. Re-reading is a minor key of everlastingness. Whatever the charisma of his oral teaching, Plotinus is, as Kant or Hegel will be after him, a "book-thinker" whose elaborate style, whose dramatization of luminous silences, are, to borrow a musical term, "through-composed." Their music of meditation is with us today.

This progress towards textuality necessarily comprised perceptions and paradoxes of authorship. Orality is grounded in the collective and the anonymous. The singer of tales varies on motifs and a narrative inventory nameless in its sources and dissemination. Via his thematic variations, the performer can exhibit a greater or a lesser force of inventiveness. The discriminations between creation and invention are tangible. Authorship is an altogether different phenomenon. Familiarity has eroded its inherent strangeness. In what sense can a writer be "the onlie begetter," the owner of a work? What were the stages of sensibility and of reception which generated this problematic concept?

Certain rough and ready distinctions seem plausible as between the lyric poet and the dramatist on the one hand and the philosopher on the other (though that division of an inaugural unison comes, we have seen, late). The producer of fictions, the artisan of the imaginary, even where he draws prodigally on extant mythological or historical matter, personalizes an idiom, a metrical rhythm, a choreography of executive motions which we call "his style." To a lesser degree, the philosopher, the dialectician, the thinker on history and politics may do the same (an awareness unmistakable in Thucydides). But what does it mean to be the author of an abstract idea, to personalize a truth, a logical lemma, whose very intent, whose claim to validation, are those of universality? The analogy would be that of the contingent, fundamentally irrelevant, attachment of some proper name to a mathematical theorem. It would not be that of the signature appended to a Pindaric ode or an Aeschylean tragedy.

Scholars posit a momentous modulation towards individual, egotistical self-consciousness and personality of utterance during the seventh and early sixth centuries. Early Greek seems to have a word for "plagiarism": *logoklopia*, "a word-theft." By the time of Herodotus, the association between an author and his works is generating characteristic manoeuvres. We find quotations from a previous source, that Herodotean "they say." *Mime-*

sis, paraphrase, transposition, even pastiche (as in Aristophanes) become familiar means. Are there seminal connections, via the Sophists, between these developments and those of coinage, with its mechanisms of proprietorship, of emblematic identification, of exchange and counterfeit? Whatever the motives, technical, geographic, astronomic, military, and constitutional inventions and discoveries are, increasingly, ascribed to illustrious individual minds. The crucial term is *heuremata:* "things discovered by thought." But what of *poiesis,* of the fictive, of the allegories in Plato? In what we have of Aristotle, an intellect so focused on instauration and definition, there seems to be no particular examination of the creation/invention dichotomy. What we do know is that certain essential philosophic terms and the chains of thought they set in motion are assigned to particular thinkers and sages. *Arche,* "beginning," "origin," is attributed to Anaximander. *Kosmos* derives from Pythagoras, Hesiod, or Parmenides.

This whole constellation of conventions and interrelations accompanies and turns on the authority (the "authorship") of the scroll, of what will become the book. From Aristotle's academy to Alexandria, the cognizance and taxonomy of mental products, whether history or philosophy, *belles lettres* or the sciences, relate immediately to the library. Its catalogue serves as the orderly house of memory. The scroll both mirrors and organizes the maps of consciousness and of fact. Inner and outer life are "read," as they will be to our day.

"To our day," but not, I conjecture, for very much longer.

I have tried to show elsewhere that the reading of the world in the image and format of the book and of the work of art as representation has been neither an unalterable nor everlasting option. The underwriting of Hebraic-Hellenic literacy, of the normative analogue between divine and mortal acts of creation was, in the fullest sense, theological. As was the wager (pronounced lost in deconstruction and post-modernism) on ultimate possibilities of accord between sign and sense, between word and meaning, between form and phenomenality. The links are direct between the tautology out of the Burning Bush, that "I am" which accords to language the privilege of phrasing the identity of God on the one hand, and the presumptions of concordance, of equivalence, of translatability which, though imperfect, empower our dictionaries, our syntax, our rhetoric, on the other. That "I am" has, as it were, at an overwhelming distance, informed all predication. It has spanned the arc between noun and verb, a leap primary to creation and the exercise of creative consciousness in metaphor. Where that fire in the branches has gone out or has been exposed as an optical illusion, the textuality of the world, the agency of the *Logos* in logic—be it Mosaic, Heraclitean, or Johannine—becomes "a dead letter."

More concretely, the encoding of knowledge and of imagination, such as in the truths of fiction, in the scriptural, in the scroll, the parchment and the book, together with the inference of creativity and inventiveness, has had its specific psychological and social matrix. What I have often referred to as "the classic act of reading and of receptivity" is made practicable by a vital triad. It is that of space, of privacy and of silence made iconic by St. Jerome in his study or Montaigne in his tower. Inevitably, this privileged congruence related to the clerisy, the mandarinate, the educated and economically enfranchised in Western societies. To read in silent privacy, to own the means of such reading, the book and the private library, is to benefit from power-relations of, in the broadest sense, an *ancien régime*. We have seen that the decay of that régime long predates current transformations and is inwoven with the *Sprachkrise*.

It is some of these transformations I want to look at. In what ways will they affect those "categories," as Kant might have called them, of individual creation, i.e. authorship, of originality, of aspirations to lastingness, which are the theme of this inquiry. What will it mean to "create" in the cyberspaces of democracy? Will such creation necessarily become "invention"?

4

In accord with Hegel, the owl of Minerva does indeed take flight at twilight.

Over the past decade, more public, national libraries have been built and inaugurated than in any previous period. The new British Library will house approximately seventeen million books, be open to some four-hundred thousand readers annually and add more than one-hundred thousand new titles over any twelve-month period. The new German National Library is under construction in Frankfurt. In Paris, the Bibliothèque Mitterand contains in excess of twelve million volumes stacked in four-hundred and twenty kilometers of storage space and moving, when called for, along eight kilometers of transmission belts. The Mitterand is prepared to serve two and one-half million readers *per annum* and to catalogue some two-hundred thousand acquisitions each year. Its four towers spring, almost directly, from that one tower in the Louvre in which Charles V deposited one thousand manuscripts in 1368.

The Library of Congress in Washington dwarfs even these statistics. Its holdings exceed thirty million books and some eighty million articles, offprints and pamphlets on eight-hundred and fifty kilometers of shelving. The Library employs four thousand five-hundred men and women seeking to cope, via a constellation of intermediate clearing houses, with c. seven thousand new items received *each day*. The yearly budget runs to more than four-hundred million dollars.

The social, intellectual motives which underwrite these colossal edifices and investments are multiple and contradictory. The written word, also in print, has proved vulnerable. By far the major part of texts produced in the ancient world has perished. A ship-wreck virtually in sight of Venice has erased forever classics of literature and philosophy which were being rescued from the ravaging of Constantinople. Libraries have been burned, at Alexandria in 642 A.D., at Sarajevo in 1992 (a piece of barbarism which annihilated medieval manuscripts as yet unedited or reproduced and incunabula not yet reprinted). The balance between tenacity and fragility is at all time unstable. This instability has been aggravated by the development of weapons of mass-destruction, though the neutron-bomb, fatal only to human beings, may turn out to be the librarian's dream.

An obsession with conservation and custodianship is paradoxically instrumental in modernity. Archaeology, the uncovering, preservation, and restoration of the faintest marker and scrap out of the past, has become impassioned. The realisation of the mortality of all cultures, as Valéry put it, laid bare by two world wars, has generated a deep-lying anxiety. An inventory must be made, remembrance must be documented and ware-housed before it is too late (Hegel's twilight). An obscurely felt eschatology and sense of an ending are operative.

But so are futuristic intuitions and technological innovations. An equivalence is posited, often without closer scrutiny, between knowledge and power, between access to information and its social-economic appliance. In their very architecture, the new libraries are like mammoth generators and power-stations designed to transform what is taken to be knowledge into intellectual and social yield. This process, this "fast-breeder reactor," develops its own inertial thrust. Collections must be made complete, acquisitions open-ended. There is always more potential fuel to be stocked. Who knows whether the next tract or seemingly ephemeral periodical does not contain some key to the universe? Both legends and learned conjecture ache with the possibility that precisely such keys have, in the past, been lost by destruction or inadvertence.

It is these collaborative contradictions between the archival and the forward-bound, between museum and laboratory, which endow the leviathan libraries recently inaugurated or in progress with their uncertainties of purpose and planning. These vacillations do seem to render these ziggurats of marble, brick, and glass so strangely off-balance, even transient. Like titanic toys destined to be broken. For it is obvious that the Mitterand, the British Library, the addenda to the Library of Congress are obsolete even as they are opened. The dilemma is that of the format and future of the book.

In their design, these libraries articulate a logic of unavoidable uncertainty and indeterminacy. They are centaurs, part shrine, part futurama. Their treasures out of the past are, literally, enshrined in hushed, dimly lit sanctuaries of safety-glass and precious woods. They are hardly meant to be touched, let alone consulted. Statistically, our libraries both on the national, monumental scale and throughout the literary-academic sphere are warehouses of collected recollection, classified archives of the scripts of revelation, argument, imagination, tabulation for that part of human history which has committed life to writing. Million and ten million-fold, successive modes of textuality, from the tablets of Sumer to printing and beyond are housed either underground or, more recently, in lofty towers out of Babel (where these opposite vectors are, indeed, charged with symbolic and iconographic indices). The bulk of this material is never, or only very rarely, disinterred for current use. No scholar, no Coleridgean "library cormorant," no general reader can hope any more to acquaint himself exhaustively with more than a fraction of the available sources in even a more or less confined speciality. Yet the unread, the untouched, in the dusty silence of the stacks and reserves does exercise a pressure of incipient presence and readiness. It is, like the ghostly armies excavated in Chinese imperial tombs, on call (now "on-line"). The tôme, the pamphlet, the periodical might one day be summoned to the light. The cracked spine might be opened to the foxed page. Also the obscurest of monographs possesses its potential for resurrection. Lazarus is patron saint of library stacks.

At the same time, the new libraries must cater to those revolutionary means of publication and reading now in almost uncontrollable progress. Some two-thirds of the entries in the catalogues of the Library of Congress are soon to be in formats other than those of the book as we have known it. As he enters the Bibliothèque Mitterand, the "reader"—a rubric already in need of qualification—is invited to use either an *iconothèque,* a *sonothèque,* or a *médiathèque,* with their electronically listed and transmitted wealth of pictorial, auditive, periodical, and audio-visual material. The audio-visual hub will have on offer a choice, frequently updated, of 3,500 films, of ten thousand recordings and more than one-hundred thousand photographs from Daguerre onward. One-hundred and ten on-line terminals provide access, via CD-rom, to a selection, also renewable, from two-thousand hours of television and eight-hundred of radio. The main book catalogue, comprising c. ten million titles, will be wholly automated and consulted on the screen. By early in the millennium, it is hoped that the Mitterand, like its peers, will be connected electronically to the rest of the planet's deposit libraries and specialized collections. Thus will be realised the Leibnizian dream of a *Bibliotheca universalis,* putting the sum of recorded human memory and knowledge in reach of a desk-top terminal, wherever it may be located. In a perfectly practical sense, libraries will be synapses, electronic nerve-points of exchange in a global net.

It is this co-existence of and relationship between the oldest and the newest, between the clay tablet or papyrus and the electromagnetic tape, in a moment of fantastically accelerated technical development, which is difficult to build and plan for. Arguably, the British Library and the Mitterand were out of date on the day they were opened. They are, in large measure, sumptuous mausoleums to which there adheres, even where they are architecturally modernistic and assertive, the aura of the sepulchral, of solemn stasis, inseparable from the very concept of a museum and archive. They tower as vast treasure-troves of the embalmed on the verge of an altogether different consciousness which they must labour to anticipate and respond to.

It is the lineaments of that consciousness and the place in it, if any, for those ideals of creation sanctified by the book, the concert-hall, or the picture-gallery, which are now beginning to emerge. It is the relations of time to the canonic, both in regard to recall and future survival, which are now under unprecedented social and psychological pressure. As one of the most sober of philosophic analysts puts it: "There is reason to think the future of cyberspace will bring metaphysical novelties—that virtual reality interpreted via the virtual community is to some extent a new world and one that we are on the edge of."[1] The issues are a minefield for the layman, but one must try to understand what is at stake.[2]

How can we discriminate between technologies which are, however spectacular, in essence extensions, accelerations, magnifications of previous means—as was the printing press—and those which constitute a "quantum leap," which open vistas of another order than any precedent? Not only is any such distinction fluid, but the reasons given for it are, in part, ideological. They voice more or less express convictions as to what truly matters, as to the ends to be realised, in consciousness and society, both in theory and *praxis*. Marx's dictate that at a determinant point quantity becomes, transforms into quality is helpful. If, as experts predict, some two billion users will be on the Internet by 2005, using computer-driven feedback loops to communicate and transact virtually every mode of human enterprise, funda-

1. Gordon Graham: *The Internet* (1999), p. 163.

2. The literature is already extensive. I have found the following of particular guidance: R. Sheilds, ed., *Cultures of the Internet* (1996); F. Dyson, *Imagined Worlds* (1997); M. L. Dertouzos, *What Will Be: How the New World of Information Will Change Our Lives* (1997); S. Johnson, *Interface Culture: How New Technology Transforms the Way We Create and Communicate* (1997); M. Heim, *Virtual Realism* (1998); S. Horn, *Cyberville* (1998).

mental categories of community, of participatory politics, of the exchange and codification of knowledge and desire will have altered. The analogy will not be one of expected and gradual adaptive change, but of mutation.

A second obstacle to responsible foresight relates to the underlying model and engineering of the new electronic media. In ways which differ qualitatively from Pascal's or Babbage's mechanical calculators, but also from the first generations of even the most rapid and capacious of analogue and digital computers, the "mind-machines" now being programmed (software designing and generating software) and now pragmatically forseeable, are something other than passive tools. They are far more than titanic slide-rules and number-crunchers. They aim to simulate, to mime the cerebral processes which have brought them into existence. They are, though at a reductive level, facsimiles, as it were, of what we believe we know of the human cortex and of the electrochemistry of its neurological reticulations. There may, to be sure, an epistemological trap here. What we assume to be the mimetic capacities of these machines could reflect the inadequacies, the innocence of our own conceptions of the brain and of consciousness. None the less, it is from intuitions of similitude that arise the allegories, the mythologies of fascination and of fear which surround the hyper-computers currently being developed. Almost enforcedly, we attribute to the humming monster mirrorings, counterparts of human thought. When these parallels manifest analytic, performative capabilities exceeding our own, the psychological-social impact can be unnerving.

The victory of IBM's Deep Blue over Kasparov raises question well beyond the shock of the occasion. In one of the formally profoundest, most entrancing and inexhaustible of human pursuits, no living person can, henceforth, be regarded as supreme. In "the last analysis," a betraying phrase, the machine will prove stronger (and stronger). I find this at once mesmerising and deeply sad.

But the most challenging uncertainty lies at the borders between the psychological and the philosophic. A number of players who have encountered computers, who have been involved in their programming, have wondered at what point speed and ramification of calculations shade into "something else." The sceptical answer would be that our conventional differentiation between calculation and thought needs to be revised. In a rule-bound context such as chess, calculation *is* thought. But is that reduction altogether convincing? Are there spatial conceptualizations and foresights generated by the computer which seem closer to "thought" than to calculation, an automatic process however arduous? Is there more than anthropomorphic exasperation to Kasparov's reported remark, concerning a phenomenal sequence of moves in the fifth game of the match, that Deep Blue was "thinking"?

Yet even these questions and their empirical matrix will seem rudimentary as the new worlds of cyberspace, the planetary Web, and Virtual Reality evolve, at a rate and on a scale (the Marxist crux) hardly intelligible. Here the relative temporalities come into play. So far as we can make out, the evolution of the human brain and nervous system is an exceedingly slow biogenetic process. Until now the genesis of consciousness and of language, let alone their evolution along lines of natural selection, eludes our understanding. In contrast, the improvement of successive families of computers and soft-ware is taking place at extreme speed. We have seen that the computer breeds; the next generation of micro-chips and wiring operates more rapidly, accurately and inclusively than the one which came before. There are no throw-backs. Thus there exists the distinct possibility, anticipated by Turing, that computers, designed and programmed by computers, will outstrip exponentially certain human capabilities and, indeed, cognitive insights (was the Four Colour problem, a classical conundrum, finally solved by the computer or its questioning programmers?). Optimistically, on the other hand, we may postulate that ever-increasing interactions between minds and machines on the interface, between eye and holographic, computer-generated imagery, will enrich and strengthen our mental resources. The dialectic of the feed-back can be intensely educative. Already, children are setting out on great voyages.

The concepts, however, the idiom of what have been regarded as quintessentially human acts of creation and invention, are now in flux. The issues are crystallized by the case of the book, of its composition and reception.

5

The layman can cite and reflect only on what the experts tell him. It is today a commonplace to invoke "a new universe," to point to fundamental alterations not only in the means of information, knowledge, and transmission but, in inevitable consequence, to transformations in the modes of human thought and feeling. Take the example, at once so powerful and ready to hand, of a newspaper. Already a reader can choose to compose his own newspaper on his screen, interleaving any number of articles from any number of sources. He can "surf" immediately to any outlet and product and illustrative material referred to in the text. On the Web-page, any reporter or columnist can bypass

proprietors and editors, assembling his or her own public, inter-
acting on a planetary scale with other writers and the answering,
questioning responses of on-line readers.

Even this is only a rudimentary beginning. Soon there will be a
critical mass of cable modems. Not only will these generate high-
definition television on your computer screen; they will do so at
a speed exponentially greater than that of the Web. We will scan
a reportage or editorial comment about, say, Indonesia, call up
illustrations of unprecedented graphic clarity and down-load any
of this material we wish to store or make use of from its television outlet. As one observer has put it: "Just as newspapers and
editors will largely disappear, so will record companies and the
BBC." In regard to license of speech and representation, of direct
dialogue and the formation of interactive communities of shared
concerns, interests, ideologies, and passions, the changes before
us come near to being incalculable. The Net "provides the first
totally unrestricted, totally uncensored communication system
—*ever*. It is the living embodiment of an open market in ideas."[3]
It may come to rank as "the most remarkable thing human beings
ever made." The hyperlinks which will enable any number of
computer databases to exchange information, which, at the touch
of a finger, give mankind access to a library of libraries, to an
all-inclusive picture gallery or science museum (Malraux's Napoleonic and universalist dream), to a planetary noticeboard open to
everyman, make for what can soberly be qualified as a new world.

These are no science fictions. The number of classified documents accessible on the Net in 1998 was estimated at four-
hundred million; this figure will have doubled at the start of the

3. John Naughton: *A Brief History of the Future* (1999), p. 22.

millennium. Even now, schooling, economic analysis, and programming, commerce, aspects of medicine, the arts of war are
being revolutionized:

> A force of unimaginable power—a Leviathan, to use a Bibli-
> cal (and Hobbesian) phrase—is loosed on our world, and we
> are as yet barely aware of it. It is already changing the ways
> we communicate, work, trade, entertain and learn; soon it
> will transform the ways we live and earn. Perhaps one day it
> will even change the ways we think. It will undermine estab-
> lished industries and create new ones. It challenges tradi-
> tional notions of sovereignty, makes a mockery of national
> frontiers and continental barriers and ignores cultural sen-
> sitivities. It accelerates the rate of technological change to
> the point where even those supposed to be riding the crest
> of the wave begin to complain of "change fatigue".[4]

If we bear in mind that these predictions are offered at a point
when the Internet is still in its pioneering stages, we may indeed
expect that cyberspace will provide what Gordon Graham calls
"metaphysical novelties." The maps of consciousness or, more
precisely, our reading of thse maps will construe a New Atlantis,
in Bacon's spirit but immeasurably beyond his reasoned imaginings. It is, moreover, essential to bear in mind the irreversibility
of these mutations. Its elements cannot be dis-invented. They can
only multiply and reach into every cranny of our individual and
social lives.

Can we make out the impact of this *novum organum* in the
arts—where the concept of creativity may have to be re-thought?

4. *Ibid.*, pp. 44–45.

Paradoxically, the pursuit in which the question first arose has proved doubtful. It is that of electronic music. Synthesizers, sine-wave generators, ring modulators, as in Stockhausen, and certain American minimalists, have produced music of a certain interest. In the hands of a Boulez, the resort to electronic aids and computational algorithms has generated—for once the appropriate term—memorable effects. As have combinations of the electronic with actually played instruments and with the human voice. Psychologically, socially, and pedagogically, the chance for a composer to test, to listen to his or her music without incurring the expense and hazards of live performance, so routinely denied to experimental scores, has obvious value. More subtly, the availability of unlimited *collages* and mixtures of sound has enriched the composer's palette. It contributes to that aesthetic of totality, already seminal in Varèse, which is vital to late-twentieth-century acoustic sensibility. All sound can be incorporated within, can be made music. Yet is it myopic to say that, till now, the hoped-for masterpieces, the new registers of expressive feeling, have not been forthcoming? Have we progressed beyond Stockhausen's *Song of the Young Men,* now half a century old and among the very first of its kind? And does the undoubted poignancy of that composition spring not from its technical innovations but from classic means of text, human vocalization, and a tragic historical context?

This is emphatically not the case in regard to Pop, to Rock and the new sound-worlds around them. Electronic magnification and enhancement are strictly inseparable from these genres. Sheer volume is a complex, not altogether understood, force. It alters every executive and aesthetic fibre in the musical experience. In a paradigmatic Marxist sense, the quantity of decibels becomes a qualitative whole. Loudness, notably in Rock, is, as I have tried to argue, an ideological-social strategy charged with the conflict between generations and life-styles, brimfull with anarchic reprisal and ecstatic communion. The dialectic between Pop, Rock, Acid House, Hip-Hop, Techno, on the one hand and the cultures of narcotics, of racial stress, of urban rivalries on the other, are self-evident but also resistant to any unitary, simplistic analysis. Coming after jazz, itself in so many respects a classical form, Pop and Rock have, as it were, changed the beat of city life, of adolescent eros, of ethnicity. The concatenations are simultaneously local—sub-cultures, underground(s), hypnotic privacies flourish—and tidal on a global scale. A recent Ricky Martin record is thought to have sold more than twelve million copies world-wide. Digital television, with direct access to its holdings and presentations, will open a virtually unlimited gamut of new music to those who have never set foot in a record shop. The viewer-listener will be able to meld, to re-combine tracks from different recordings. "Tribal" distinctions will lose their edge: the laptop empowers one to move with autonomous taste and choice between, say, mod, punk, New Romanticism, Latin American, and what have you. What political myopia can prevent the Cuban sound from invading and entrancing the United States? At last count, fifty-seven countries can log in a live Internet show, bypassing radio and television. At each of these synapses, as, perhaps in the reticulations of the human cortex, technology is the crux:

There's a system called Kyma that morphs sounds together in the way they morph two images together. . . . I've got a laptop, and I make a lot of sounds on it. Eventually, I'd like to be able to sit under a palm tree on a beach and send by digital phoneline a track back to London.

Will this symbiosis between composition, performance, transmission, and reactive reception widen further the gap between classical music, taking "classical" in a generic sense, and Pop, Rock, or their progeny. Musicologically and in actual performance, the bridges, the reciprocities of inspiration between jazz and the classical were never broken. Virtuosi could star in both. Though live realisation is indispensable also in Pop and Rock, it is machine-enhanced and propelled. Via the amplifier and the strobe-lights, moreover, such performance demands from language, often intentionally distorted and inaudible, a submission altogether different from that in a *Lied* or libretto. The scream of flayed Marsyas prevails over the articulate rhetoric of Apollo. If there is to be a next step involving a mutually stimulating co-existence of the chamber-music recital and the rave, it too will arise out of electro-magnetic technologies as yet barely discernible.

Architecture takes us to the border. It has perennially busied the philosophic imagination, from Plato to Valéry and Heidegger. More insistently than any other realisation of form, architecture modifies the human environment, edifying alternative and counter-worlds in relationships at once concordant with and opposed to nature. Even fragmented, its vestiges are a catalogue of time, legible to the eye and hand. Only braille is as tactile a script. The sinews which connect architecture to matter are organic, even beyond those of sculpture which can, itself, be regarded as construction. A building is kindred with the earth on which it stands; its foundations penetrate (and bury) that earth. A building can defy or ironize this relation by means of elevation, arching detachment, or vertical thrust. It is made of natural components and their derivatives, of wood, stone, and metals. The edifice gives to these elements a second nature whose relation to their primary state is one of dynamic continuum and counter-statement. Rocks grow into portals and pillars; the branching tree modulates into the fan-vault. But the master-builder will often deny or parody the claims of the organic. He can make marble translucent, making it seem an almost weightless membrane of light and rippling water. He can endow wood with the felt weight and glow of bronze; he can make steel as aerial, as tenuous as lace (cf. a Santander bridge).

With potent, partly metaphoric subversion, the theory and practice of the architect draw on the aesthetic categories of the other arts. A building can draw on statuary, painting, mosaics, and the decorative arts. More obliquely its spaces will enact the music to be performed within them. When architecture adduces "harmony," "proportion," "fluidity," "drama," "figurativeness" and neighbouring rubrics, it borrows from music, painting, and literature. But the commerce is mutual: monumentality or intimacy of scale, angles of incidence and surprise are as vital to the poet, composer, or graphic artist as they are to the builder. A device such as purposed irregularity and asymmetry, such as in the alignment of an Attic colonnade or baroque facade, will engage poetics and the psychology of perception as much as the empirical skills of the draftsman and mason.

Architecture has always been at home in the house of mathematics. Early geometry may have sprung from architectural problems. Architecture is intimate with technology, engineering, and the earth sciences. It is both *poiesis* and *technē* or, as Valéry would have it, geometry and metrics. This duality is crucial to the Platonic hypothesis of ideal Forms, to the lyric mathematicization, if one can put it that way, which animates the Greek sense of space. Theoreticians of beauty in the renaissance will seek to fuse the architectural (out of Vitruvius) with the mathematical, making of both the expression of a rational music as they were thought to have been in Pythagoras. With the development of new and hybrid building materials, notably after the industrial revolution, the disciplines of the architect and of the engineer, of the "imaginer" and the metallurgist, grow ever closer. Prophetically, Hart Crane celebrates this fraternity and its life-transforming potential in "The Bridge":

> Wall, from girder into street noon leaks,
> A rip-tooth of the sky's acetylene;
> All afternoon the cloud-flown derricks turn . . .
> Thy cables breathe the North Atlantic still.

Now one senses that the power relations between conceptualizing intuition and feasibility are shifting. It may well be that the sophisticated trial-and-error methods which made possible the (imperfect) realisation of certain unprecedented novelties of structure, curvature and use of materials in the Sydney Opera House are already dated. Over these last years, the rôle of the computer, of computer graphics and holograms and of its sheer force or calculation, have expanded dramatically. The techniques used by Frank Gehry in the Guggenheim Museum in Bilbao originate, for a large part, in aeronautical engineering. Robotic arms trace the shapes of hand-made models and relay the information to computers. These, in turn, analyse multiple variants and combinations so as to exploit all possible economies of stress, to map

desired sight lines, to achieve linear programming for the potential flow of visitors through gallery spaces. The computer determines what is and is not possible in terms of building materials,
such as the titanium never before used on Gehry's scale. Simula-
tions achievable solely on the computer test the visions of Daniel
Liebskind, both in his Jewish Museum in Berlin and in his proposed extension to the Victoria and Albert in London.[5]

It is, to be sure, the reciprocal suggestions and questionings
that matter. It is Gehry's multiple sketches of sea-anemone deployments and unfoldings which testify to the seminal act of
imagining, which generate the programmes for computation.
Liebskind has cautioned against any uncritical adulation of the
computer's functions. He remains persuaded that it is an architect's drawings and maquettes which lie at the heart of the constructive process. But the overlap is growing dramatically. Antony
Gormley's projected "Quantum Cloud" is too complex for purely
"human" engineering. The sculptor used a state-of-the-art scan-
ner which, in twenty seconds, created an image consisting of
thirty-thousand digital co-ordinates in three dimensions. This
"image" of his body was then transferred into specially designed
software matching the artist's vision to parametres of material
feasibility. The programme contained 75,000 lines of commands
to help achieve "an energy field in flux. It is a symbiosis of old
physics and new, of art and science."

In the architecture (and sculpture) of today and tomorrow, discriminations between human creativity, technological invention,
and controlled experiment, such as they operate in the sciences,

5. Cf. the subtle discussion of Liebskind's intentions in Andrew Benjamin:
Philosophy, Architecture, Judaism (1997).

are being blurred. The brilliance of this blurring poses philosophic conundra of the highest interest.[6] Should the gold medal go to the builder or the software?

What, then, of authorship?

6

The notion of authorship has varied across history and cultures. It passed out of the collective anonymities of the archaic into individuation and the exalted personalism associated with the renaissance and romanticism. But this evolution has never been uniform or absolute. Summits of textuality as in Scripture, notably in *Job,* as in the Homeric epics or, in unresolved measure even in Shakespeare, resist any categorical bracket of authorship. The individuality of the voice contrasts with the inacessibility, material or psychological, of the begetter. Where canonic literature and utterances are concerned, the source in a single, biographically ascribed writer can be reductive. The teller may be so much slighter or less attractive than the tale. Do we not know too much about, say, Byron or Heine or Proust, such knowledge being knowingness and a diversion? Yeats's disjunction remains a warning: "perfection of the life or of the work." The issues are further bedevilled by the intuition, old as Plato, new as Freud, that creativity and the pathological are close-knit, that the most energized acts of imagining and projection are somehow grounded in disorders of sensibility, in deviant appetites and even conduct. The *dramatis* persona of a Wagner, a Dostoevski, or a Proust may pose barriers to our expectations of any harmonious correspon-

6. Cf. Neil Spiller, *Digital Dreams: Architecture and New Alchemic Technologies* (1999).

dence between the ego and the art, between sadism and grace, infirmity and life-giving radiance.

But whether it originates in the serenity of the unnamed or in the drama of the declared, public self, authorship, as we have seen, has served as the principal analogue for creation itself. This is true of all formative modes but most concentratedly, perhaps, of the crafts of language. We have seen also that "the book," as object and symbol, as allegory and metaphor, has, throughout the Hebraic-Hellenic and Christian traditions, been the medium of significant life and revelation. Whether it be the Bible or the *Commedia,* the First Folio, or Darwin's *Origin of Species,* it is the book that narrates, that transmits and interprets the "background noises," the pulse or distant peal of thunder of what we suppose the *fiat* of creation to have been like (it is the informing irony of Darwin's text that it subverts precisely this supposition). A lasting work of art, of music, of literature contains within its executive means a miniaturization, a charged particle, as it were, of the coming into being of being. In Heideggerian language, it refers *das Seiende* to *Seyn,* the existentially contingent to the primacy and enigma of the fact "that there is." Profitable, instrumental, exhibitionist artifacts—the vast majority in every genre —are ephemeral because they are at home in what is worldly and domesticated within their own generative mechanisms. They are, at the trivial or ostentatious level manufactured (one recalls Stalin's "engineers of the soul"). In contrast, serious and major work is never at ease in regard to the unclarities of inception to which it owes its necessarily incomplete, imperfect genesis and performance. It endures because it carries with it the "striations," the lava-scars left by an inward incandescence and often self-destructive surfacing. In ways difficult to classify yet obvious to the active reader or listener or viewer, the ephemeral, the opportunistic in thought and the arts remains static. It emits the flaring brilliance of the moment (it is "a hit," "a blockbuster"). The classic is in perpetual unfolding and metamorphosis. The great winds of initial creation are at its back.

The technology, the uses, the material format of the book are today in transformation. Electromagnetic facilities for transcription, dissemination and storage have already revolutionized most elements of textuality and the "scriptural." I have written of the changes in the nature of the new libraries, of the possibilities of open-ended and combinatorial exchanges between writer and reader. The reach of both eye and ear in the conveyance, montage, digitalization of word and image, of message and audio-visual accompaniment, will be extended in directions we can barely begin to imagine. *Of course,* books as we have known them since Gutenberg will continue to be written, published, marketed, and read. Very probably the number of titles in traditional formats will increase for some time to come (at the current rate, in fact, the mass of the unread may collapse inward). *Belles lettres,* literature for pleasure and consolation, will, during the foreseeable future, appear in traditional guise. The portability, the tactile presence, the secrets of companionship inherent in books as we have grown accustomed to them still look to be irreplacable. But whether this will obtain for generations now achieving literacy in cyberspace and on the Internet is not at all certain. Nor is that the question. Will these transformations and the headlong changes in culture at large modify fundamentally the concept of authorship and the analogies between *auctoritas* and the grammars of creation?

We know that even the most isolated and solipsistic of makers in enmeshed in a spider's web of social, historical, and pragmatic pre-conditions. There can be no blank start. However much he strains to personalize, to reshape and modify the language, the writer is heir to an instrument not his or her own. As are the painter and the composer. The legacy of the inherited and, to a greater or lesser degree, contemporaneity crowds the most jealously guarded of retreats. I believe that this pressure, that the intrusion of external determinants have increased massively, that the interventions out of society, out of the historical-political circumference, thrust more undeniably, more clamorously into the house of consciousness than ever before. They busy not only the surfaces of perception; they demand access to the innermost of sensibility, to the formative threshold of the psyche. Such an hypothesis is difficult to formalize, let alone demonstrate in any quantifiable sense. It can be objected that "the world was always too much with us," that it weighed on the classical poet, so urgently in quest of bucolic apartness, no less than on Montaigne in his tower and Marvell in his garden. Assuredly, we are dealing with a question of degree, of accelerating process and enforcement. But the sense of an historical hinge, of a new penetrability of the ego, certainly in the West, can be documented. The "noise-levels," the dynamics of interference, augment enormously with the industrial revolution, with urbanism and the claims made on everyday existence by historical-political demands after the mid-eighteenth century. Time, as psychological and existential experience, quickens dramatically. Spaces around the once private individual are compressed by the novel technologies of communication, both in regard to transport and to information.

Much of Rousseau's ideological pastoralism, pedagogy, and mappings of self-consciousness seeks to stem the onrush of the new hammering. Rousseau strives, often at the edge of hysteria, to fence off what he can of a refuge for the deafened, mobbed self. His educational blueprint, his idyllic fiction, the reveries of the *promeneur solitaire* are an endeavour to articulate, to make scenic and exemplary, the breached values of inwardness. Rousseau is the ecologist of the ego. Wordsworth observes closely the on-rush of a new world-order rendered social, collective, urban, and invasively ideological. He registers its symptoms—the power of the cheap press, the tentacular metropolis, the strident loudness of daily life—with worried precision. In Wordsworth's lyrical and self-examining poetry, there is an almost muscular counter-pressure to the crowding from without. The sheer weight of the text seeks to bar the door against break-ins. Goethe had identified the battle of Valmy and the victory of a populist conscript army as the start of a new era, of history as mass-experience. Acutely, he charted in his memoirs, in *Faust,* in the counter-idyll of *Hermann und Dorothea,* the mutation of the daily into the journalistic. He saw how Hesiod's "works and days" or the *très riches heures,* often paced only by natural, seasonal pursuits, had turned into the journalistic. Days had become *journées,* which is to say the factitious twenty-four hours of the *journal* (German imported the word from French). Nietzsche's virtuosities of isolation act out a reflex at once programmatic and therapeutic, discursive and obsessed, in the face of mundane encirclement—familial, professional, political.

These several strategies were rear-guard skirmishes, however fruitful. No more than Kierkegaard's "live burial," could they arrest the tide of actuality. No one can calculate the engulfing volume and rate of news, of information, of verbalized and imaged suggestion which pound individual reception, emotions, and memory from the coming of the mass-media in the romantic age to the dam-burst of the Internet and the planetary Web. The pseudotechnical term "hits" is revealing. The impact on the antennae of awareness is incessant, the noise focussed on consciousness inescapable. It now searched out and seeks to deafen the sub-liminal. The strobe-lights of immediacy, whether they are those of sensory stimulus, of information or the imaginary, blind the recesses of vision inside us. What is monstrous in global affairs is made the more so by instantaneous, graphic transmission. Attempting to ensure such material and the "entertainments" which would match and outdo its horrors, we grow numb. It is this "numbing-down" that sickens the nerve-centres of creativity. In the pornography of noise, calm privacies have become a privilege of the fortunate or the condemned. Psychiatry regards much of the current incidence of mental collapse as an attempted flight and escape from the stress of uncontrolled input generated by the clamour and voltage of daily reception. It is no longer one "person from Porlock," the alleged disturber of Coleridge at work on *Kubla Khan,* who is the archetype of interruption. It is reality itself made leviathan and legion.

The correlations between silence on the one hand and creation or invention on the other are multiple. They differ from case to case. Bach seems to have composed some of his most intricate scores amid a welter of domestic disturbance. So did Schoenberg when orchestrating, in Barcelona, the fearsomely complex orgiastic dance of his *Moses und Aron*. Noise maddened Proust and made writing impossible. Kafka's last parable, *The Burrow,* details the terror of even the faintest sound when it penetrates the artist's asylum. Objectively, noise-levels, the volume of acoustic and amplified phenomena which envelop us, have increased exponentially. In the night-city, silences are disappearing. Like crazed locust, the cellular phone eats up what is left of silence, both private and public (in a marvellously telling allegory, cellular phones have been heard to ring from inside a coffin). On the very simplest level, therefore, conditions of tranquillity which may have been instrumental for intellectual and aesthetic production, are today either very difficult to ensure or altogether unavailable.

But the legacies and modes of silence I have in mind are more resistant to definition, let alone statistical measurement. They are primarily internal. They guard and empower habits of concentration, of compacted attention, of withdrawal from the "impertinent"—meaning both the trivially obtrusive and that "which is not pertinent"—of which the total in-gathering of masters of meditation or of chess is an instance. Such orders of closure to the outside, of contradiction to mundanity, where "contradiction" is, very precisely, an articulate but unvoiced "saying against," are in part the consequence of schooling, as in monasticism both Western and oriental. They flourish in a certain historical-social ambience. They follow on the training of directed attention and ordered memory, a training expressive of the ideals of a given milieu and made possible by the availability of an undisturbed locale (the hermitage, St. Jerome's emblematic study, the winter-isolation in which Descartes meditates, Kierkegaard's nocturnes or Heidegger's forest-hut out of worldly reach). There have, in Western history, been privileged epochs of silence. The philosophic techniques, the poetics of the seventeenth century, the self-cloistering of a Pascal or a Spinoza will culminate in Malebranche's celebrated equation between attention, the mind's concentrated scruple, and "the natural piety of the soul." All that distinguishes such an attitude from modernity is contained, with awesome ironic concision, in Marvell's couplet:

> Two paradises t'were in one
> To live in paradise alone.

It is this harvesting of the self and dismissal of the outside world, this "bursting upon a silent sea," which may, in most cases, be required for thought and imaginings of the first rank. The postulate of alternative being, the innovations which alter and enlarge our horizon, the acts of expressive counter-factuality which both define the analogies with and the dissent from the original *fiat*, seem to me to arise out of a listening inward of, as it were, breathless acuity. The receptivity of the systematic thinker, of the artist, of the mathematician is open to, is brought to bear upon, a crucible of nascent instigations, of triggering impulses only partly conscious. His or her perception has a finesse of hearing, a perfection of pitch in respect to the advent of potential relations, forms, executive potentialities, beyond the ordinary. He or she hears deeper. Pressed to the ground of being, the inner ear of the thinker or poet or master of metaphor seems to apprehend the charged silence which precedes the first lightning-flash of incipient form. The clamour of communicative sociability, of gregariousness, the stridency of the everyday and night which now prevail make such listening more precarious. We are less and less trained to hear ourselves be, where such hearing may be the key precondition to the creative.

Unmistakably, the gifts of silence which I am trying to deliniate do attach to various modes of religious experience and practice. There is a sense in which all extreme concentration could be seen as related to the theological. It seeks out the as yet unknown, it presses on the bounds of the empirically evident. The inner voices heard by the poet, the tensions of unresolved relation edging towards consciousness in the composer and mathematician, come out of that loaded silence towards which the mind and spirit bend their attentiveness. Throughout this study, we have seen that it is virtually impossible to explore these "inclinations," in the strongest sense of the term, without adducing theological dimensions or, at the least, the idiom which these dimensions have generated. Today, this idiom and the reflexes of recognition derived from it are largely ossified. They have grown conventionally pallid and have ebbed from serious engagement. A passage from Coleridge's *Aids to Reflection* helps measure the gap:

> The Chamelion darkens in the shade of him who bends over it to ascertain its colors. In like manner, but with yet greater caution, ought we to think respecting a tranquil habit of inward life, considered as a spiritual *Sense,* as the Medial Organ in and by which our Peace with God, and the lively Working of His Grace on our Spirit, are perceived by us.

Note the crucial hint of a "spiritual sensuality" in relation to the vital ("lively") forces within us. A few lines further, Coleridge invokes "the darkness of desertion." At stake is the fragility of the creative within us, the blighting ease with which we take leave of our creative selves. Which, in turn, pivot on those tranquillities now so hard come by. But already, any such vocabulary and the configurations of the human psyche which it argues have themselves become obsolete.

Solitude and privacy are cognate to silence. Their informing rôle in the creator's work-shop is intuitively convincing; but, again, difficult to demonstrate. Here, also, two levels are implicit: the empirical and the internalized. Solitude has, in our societies, become rarer and indeed suspect. The bias towards the communal, the participatory and the collective is insistent. The crowd, in a well-known phrase, may be lonely, but it is a crowd. A dread of solitude, an incapacity to experience it productively, haunts the young. Background music switches on when the door of the elevator closes in American buildings lest the moments of aloneness prove threatening. Democracy and mass-consumption, with their ideals of uniformity, of "peer-group" acceptance and approval, condemn solitariness. A sensibility apart, a "loner" in thought and imagining, is the most telling dissenter from democratic, populist collectivities and majority rule. There is in solitude a natural aristocracy, a refusal of belonging. This abhorrence of *profanum et vulgus* endows a philosophic lineage extending from Heraclitus to Spinoza, Nietzsche and Wittgenstein its "mountaintop" lustre. There are magnitudes in poetry, Hölderlin's for one, otherwise implausible. If there is, however, one change of feeling and of usage which comes near to defining modernity, it is an accelerating erosion of both solitude and attendant privacy.

Ezra Pound saw it coming: "a frankness as never before," a "tawdry cheapness" via the exposure of even the most intimate of human acts and relations. What refuge is there now from voyeurism, from a lust for disclosure and self-disclosure which fuels the appetites of the media and their public? There is no domain, be it erotic, financial, medical, familial that is not invaded (an invasion of utmost menace to representative democracies in that it bars from public life and its nakedness the more gifted, the more complex in the community). But there is little need of eavesdropping and the concealed lens. The confessional, the strip-tease of the self, the publication of daily and nocturnal pursuits in graphic detail, are on voluntary, eager offer. The camera of the *paparazzi*, the questionnaire of the sociological inquirer, the bug and the psychoanalyst's ear, diverse as they may be in technique and context, add up to a monstrous quiz-show. A prodigality of literary avowals and exhibitionist indiscretions saturate the climate. Thus we inhabit an echo-chamber of interminable gossip, a confessional wired to loud-speakers. In its demands for "freedom of information" and transparency—demands often legitimate— populist democracy must devalue privacy. The truly private spirit, the guardian of the silent gravity which we call a secret, and which Kierkegaard found supremely in Antigone, are feared. In sum: it is difficult to make out where in cyberspace, under what license, solitude and privacy will find breathing-space.

This collapse of an *ancien régime* of aloneness and reserve —*pudeur* defies modern translation—affects inner creative resources just as does the eradication of silence. Kabbalistic fantasies have it that God's bout of creation sprang out of a solitude so absolute that He himself found it vexing. It is out of a tautened solitude and privacy of dormant, then woken powers that the maker peoples his perceptions and recognitions, where "peoples" comprises as well the tonal constructs of the composer and the shapes "bodied forth" by the artist. The germinating surge out of solitude and the sanctuary of the self is of the essence. It allows the sub-conscious right of access to its receptors and, as it were, watch-towers prior to visible, audible phenomenologies. Shakespeare's Richard II, as we saw, puts it memorably:

> And for because the world is populous,
> And here is not a creature but my self,
> I cannot do it; yet I'll hammer it out.
> My brain I'll prove the female to my soul,

My soul the father, and these two beget
A generation of still-breeding thoughts:
And these same thoughts people this little world . . .

Clearly, solitariness and privacy of this order, an order at once metaphysical and existential, had its religious pre-suppositions and configurations. The domain of privacy is, at the last, that of the dialogue, imaginary, conceptual, ritual but no less functional with the first or other maker. It is that of the encounter, filial or agonistic (or both), joyously mimetic (the *imitatio*) or jealously polemic, which I have emphasized throughout. Our growing remoteness from the felt actuality of this solitary, autistic if you will, rendezvous with the transcendent or the demonic, is directly proportional to the fish-bowl exhibitionism of modern ways. What "leaks" out of inner life is far more than any mundane secret. It is a confidentiality of being, where the etymology of "confidential" encloses a triplicity: there is trust ("confiding"), there is hope ("confidence"), and there is faith (*fide*). Words do remind us unnervingly of our losses.

This shrinkage in the spiritual and social-material matrix of the creative process accords closely with the overall displacements from individuality to the collective. The figure of the artist as Promethean or Faustian maker, of the composer or writer practising his mystery in an aura of heroism and suffering, now embarrasses. In their life and writings, Joyce and Thomas Mann may have been its final exponents, and Mann's *Doktor Faustus* its self-conscious epilogue. Characteristically, the "titanic" in Picasso ends up by being that of money. The spirit of our age is one of "interface" and participatory immersion in *communitas*. John Updike puts a novel onto the Internet inviting his "surfers" to complete successive chapters. The distance between begetter and recipient, between author and audience, is being blurred and "politically corrected." By its very nature, the globalization of the communicative Web brings with it aleatory, re-cyclable, open-ended aesthetic and discursive genres. These are, at numerous points, the antithesis to *auctoritas*.

Incompletion and the fragment, not the monumental, are the pass-words to modernism. If, as Adorno has it, "totality is the lie," the concept of the *magnum opus* becomes a delusion. The myriad-facetted, coherent entirety which Mandelstam celebrates in his essay on Dante, the architectural summation striven for by Proust are of the past. As in the case of the book itself, there will, to be sure, be complete editions of a modern master and attempts, more or less openly blazoned, at the "Great American Novel." But these phenomena will display an archaic, nostalgic resonance. They will be murals in a more or less deserted basilica. I have cited the example before: a recent major paper in nuclear physics carries some fifty signatures. Our representative forms and scenarios are choral as they were before the enigmatic leap into heroic, doomed egotism in Greek tragic consciousness and Hebraic narrative. Democracy and the Internet bid us "join in."

Beyond these sociological and psychological revaluations lie conjectures at the near edge of science-fiction. Organ-transplants, cloning, the initiation of organic life *in vitro* must inevitably alter the status of the self, of the first-person singular. As will the implantations in the cortex of electrodes and fibre-optical terminals. At what point does an individual cease to be identifiable as such? At what stage, his or her vital organs replaced, his or her consciousness electrochemically re-energized, will a man or woman enter what has been labelled "the bodynet," becoming a sequence of his or her previous incarnations in what could, theoretically be an unbroken molecular chain? (The seduction and horror of the project inhabit a number of fairy-tales, the Makropoulos fable and Janáček's inspired operatic version among them.) In what ways could we even begin to relate the "smartroom" minds and bodies of the explorers of Virtual Reality to any hitherto-known concepts of authorship and *poiesis*? Science can advance at ease with these prognostications. Can the arts and humanities?

Yet even these futurities are themselves symptoms. They tell of a fundamental mutation. Something altogether more radical is at stake.

7

This book has tried to elucidate aspects of "creation" and of "invention" and of discriminations to be made between them. This attempt leads me to a central hypothesis. I believe that the status of death, certainly in the West, is undergoing fundamental transformations. If this is so, both what we mean by "creation" and by "invention" will have to be rethought.

Death has its history. This history is biological, social, and mental. Biologically envisaged, the universalities and physiology of the death of the individual in our species have not altered significantly over the relatively brief span of human evolution. The growth of medical, therapeutic resources, the gerontology which may prolong average life-expectancies in the more forunate societies are, however dramatic, marginal in their effects. Sooner or later, what we are genetically programmed to experience as death overtakes each and every one of us. Elixirs of immortality—a hellish thought—have not yet been brewed. It is the other end

of the stick which is being revolutionized. Artificial insemina-
tion, the freezing and implant of human eggs, the conservation
of sperm, the not too-far-distant prospect of embryonic growth
outside the womb are indeed changing certain realities and symbolic images of birth. Dialectically, such a change should be mir-
rored in our perception of death. Such revisions may become perceptible; until now, however, death has retained its often mute
finality. The notion of "immortality" or resurrection via the deep-
freezing of the departed, a notion in counterpart to the treatment
of embryonic material, is merely embarrassing.

Every historical era, every society and culture have had their
own understanding, iconography, and rites of mortality. It may
well be that all mythologies and religious or metaphysical systems and narratives are a mortuary, an endeavour, often inge-
nious and elaborate, to edify a house for the dead. From it, the
living are meant to emerge with bearable grief, with consolation
and compensatory hopes. Death-bed etiquette, practices of exposure, interment, or incineration are as various as are human
communities, ethnic identities and local circumstance. Statistically estimated, the number of the dead since the last Ice Age
outweighs that of the living. We are still a planet of the dead.
But we owe to this fact our prayers, our ontologies and much of
our art, music, and literature. It is the creation of these articulate fictions, of their striving to contain and even overcome death,
which will alter if our experience of death itself alters. The links,
the fibres of interrelation which attach philosophic thought—defined by Seneca, by Montaigne as "learning to die"—and aesthetic
performative acts to the fact of death, are organic. We think, we
shape, in intimate companionship with and contrariety to death.
Even where the idiom of religious faith, of philosophic stoicism

or lyric invocation solicits and welcomes death, such welcome is an attempt to assuage, to domesticate its terrors. "Death, where is thy sting? Ding-a-ling-a-ling." Brendan Behan's ditty out of 1914–1918 sounds defiantly chirpy, but rings hollow.

When we ask what it is that may be redefining our sense of death, conjectures and intuitions lie to hand.

Historians concur that the twentieth century has been the most murderous on record. Some put at one hundred million the number of victims of war, famine, deportation, concentration camps, and genocide between August 1914 and the slow termination of Stalinist rule. From Madrid to Moscow, from Narvik to Messina, Europe and western Russia have been a charnel house, a setting for atrocity. No one knows the exact toll of Mao's crazed "great leap forward" (ten million, twenty million?) or of the tribal blood-lust in Rwanda, in Indonesia and, of late, in the Balkans. As never before, the mass media have saturated our awareness and memories with images of organized horror. It is the bones and ash of the Nazi death-camps, the pyramids of skulls in Cambodia or the foul burial ditches uncovered in Bosnia and Kosovo, that are the emblem, the icons of recent history. Millions among these hideous deaths remain anonymous. The names were wiped out as well as the human beings. Acres of unmarked crosses stand voiceless in the war-cemeteries of north-east France and Flanders. Where are the starved, tortured inmates of the Gulag, of the Kolyma mines and ice-forests buried? "Known only to God": a presumption made less and less plausible, less and less comforting, to modern rationalism.

It cannot but be that this long march through blackness has devalued death. The mind cannot take in the relevant statistics: the thirty-thousand slaughtered during the first days on the Somme, the two-thousand death sentences signed *per diem* in the Kremlin during the Purges, the hackings to death by giggling tribesmen in east Africa, the sum of the blameless incinerated in Dresden, Hiroshima, and Nagasaki. Feelings, understanding are made numb by the flourishing of torture throughout our political ideologies and nation-states. To these phenomena there has been no response, even faintly adequate, from theology, philosophy, or the arts. How could there be? At best we have the startling but stylized cunning of Picasso's *Guernica,* the witness of Primo Levi or the riddling poems of Paul Celan. But what are these in "the great winds from under the earth"?

Thus the sheer scale of death, its obscene technologies (some would say: "industrialization") and its namelessness have become paramount. Together they have, in some sense, trivialized the very concept. This trivialization may itself be a defense mechanism in the face of the incomprehensible and the unendurable. But it has, I believe, modified the aura, the dignity of death in our culture.

To any such modification, the abrogations of silence, solitude, and privacy which I have cited are directly germane. Two contrasting yet congruent tendencies are at work. Where massacre and economic-social misery prevail, death withers to naked routine. No especial significance honours the victim, so often skeletal in his or her trashed existence. Where superfluity obtains, death is sanitized and gentrified. Medical care and technology—those tubes, those softly lit rooms—privilege the moribund party. At the same time, however, death is absorbed into an almost commercial process and sweet-and-sour uniformity. California manuals for parents of younger children suggest that death be made reassuring by the flushing of gold fish down the toilet. This roseate exit and strategy of the cosmetic occur, as by the logic of paradox, in midst a society whose appetite for extreme violence, for representations of murder on the screen and in the comic, is unquenchable. Put enough rouge on the dear departed, let the electric organ croon, and soon death may become only a virtual reality.

Under these dispensations, it is becoming difficult to die one's own death, to meet that most intriguing of obligations in freedom. Kierkegaard foresaw the difficulty and Heidegger analysed it. The implacable invasiveness of modern clinical usage, the keeping alive by demeaning plumbing of those for whom death would be a release, makes of suicide the sole guarantor of privacy, of the autonomy of the self. Suicide is the critical act *par excellence*, the ironic dissent of the spirit from *kitsch*. It alone negates the tranquillizer rhetoric of what has been called "the American way of death" (an unfair labelling in as much as these practices are today more and more conventional throughout economies of conspicuous consumption).

The concept of death has entailed that of immortality. A mutation in "death" alters both poles. Devalue death and immortality loses meaning. Banalize dying or make of it a social taboo, and immortality erodes to an outworn "conceit"—allowing that word both its rhetorical and its moral-psychological meanings. Only death, when it is at the heart of being, can validate the pursuit of the undying. Light and dark, extinction and survival being, as Heraclitus observed, inseparable twins.

Men and women have committed their lives to raising what Yeats called "monuments of unageing intellect." They have produced texts, composed music, painted pictures to last beyond their own biological lives. Either in the secrecy of their hearts or in proud utterance, the thinker, the maker, the masters of form have aimed at perdurance (the word is archaic, but perhaps stronger than any other). In rare cases, they have been indifferent to the perpetuation of their own names and signatures (the Shakespeare riddle). In the overwhelming majority of formative acts, however, they have hoped to transmit to the future their identity. They have hungered after immortality, within the bounds which saddened common sense assigns to this promise.

At every point in this study, the architects of philosophic constructs, the poets, the builders have borne witness to their wager on lastingness, to the contract they hope to have signed with tomorrow. Some have done so in clearsighted realisation, at once sovereign and fearful, of their rivalry with God (a Michelangelo, a Tolstoy). Many, a Keats for example or a Schubert, have been harried by the fear that their works might perish and their names be "writ on water." There are those, Flaubert most eloquently, who have raged at the paradoxical survival of their creations, of their fictions beyond the brute fact of their own deaths. Often the most inspired have understood their own powers as mimetic, as reverently analogous to those of the divinity. In Dante, in Bach, or at a more complexly psychological level, in Beethoven, in Mahler (the contrast being the pious servitude of Bruckner), this enlistment of a transcendent precedent and exemplar is manifest. Less frequently, as we have seen, the relation, vitally felt or metaphoric, is one of challenge, of defiant competition. The artist, the man of self-acknowledged genius (a Balzac, a Wagner) constructs thronged worlds, immensities of design whose originalities of insight match, surpass (?) the craftsmanship of the Deity. At some level, awake or sub-conscious, the mortal maker senses that his or her death is God's self-defense, God's insurance, too often bitterly unfair because premature, against that Promethean "storming of the heavens" (a *topos* ancient as Aeschylus). Thus the preeminent poet or composer or artist dies young lest creation itself be rivalled or overshadowed.

Across the spectrum of these "immortalities," of the *exegi monumentum* which I have referred to throughout, death is an essential player. It is the capacity of certain human intellects and sensibilities to give life to their conceptions, to "conceive" in the full sense of that overcrowded word. This pregnancy—we recall Shakespeare's Richard II—draws death. It endows death with its devastation, its laying waste. Death, as it were, smells out its creative quarry. Keats's, Kafka's terminal pronouncements testify to this fatal scent. A primal violation is avenged. Contrary to the prohibition on the making of images, where such making may be taken to include speculative thought as well as the totality of the aesthetic, we have laboured to outwit death, to be "for all times." The wrestling match with the dark angel, as graphic in Dunbar's lament for his fellow-poets as it is in the art of Rembrandt or in Rilke's *Duino Elegies,* has been archetypal of human creativity despite, because of its foreordained outcome. The loser is annihilated but prevails. This archetype, this shorthand for an immensely complicated set of motives and values, depends very precisely on substantive apprehensions of death, on men and women as free and private agents in the face of death. It depends, in turn, on contiguities between animate death and a theological or metaphysical dimension. It is these contiguities, I am arguing, which are waning, which are receding over the horizon of reason. With this recession, with the transit of our culture and informing vocabulary towards a new code of the collective, the replaceable, the ephemeral, the trope of immortality, crucial to what we have known as thought and art of the first order, is growing more and more suspect. Today, I venture, even the most charismatic of philosophers, even the most self-dramatizing of writers, painters or composers, find embarrassing, if not downright ludicrous, the claims to perdurance which have been the rallying cry since Pindar, Horace, and Ovid. Only the French Academy will continue to count its *immortels*. The duel with death that lay at the hungry heart of human creations will have become shadowboxing. Immanence will prevail.

As in the critique of language, there are seminal moments. The synchronicities are striking. Dada erupts in 1916. Confronted with the insane hecatombs on the western front, Dada heralds the demise of reason. It empties language and syntax of ascertainable meaning. Hugo Ball sings out

> hollaka hollala
> blago bung
> blago bung
> bosso fataka
> ü üü ü

in derision of any reasoned discourse or rhetoric. Dada mocks the pretentions of the arts and of literature to humanize. It grimaces at their utter bankruptcy in the face of political and social bestiality. The monumental, the classic, the canonic are held up to fierce ridicule. In the apocalyptic slapstick of the Café Voltaire, the mere notion of a formal masterpiece, of an aspiration to immortality is excoriated (there are a third of a million corpses unburied at Verdun). As with the paintings of Ensor, death itself is made grotesque and oddly perishable. Only nonsense, only the most ephemeral of gestures are allowed their momentary truth, and even they are seen to be uselessly self-indulgent.

Acknowledged or not, the legacy of Dada has been immense. There has been since no significant movement in Western art, literature and aesthetic debate that does not come out of Dada. Deconstruction and post-modernism are Dada translated into academic-theoretical jargon—a jargon often as impenetrable as were the glossolalia of Dada itself. The cult of the absurd in existentialism derives from Dada, as do the anarchic rituals of the flower child and masked protester in the capitalist street. "Happenings" were pure Dada. When Russian futurists exhort us to burn down all libraries so as to emancipate the senile spirit from the dead weight of the past, from sclerotic idolatries of magisterial survival, they are joining in the Dada chorus:

> echige zunbada
> wulubu ssubudu uluw ssubudu. . . .

Dada's influence is not yet fully reckoned with. But whatever their artistic genius, figures such as Picasso and Matisse belong to an Olympian past. In their undisguised striving after futurity, after the consecration of the museum or the pantheon, these painters are disciples of Giotto. Henry Moore links hands directly with Pisano and Michelangelo. In Stravinsky, in Schoenberg, the pride of inheritance and canonic inclusion is as manifest as it is in "Homeric" Joyce or in Thomas Mann's identification with Goethe. It does seem to me that the seers, the clairvoyant gravediggers of "immortality" are not to be found among the classics. The outriders to the age on which we are now entering are Marcel Duchamp, Kurt Schwitters, and Jean Tinguely.

Has there been, after Leonardo, an artist, a contriver more *intelligent* than Duchamp? Whenever we view, in a museum or gallery of contemporary art, those bricks on the floor, the eviscerated calves, the soiled bed linen, the burlap bags hung on bent hooks, or the splatter of elephant dung on canvas (a motif known to Dada), we are entering Marcel Duchamp's kingdom. Where constructivism and deconstruction play their kindred games, the ground rules are Duchamp's. As are, since *Nu descendant un escalier* of 1912, efforts to bridge the gap between painting or sculpture and the cinematic, to set seemingly arrested forms into kaleidoscopic motion and mobility. When, in the summer of 1913, Duchamp purchased a funnel used to bottle Norman cider and signed it, he dismantled at a stroke the definition of Western art as original creation, as authorship. The *objet trouvé*, the urinal reversed and made fountain, the bicycle wheel set to spin on a chair, is or is not, as the case may be, given a displacing title and signed either pseudonymously or *in propria persona*. The implications are seismic, if wit can generate earth-quakes. Designated, looked at as "art," just about any object, however utilitarian, familiar, unprepossessing, is made art. The artifact is made an "art fact." It is now entitled—those Dadaist Duchamp titles—to be and to be experienced as art. The signature, factitious or not, cannot be challenged and puts in doubt the claims to propriety, to the glory of the creative ego, as these have been taken for granted since Phidias and Apelles. Duchamp's profound gags make of *all* forms an aesthtic potential and accident, an occasion, perfectly arbitrary, for beauty or pathos or terror in the beholder's jolted eye. No so-called work of art should be guaranteed reverence and fixed repose. It is in fraternal, teasing salute to Leonardo—Duchamp's laughter is precise—that a moustache is added to the Mona Lisa.

Capital distinctions are being eradicated. It is in the autumn of 1912 that Duchamp visits the Aeronautics Salon at the Grand Palais in Paris. He is in the company of Fernand Léger and of Brancusi. Turning to the latter, Duchamp challenges: "Painting is finished. Who could do better than that propeller? Tell me, could you make that?" In that instant, fundamental permutations occur. The craftsmanship, the formal elegance of the mechanical device is elevated to, and above that of art. Technology is shown to be the act of *poiesis* (as it will be in Leger's paintings). Art can no longer rival, let alone excel the *technē* of the engineer. *Invention is identified as the primary mode of creation in the modern world.* It follows that art is becoming amateurish indulgence, that a Marcel Duchamp is better employed at chess. Here also, if the pun is allowed, the move is perfectly calculated and significant. Like art, poetry, or music, chess is transcendentally trivial. It exercises no formative power over human affairs, now more and more governed by technology and the sciences. The chess master (Duchamp played second board for France just behind Alekhine in 1930) is a high priest of the irrelevant. The Surrealist indignation that so important an artist as Duchamp should have relinquished art for a board game wholly missed the point.

Literature is made of language; painting and sculpture of natural or recombined ingredients; music is made out of the raw material of sound. We inhabit a world whose components are, in essence, what Duchamp famously called "a ready-made." Only God is deemed capable of making out of non-being. Only He can innovate out of nothingness. Human experience is a response to factualities, to prior existentiality. This, we have seen, is true of all representation, of all means of understanding and interpretation however abstract. Whether pure mathematics embodies an exception remains an unsolved question (perhaps *the* question). If art is constructed of the ready-made and the *objet trouvé*—what else do we perceive, what else do we manipulate and re-combine?—all its feigned creations are a collage of reality. All imaginings, inner and outer, are a process of selection and assemblage.

Kurt Schwitters emerged out of Dada. But he dreamt of a *Gesamtkunstwerk,* of a representational totality which would both extend and mock that of canonic and Wagnerian monumentalities. His collages were to be huge metaphors, yet the objects and images brought into contiguity were to affirm their disparity, their anarchic resistance to any harmonic, signifying resolution. The *Merzbau* was projected in 1919 and begun in the early 1920s. It was to be a mosaic, though that rubric is too orderly, of the detritus of everyday life: used tram tickets, cloak-room tokens, beer mats, scraps of newspaper, candy wrappers, splinters of glass and metal, woodshavings, chicken-wire, bits of discarded string. Independently, Schwitters set out to fulfill Walter Benjamin's programme of messianic retrieval, of the recuperation from oblivion of what is humblest. Using even the most soiled props out of the refuse of modern life, Schwitters professed that "even garbage can cry out" against war and economic oppression.

Incomplete by definition, the first *Merzbau* perished in an air-raid on Hanover in 1943. A second version went lost in Norway to which Schwitters had fled. An attempt to re-compose "my life's work" in England after 1940 ended in total isolation and frustration. This destiny was wholly apposite. The *Merzbau* is a continuum, defiant of any circumscription in time and place, let alone in the burial-ground of the museum. There is always new material to be glued on, to be juxtaposed. Thus, although it is in any ordinary sense non-existent, indeed *because* it is non-existent, the *Merzbau* not only seems more figurative of our age than a *Guernica* or a *War Requiem*, but has exercised immense influence. It is the absent guest at the ghostly revels of classical and romantic aesthetics.

One step remained to be taken. In 1960, in the forecourt of the Museum of Modern Art in New York, Jean Tinguely set alight his intricate, soaring *Hommage à New York*. The metal construct collapsed in brightness ("a brightness falls from the air"). Other "self-destructs" were to follow. Welded of scrap-metal, of pieces of discarded machinery in Tinguely's iron-mongery and forge, these composites, baroque in their delicacy but industrial and technological in their elements and manufacture, gyrated and shook themselves to rubble. Their presentation was to be a "happening," an experience of pure singularity, unrecapturable and, therefore, immune from any subsequent compromise or exploitation. Tinguely's is a genuinely philosophic sensibility. Witness the incisive lampooning in his series *Les Philosophes*, whose ratchets, tubes, wheels and wrought-iron pincers evoke, uncannily, the stance of a Rousseau, a Wittgenstein, and a Heidegger. The "self-destruct" is a metaphysical prank designed to enforce a terminal logic. Only self-annihilation can dispell the millennial mists of aesthetic pretense. Only a "self-destruct" can validate acts of renewal freed from illusions of permanence, from vainglorious rivalry with death. Art is high or low entertainment, a carnival for the hour. In its festive suicide, the "self-destruct" does more to disarm death than any ode to immortality. The last laugh is truly the best.

Dada and these three grave jesters, Duchamp, Schwitters, Tinguely, mark the end of the concept of *poiesis* as it has prevailed since antiquity. Hegel had anticipated and conceptualized this ending. Such a finding is no mystical, teutonic chatter. It has a rigorous, if also metaphoric, meaning. It tells us that there is no more re-insurance for poetics and the arts in the analogy drawn with divine making. It suggests that the conceit of immortality central to our aesthetic and intellectual ambitions is just that. Death is no longer the ennobling, paradoxically sustaining adversary. Dada and its inspired ministrants *have re-invented creation*. They have made of it nothing more and nothing less than a rhetorical tactic. It is now the notorious ghost in the machine, where the machine frequently exhibits a conceptual sophistication, a quality of making and even of formal beauty equal to, if not surpassing those, in the arts (again, architecture and music are at the border line). "Creation," in its classic sense and connotations, turns out to have been a magnificently fruitful invention. Some cave-artists at Altamira or Lascaux wished to be regarded as more than an adroit mimic and reproducer of the ready-made world, of that *objet trouvé* which is a bison.

What is labelled "art" will continue to be produced, exhibited, and enshrined. There are enough soiled sheets and bisected calves to go around. But it will not be called upon or wish to "think itself through." It will not re-evaluate the ontological fictions that remain open to it after the ebbing of the theological and the melting-down of transcendentality. A Duchamp urinal, a Schwitters collage, a Tinguely "self-destruct" can co-exist with and engage these recessions. Consciously or not, what now excites our curiosity in the art gallery will illustrate them. The "masterpiece" as we have known and dreamt it cannot, in honesty, do so. "*C'est fini la peinture.*"

CONCLUSION

It is difficult to believe that the story out of *Genesis* has ended. The play and counter-play between "creation" and "invention" has always been, in part, subjective and flexible. To Alexander Pope, "invention" is the highest capacity of man, a near-divine attribute: "Homer is universally allowed to have had the greatest *Invention* of any writer whatever." Paul Celan regards "invention" as tantamount to falsehood. The inversion of the two terms in Dada is arrived at by parody and negation. Yet these two modes are themselves intensely creative. They invite further reflection, however speculative.

We are entering on a planetary culture and hierarchy of values increasingly dominated by the sciences and their technological application. These are in perpetual progress as knowledge breeds knowledge. It is precisely the limitlessness of this forward motion —only the extinction of the human mind could bring it to a halt— which is replacing the category and similes of the infinite which characterized the God of Aquinas and Descartes. We saw that the exponential rate of specialization in the sciences, together with the volume of new information which this branching generates, could conceivably lead to a crisis. It could bring on a kind of implosion or inward collapse. At present, however, such negative entropy looks unlikely. In terms of cerebral energy and social prestige, of economic resources and practical yield, the sciences and technology have before them an unbounded tomorrow.

We saw that the relation between the epistemology of the sciences and the notion of "creation" has always been equivocal. To most scientists throughout history the term of reference has been "discovery"; technology has aimed at "invention." The new cosmologies regard "creation" as being ambiguous, mythological, and even taboo. To ask what preceded the Big Bang and the primal nanoseconds of the compaction and expansion of our universe is, we are instructed, to talk gibberish. Time has no meaning prior to that singularity. Both elementary logic and common sense should tell us that such a ruling is arrogant bluff. The simple fact that we can phrase the question, that we can engage it with normal thought processes, gives it meaning and legitimacy. The postulate of unquestionable ("not to be questioned") nothingness and intemporality now made dogma by astrophysicists is as arbitrary, is in many regards more of a mystique, than are creation narratives in *Genesis* and elsewhere. The reasoned intuition of a coming into being which we do not understand, but whose efficacy suggests itself via the analogies of human creativity, has lost none of its challenge. What this book has tried to show is the ways in which a resort to these analogies can become an empty, even corrosive convention when assumptions of faith and of a transcendental metaphysics are discarded. The God-hypothesis will not be mocked without cost.

But as the great mathematician and astronomer Laplace caustically put it, it is just of this hypothesis that the sciences (and technology) have no compelling need. It is scientific discovery and technological invention which will, more and more, marshal our sense of social history and of the idiom appropriate to that history. Already, so much of elegance, of aesthetic adventure is to be found in architecture, in industrial design. These are the synapses between the arts in any traditional sense, the algebra of the engineer and the virtuosity of the craftsman (Cellini would have delighted in a Ferrari). In this symbiosis, the partitions between the created and the invented have lost definition. Having listened to Duchamp, Brancusi incorporates the dancing curvatures of the propeller within his sculpture. One senses that in the arts this will be the next chapter.

Yet human exultation and sorrow, anguish and jubilation, love and hatred, will continue to demand shaped expression. They will continue to press on language which, under that pressure, becomes literature. The human intellect will persist in posing questions which science has ruled illicit or unanswerable. Though perhaps condemned to ultimate circularity, this persistence is thought made urgent, which is to say, metaphysical. An imp of demonic triviality inhabits the imperial régime of the sciences. It could be that music *knows* better, although there is nothing more intractable to definition than the nature of that knowledge.

We saw that the armature of *poiesis* has been, in a larger sense, theological; that it lies on the far side of physics (meta-physics). There is explicit engagement with transcendence in an Aeschylus, a Dante, a Bach, or a Dostoevski. It is at work with unspecified force in a Rembrandt portrait or on the night of Bergotte's death in Proust's *Recherche*. The wing-beat of the unknown has been at the heart of *poiesis*. Can there, will there be major philosophy, literature, music, and art of an atheist provenance?

Until now, authentic atheism has been rare. Nor does it mock the God-hypothesis. It can bear witness to sombre deprivation. "He doesn't exist, the bastard" (Samuel Beckett). Atheism can exact moral discipline and altruism of the severest kind. It imposes on the writer or thinker a solitide even more austere than that which our way of life has, at present, dissipated. The true atheist's assumption of the black zero in and after death makes his acts at once immanently responsible and, in a sense, hopeless. Let us suppose that a genuine atheism will come to replace the aspirin-agnosticism, the "blowing neither hot nor cold" now awash in our post-modernity. Let us suppose that atheism will come to possess and energize those who are masters of articulate form and builders of thought. Will their works rival the dimensions, the life-transforming strengths of persuasion we have known? What would be the atheist counterpart to a Michelangelo fresco or *King Lear*? It would be impertinent to rule out the possibility. Or to deny the fascination of the prospect. Currently, the search for contact with intelligent beings in outer space is close to obsessive. Is it a premonitory attempt to lighten aloneness? To forget, through the amplified whisper of the radio-telescope, the now too distant thunder-clap of creation?

We have long been, I believe that we still are, guests of creation. We owe to our host the courtesy of questioning.

INDEX